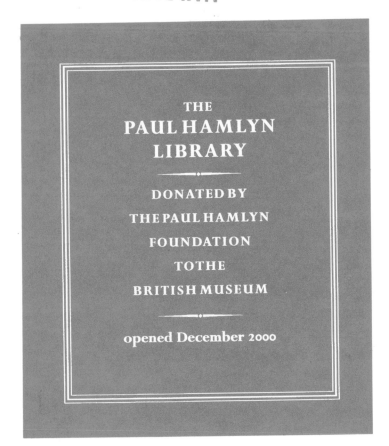

But one day of all other, the whole navy of the Englishmen made out, and purposed to set on the Frenchmen; but in their setting forward, a goodly ship of England, called the Mary Rose, *was by too much folly, drowned in the midst of the haven, for she was laden with much ordnance, and the ports left open, which were very low, and the great ordnance unbreached, so that when the ship should turn, the water entered, and suddenly she sank.*

Edward Hall, *Chronicle*, 1548

LETTERS FROM THE MARY ROSE

C.S. KNIGHTON & DAVID LOADES

SUTTON PUBLISHING

THE MARY ROSE TRUST

First published in 2002 by
Sutton Publishing Limited · Phoenix Mill
Thrupp · Stroud · Gloucestershire · GL5 2BU
in association with
The Mary Rose Trust · Portsmouth · Hampshire · PO1 3LX

British Library Cataloguing in Publication Data
A catalogue record for this book is available from the British Library

ISBN 0 7509 2839 5

Typeset in 10/14.5 Photina.
Typesetting and origination by
Sutton Publishing Limited.
Printed and bound in England by
J.H. Haynes & Co. Ltd, Sparkford.

CONTENTS

Contents

Bold figures in the Introduction and the commentaries in each chapter refer to the numbered documents that form the second part of each chapter.

PREFACE

Henry VIII's warship the *Mary Rose* had served for over thirty years when she sank before the King's eyes in 1545. This book presents a selection from the many documents which log the ship's career; chiefly, we print all the surviving dispatches written aboard during her first two periods of active service. The texts have been set within a continuing narrative which explains specific circumstances and fills in gaps for which there is no documentary coverage. The written record is accompanied by photographs of material from the wreck recovered and conserved by the Mary Rose Trust.

The project would have been impossible without the collaboration of Alexzandra Hildred and Christopher Dobbs. We are greatly indebted to them for their advice and assistance and to Andrew Elkerton and the Mary Rose Trust for providing many of the illustrations. The map has very kindly been provided by Dominic Fontana of Portsmouth University. We are very grateful to Jane Crompton and Christopher Feeney, and their colleagues at Sutton Publishing, for accepting the book and bringing it into being. For additional help we must thank Simon Adams, Lisa Barber, Aude Fitzsimons, Ian Friel and Judith Loades.

Portraits in the Royal Collection are reproduced by gracious permission of Her Majesty The Queen. The portrait of Lord Paget at Plas Newydd is reproduced by kind permission of the Most Honourable the Marquess of Anglesey. The portrait of the Duke and Duchess of Suffolk at Woburn Abbey is reproduced by kind permission of the Marquess of Tavistock and the Bedford Settled Estates. Lord Lisle's dispatch of 1545 is printed by kind permission of the Most Honourable the Marquess of Salisbury. We are grateful to Dr H.G. Wayment for supplying a print of his photograph of the window in Fairford church which he has identified as a portrait of Wolsey. Dr M.H. Rule, CBE, has kindly allowed us to use her photograph of the raising of the hull of the *Mary Rose*. For help with the documents and illustrations we are also grateful to Messrs P. Barber, S. Roper and N. Spencer (British Library), Miss S. Burdett (National Trust),

Mr R. Harcourt-Williams (Hatfield House), Messrs P. Johnson and A.H. Lawes (Public Record Office), Miss L. Nicol (Cambridge University Press), Dr E. Springer (Österreichisches Staastsarchiv), Miss S. Smith (Royal Collection) and Miss L. Wellicome (Woburn Abbey).

The documentary texts and editorial apparatus have been the responsibility of Dr Knighton; the commentary was written by Professor Loades.

C.S.K.
D.M.L.
London, August 2001

LIST OF ILLUSTRATIONS

LIST OF COLOUR PLATES

These are found between pp. 70 and 71.

NOTE ON MEASUREMENTS

In the transcribed documents Roman numerals have been rendered as Arabic, and the conventional abbreviations applied as standard; otherwise measures are given as nearly as possible to the format of the original MSS.

Currency

The pound sterling (£) of 20 shillings, the shilling (*s*) of 12 pence (*d*). The mark (13*s* 4*d*) was a term of an account, not an actual coin.

Weight

The pound avoirdupois (lb) of 16 ounces (oz); 112 lb making 1 hundredweight (cwt), and 20 cwt 1 ton (although the cwt may sometimes have still been calculated at 100 lb as its name implies).

Linear

The league was generally accepted as 3 miles. The modern nautical mile was not yet established, and 'mile' is to be understood as the standard 1,760 yards.

Dates

The year of grace is reckoned from 1 January (and not 25 March as was usual in the sixteenth century), but dates are otherwise in the Old Style (i.e. not adjusted to the Gregorian calendar). The regnal years of Henry VIII are frequently used in the documents; the King's accession day was 22 April, and the regnal year was calculated from that date, until 21 April following:

     1 Henry VIII runs 22 April 1509–21 April 1510
     10 Henry VIII: 22 April 1518–21 April 1519
     20 Henry VIII: 22 April 1528–21 April 1529
     30 Henry VIII: 22 April 1538–21 April 1539
     38 Henry VIII: 22 April 1546–28 January 1547

Date formulae in Latin have been translated.

INTRODUCTION

BACKGROUND

The *Mary Rose* was a 'Great Ship'. She has become the symbol of Henry VIII's navy, largely because a substantial part of her has survived, and was raised to the surface in a high-profile operation in 1982. She now has a museum dedicated to her, and her loss has been the subject of much scrutiny. This status, however, is appropriate for other than archaeological reasons. Her working life coincided almost exactly with the King's reign, and when she was built she was of an innovative design, signalling Henry's lifelong interest in fighting ships. She was the *Dreadnought* of her day.

In 1509 England was not a sea power, and had not been since the eleventh century. The reason for this was that the Norman and Angevin kings had also held substantial parts of France, and the English Channel was a highway within their dominions, rather than a defensive moat. This changed to some extent during the fourteenth century, and in the early exchanges of the Hundred Years War the English were alerted to the need for sea defences by a number of French amphibious raids on the south coast. In response, the English won their first major naval victory for 300 years at Sluys in 1340. This gave Edward III effective control of the Channel for a generation, but it did not change his strategic thinking, which continued to focus on winning pitched battles in France.

Edward, in fact, had no navy. He owned some ships, most notably the large cog *Thomas*, which served as what would later be called a flagship, but he raised a fleet when he needed one by the traditional methods. One of these was 'Ship Service', a feudal contract whereby certain port towns provided ships for the King's service in return for their charter privileges. Another was a variant of the Commission of Array, when a nobleman or an experienced captain was authorized to 'take up' ships for the King's service, for a given period and at a given price. This was possible because there was no significant difference between a warship and a merchant ship. The King maintained a stock of prefabricated wooden castles, which were added to the requisitioned ships to accommodate archers and other soldiers, and then removed at the end of the campaign. The advantage of this ad hoc approach was that it was cheap; not only did the King not have to invest in expensive ships, but the modest number of vessels he did retain could be serviced by a single officer, the Clerk of the King's Ships. There was no permanent plant, and the regular workforce was confined to a handful of master mariners. The King used his own ships to trade, and to carry his ambassadors and messengers, but when not in use for his own purposes, they could be leased out at a profit.

The disadvantage, of course, was that it was inefficient. If a threat appeared quickly (that is, without at least three months' warning), it was impossible to mobilize to meet it. No fleet could be kept in being for more than a short campaigning season, because the ships were needed for other purposes, and consequently 'keeping the seas' was an impossibility. There could be no defensive shield, and no means of protecting merchants against the depredations of pirates. Such a system was suitable if the only need was for an occasional 'Navy Royal' to escort a fleet of troop transports to France, and that was how Edward III operated it. The great victory at Sluys was little more than a happy accident; a chance encounter between two fleets which had been assembled for a different purpose.

The first signs of a more creative naval policy had come from Henry V in the early fifteenth century. Unlike Edward, Henry had some appreciation of the importance of sea power in its own right. He was also sensitive to the discontent that wholesale requisitioning bred in the merchant community, particularly in London, which was becoming a major factor in policy calculations. Moreover, Ship Service was in full decline as the original chartered ports lost their importance and the new ones negotiated different contracts. When Henry decided to renew the war with France in 1415, he therefore decided to build or purchase about thirty of his own ships, and to take up most of his transports in the Low Countries. He was, as is well known, spectacularly successful. His fleet was unchallenged and his armies victorious. His shipwrights also pushed their technology to its limits to build the massive *Grace Dieu* of 1,000 tons, once thought to have been a white elephant but now considered to have been useful as well as impressive. Its remains can still be seen in the Hamble estuary at low tide. However, Henry's naval vision did not extend beyond the job in hand. As soon as the war was won, the fleet began to be dispersed, and after he died in 1422 it was run down almost to nothing, on his own instructions. By 1450, everything except one small balinger had either been sold or had rotted from neglect, and the office of Clerk of the King's Ships was discontinued. In so far as Henry VI had a policy for 'keeping the seas', it was to privatize it, and a variety of methods was tried, including licensed self-help by the merchant communities of Bristol, Calais and London. Nothing worked, and the failure to control piracy resulted in the payment of substantial compensation in order to prevent diplomatic fallout. In 1449 a private fleet, under even less discipline than usual, attacked and plundered ships of the powerful Hanseatic League, and the price, both financial and political, was very high.

Edward IV, who secured the Crown in 1461, appreciated the problem, but it was not high on his list of priorities. He owned more ships than Henry VI had done, but left them in the care of 'King's shipmasters', and used them almost entirely for trade. To the extent that the seas were kept, it was by the same shambolic methods as before, although the disasters were on a smaller scale and Edward did actually fight a full-scale war with the Hanseatic League on his merchants' behalf. It could hardly be described as successful. Edward had no more idea of naval policy than his predecessors, but he did resurrect the office of Clerk of the King's Ships in 1480, and that was to signify the beginning of a new situation. Edward died in 1483 in possession of about half a dozen ships, and the brief reign of Richard III, eventful as it was in some ways, merely saw that position maintained. When Henry VII came to the throne in 1485, he continued with Thomas Rogers in office as Clerk of the Ships, and seems to have taken a thoughtful look at his modest department. The results were not spectacular, but they were immediate. Within two years two large state-of-the-art warships had been built, the first in England. These were the *Regent* and the *Sovereign*, carracks of 600 and 450 tons respectively and of the latest Portuguese design. Both these ships could be (and were) used for trade, but they were primarily intended for fighting, and mounted large numbers of the small guns called serpentines. Henry had no intention of waging war if he could avoid it, so these ships were partly a deterrent and partly a statement of power. In them can be glimpsed the first signs of a long-term policy.

For the same reason, the construction of a dry dock at Portsmouth in 1495 was equally significant. Henry V had kept his ships at Southampton, but during the fifteenth century Portsmouth harbour had been minimally fortified to guard the anchorage against French attack. Henry VII extended those fortifications, and excavated a dock close to what is now the Old Basin. This was not in itself an innovation but the accounts of the work suggest that the new facility was intended to be permanent, and it may have been connected with the difficulty of docking the carracks in the traditional way, by beaching them. Henry built storehouses and a forge at Portsmouth, creating an embryonic naval base; and he also constructed some facilities at Woolwich, within easy reach of London. He did not, however, build or purchase a large number of ships. The *Sweepstake* and the *Mary Fortune* (both relatively small) were built in 1497, but when he died in 1509 he handed on just five ships to his son, fewer than he had himself inherited. Nor had he developed new methods of keeping the seas. His smaller ships could be, and occasionally were, used to chase pirates, but the great carracks were useless for that purpose, and he did not have enough vessels to make a real impact on the situation. What he did do was to provide armed escorts (at the merchants' expense) on some occasions to 'waft' the Merchant Adventurers' cloth fleet to Antwerp. He also revived the old bounty system, whereby merchants were paid so much a ton to build larger ships than they really needed, and to make those ships available for royal service when required. Piracy seems to have been less of a problem during his reign than it had been earlier in the century, but this was because the merchants started using a convoy system which made them less vulnerable to attack, rather than because the King was intervening effectively.

So Henry VII left a situation full of potential, but with very little achieved. His last Clerk of the Ships, Robert Brigandine, was a man of skill and experience, but more important, the new King had new ideas. Henry VIII was not an innovative thinker, and most of his original actions were the unintended consequences of trying to get his own way, rather than deliberately planned. However, he has an excellent claim to being the founder of the modern Navy, and the first thing he did was to build the *Mary Rose*.

LIFE ON BOARD

The *Mary Rose* carried a crew which varied at different stages of her existence from 150 to 200 officers and men. In action she carried between 20 and 30 gunners, and between 175 and 220 soldiers. The proportions shifted over thirty-five years, but the total was always around 400. Before she was rebuilt in about 1536 there were rather fewer seamen and gunners, and rather more soldiers. The rebuild enlarged her, and increased the number of guns; moreover, changing tactics reduced the likelihood of hand-to-hand fighting. At the time of her loss she may have been carrying more than her normal complement,

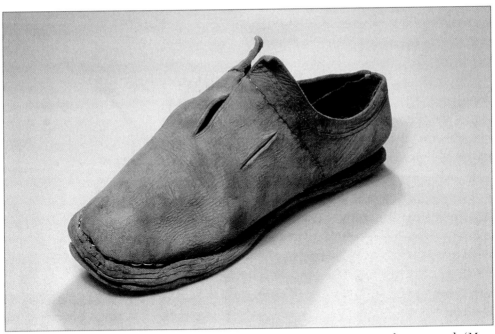

Leather shoe with a high vamp and slashed decoration, one of many examples recovered. (*Mary Rose Trust*)

because not only would her officers have been attended by their own servants, but extra soldiers would have been taken aboard to help with the kind of action that was anticipated. The contemporary figure given for the loss of life was 500, and that was probably exaggerated, but not necessarily by much.

The seamen wore woollen garments, breeches, tunics and caps, which they repaired themselves as the need arose. Although they had leather shoes which they wore on occasion, particularly ashore, wet and slippery decks meant that they worked most of the time barefoot. In anything like bad weather they must have been wet most of the time, because their rough garments would not have been waterproof. When times were good, and the pay was regular, most of them probably had spare clothes, stockings and undergarments. Such things were not luxuries, because of the living conditions, but times were sometimes hard, and both taverns and gambling houses took their toll of these items. The soldiers were similarly clad, but because they were not required to work the ship, they would normally have kept their shoes and stockings on. Armour, in the shape of morions and 'almain rivetts' (body armour) was kept in the ship's armoury, along with the bows, arrows, hackbuts and other weapons. However, most of them probably possessed their own jacks, stout leather jerkins which gave

Part of the extensive collection of tableware recovered, including pewter and wooden flagons and a pepper-mill. (*Mary Rose Trust*)

reasonable protection if nothing else was available. The soldiers were also normally provided with tabards, or loose overgarments, in the Tudor uniform colours of green and white. The officers dressed in accordance with their status. The quartermasters, the boatswain, the cook and the carpenter, and probably the master gunner as well, would have ranked as yeomen on a big ship such as this, and would have worn clothes of better quality, but not very different in design. The higher officers, on the other hand, such as the captain, the master and the lieutenant, would have been gentlemen, and would have worn fine-quality wool of richer colour and design, with silks and velvets for special occasions. All ranks would have worn such personal adornments and jewellery as they could afford, and often carried their spare cash (if any) in this form. The captain and the master had quite spacious cabins, but lesser officers, such as the surgeon and the carpenter, had little cubbyholes, and the men, seamen and soldiers alike, slept wherever they could find space for a straw palliasse, and kept their modest belongings in portable chests. It would be nearly a century before hammocks came into general use.

Food was always a problem, and drink even more so. The victuallers needed to be watched like hawks to ensure that they provided full measure, and did not recycle old stock. Ships like the *Mary Rose*, which rarely left home waters and were seldom at sea for more than two or three weeks at a time, had nothing like the difficulties suffered by the longer voyagers of later in the century, but it was tough enough. It was hard to find supplies until the system was reorganized after 1550, and harder still to get the supplies to where they were needed. The standard diet was simple, and reasonably nutritious, but it was dull and lacked certain vital ingredients. The main provisions were bread, or biscuit, cheese, butter, bacon, salted beef, dried or salted fish, and beer. The rations allowed were ample, but the absence of fresh fruit and vegetables encouraged diseases such as scurvy, and both the biscuit and the beer tended to deteriorate rapidly, even if they were shipped in good condition. The pursers of individual ships made their own supplementary purchases, and the officers and their servants bought their provisions to suit themselves. Consequently, the presence of fruit stones and chicken bones among the detritus of the wreck does not prove that such

A precise replica of the brick galley found on board. This reconstruction and experimental archaeology have shown that the structure was adaptable enough to cook plain fare for the crew and finer meals for the officers. (*C.T.C. Dobbs/Mary Rose Trust*)

superior rations were on general offer. Food was prepared in a galley, and cooked in a massive brick oven housed in the bowels of the ship, where the almost permanent fire not only guaranteed hot meals (a very important consideration), but also enabled wet clothes to be dried when there was no sun on deck. These ovens were a feature of all large ships, and needed very careful and skilled management if disaster were to be avoided.

A large warship such as the *Mary Rose* carried a barber surgeon, who also had to double as a physician, and the formidable equipment of this gentleman is one of the best-known features of the Mary Rose Trust's museum. He was there primarily, of course, to treat the injuries suffered in battle, but it is clear that he also had a general responsibility for the health of the crew. Tudor medicine was primitive, but not totally ineffective, and there are very few references to outbreaks of disease on this ship. We know that plague broke out on Lord Lisle's ships in 1545, and even more severely at the end of the Armada campaign, but there are no records of similar outbreaks on the *Mary Rose* during its working life. This has probably got most to do with never operating far from base, and putting sick men ashore as soon as their condition was known, but it may also have been a result of generally good discipline. Hygiene was little understood in theory, but an experienced seaman knew that keeping himself and his immediate environment as clean as possible was the best way to stay healthy. With so many men cramped together, waste disposal of all kinds must have required constant vigilance. There was no difficulty about where to put it – it went over the side – but making sure that the containers were regularly emptied, and cleaned after use, must have been one of the ship's more necessary and less desirable jobs. Even so, there were limits to what could be achieved. It's known that the ship had rats and that the men had fleas, but that would have been equally true of houses ashore. By modern standards the living conditions would have been squalid; but as the men did not desert, and showed no marked reluctance to serve in her, it must be assumed that she had the reputation of being a reasonably good ship.

Although a carrack was a labour-intensive ship, the men did not spend all their time at work or asleep. Apart from the officers, very few would have been literate, but the survival of dice, gaming boards and musical instruments provides evidence of how they passed their leisure time. It is also clear that many of them were devout. Rosary beads and small votive objects testify to a flourishing traditional piety. There was probably no priest on board the *Mary Rose* when she sank, but that would have been because she had only just left harbour, and was not expected to be out for long, rather than because there was no need of one. Normally a large ship that was to be at sea for more than a few days would have carried at least one cleric, capable of saying mass, hearing confessions and administering the last rites. There would have been no specially dedicated place for the performance of these rituals; a space was cleared on an appropriate deck when any significant number of men gathered together for that purpose. When the remains of one of those who perished in the wreck had been recovered, he was appropriately interred in Portsmouth Cathedral with the Sarum rite in use in 1545.

The Ship

The *Mary Rose* was a four-masted ship, of the type known as a carrack. This design had been pioneered in the previous century by the Portuguese, and was used particularly for their large East-Indiamen. The main characteristics of the carrack were its deep draught, and its high-built castles, fore and aft. In the days before the general use of heavy guns, these castles were valuable bases from which to launch boarding attacks down onto an enemy deck, and were easily defensible. Carracks still had their advocates as late as the end of the sixteenth century, because they were so hard to board. At the same time, the castles made them unweatherly, and difficult to handle in a high wind. The praises heaped on the sailing qualities of the *Mary Rose* were relative, and should be taken with a pinch of salt. This design was not new to England, as the *Regent* and the *Sovereign* had pioneered it over twenty years previously, but there do seem to have been some new features. It is now thought that the *Mary Rose*, unlike its predecessors, was carvel-built from the start, that is to say that the planking of her hull was laid edge to edge and caulked, instead of overlapping, or clinker-built. Such a method was not traditional to northern shipwrights, and had been borrowed from the Mediterranean. To accommodate the guns listed in the 1514 inventory, she must have been built with a number of gunports. Such ports create difficulties in a clinker-built ship, where the hull depends for its strength very largely upon the integrity of its planking shell. However, they raise no problems with a carvel build, because the strength derives entirely from the frame.

The displacement of the original ship was somewhere between 500 and 600 tons. It is difficult to be sure because, of course, the surviving hull is that reconstructed in about 1536. This 'new building' seems to have been fairly drastic but (as was often the case) not to have resulted in what was effectively a new ship. The tonnage was increased to about 700, but this does not appear to have been achieved by lengthening or widening the hull. Rather, the hull seems to have been strengthened, a substantial number of new gunports added, and the castles raised. The result was to make the *Mary Rose* a much more formidable fighting machine, but to reduce her sailing qualities still further. She may have become less tolerant of extreme angles of heel, or shifts in the distribution of weight, and it is perhaps significant that there was no further praise of her handiness after the rebuild. Instead, on 18 April 1537 Vice-Admiral John Dudley reported to the King that some of his ships were proving unweatherly, and that 'the ship that Mr Carew is in' was a particular offender, which might have to be withdrawn. George Carew was captain of the *Mary Rose* at the time of her loss eight years later, and Dudley clearly thought that his news would upset the King. None of this proves that the unweatherly ship was the *Mary Rose*, but the King might well have been upset to discover that he had ordered modifications to a prized ship which had made her potentially vulnerable.

We have ordnance inventories for both 1514 and 1546 (the latter being the Anthony Roll, compiled the year after the sinking), so it is relatively easy to work out what difference the rebuilding had made to the ship's firepower. In 1514 she carried 77 guns, but only 6 can be classed as anti-ship rather than anti-personnel weapons: the 5 great curtals and 1 murderer. In the 1546 inventory she is listed with 91 guns, of which 26 can be classified as anti-ship; these comprise 14 cast-bronze guns from the cannon and culverin classes, and 12 large wrought-iron port-pieces. All were put on board after 1535, because they bear subsequent dates. However, the Anthony Roll inventory may not be an accurate record of the armament on board when the ship was lost. She was also there said to be carrying 250 longbows (as opposed to 123 in 1514), 50 handguns (or hackbuts) and 30 swivel guns.

For about three years the *Mary Rose* was the 'star' of Henry VIII's navy. She was not the largest ship, but she was new and state-of-the-art. Then in 1514 she was eclipsed (too late to affect her role in the war) by the massive *Henry Grace à Dieu* of 1,200 tons. Thereafter, this ship, popularly called the *Great Harry* was the natural flagship when the navy was deployed at full strength. However, she was too large, and too expensive, to be used for routine duties, and the Admiral's flag continued to be carried on the *Mary Rose* for many operations. In spite of her rebuild, she was no longer a modern ship by 1545, and was just one of six or eight large warships which the King could deploy, but Henry retained a soft spot for her, and was considerably upset by her loss.

THE LETTERS

At the core of this collection are twenty-one letters (beginning with **12**) and one other document (**34**) specifically dated aboard the *Mary Rose* on active service during the wars of 1512–14 and 1522–3. Another seven letters are presumed to have been similarly written; a few related despatches are also included. All this material is printed in full, much of it for the first time. There are no letters from the *Mary Rose* during her last campaign in 1545; we do, however, have several concerning the original salvage attempt, from which all relevant extracts are given here. Of the mass of accounts, warrants, bills and other documents in which the ship is mentioned, we can present only a representative selection. Almost all the texts here are taken from original manuscripts in the Public Record Office or the British Library. With a few exceptions (**7, 44, 57–8**) these sources are calendared in the *Letters and Papers, Foreign and Domestic, of the Reign of Henry VIII*, published between 1862 and 1932, or in other guides to the

An inkwell made of horn, recovered from the wreck. (*Mary Rose Trust*)

State Papers. Those versions are, necessarily, only editorial summaries of the letters, and much more abbreviated listings of the accounts and other papers. A few of the early letters were printed in full and in original spelling by Sir Henry Ellis in his *Original Letters Illustrative of English History* (1824–46). Some were similarly given by Alfred Spont in *Letters and Papers Relating to the War with France, 1512–13*, issued by the Navy Records Society in 1897; Spont also included many documents from the French archives, not in *Letters and Papers . . . Henry VIII*. A collection of documentary and literary sources for the history of the *Mary Rose* herself was first assembled by S. Horsey; his *Narrative of the Loss of the Mary Rose* was published at Portsea in boards made from timber recovered from the wreck. The original edition is dated 1842, but appears to have been issued two years later. An undated 'second edition' (identical in content but in larger format) followed. Horsey received assistance from Sir Frederic Madden, Keeper of Manuscripts at the British Museum, and himself a Portsmouth man. Madden was to be instrumental in securing for the Museum the second section of Anthony Anthony's illuminated inventory of Henry VIII's fleet and its ordnance, completed in 1546. The first section of this MS, now in the Pepysian Library at Magdalene College, Cambridge, contains the only contemporary illustration of the *Mary Rose* (**58** and colour plate 7). Horsey's little book was reprinted by the Clarendon Press, Ventnor, in 1975, but has long been unobtainable.

While the present edition is indebted to these earlier works, it aims to make a much larger body of material more widely accessible. All the texts are given in modern spelling, including place and personal names where established; this treatment is used for the extracts from contemporary printed books as well as in transcribing the MSS. In making these modernized versions, all the originals have been consulted, and occasional improvements have been made to the texts given in Spont and elsewhere. A few simple archaic forms (as 'hath', 'cometh') are retained where they do not readily convert to the rhythms of the modern language, or if (as 'Hampton' for Southampton, 'Preer John' for Prégent de Bidoux) colloquialisms remain appropriate. Words confidently supplied because of damage to the MSS are printed in roman type within square brackets. Words in italic within square brackets are editorial insertions which identify individuals or places, explain what may be unfamiliar in vocabulary, or supply what may be defective or difficult in the syntax. Italic is also used for words which can only be conjectured from a damaged original. Otherwise dots are used within square brackets to show where text is lost. This applies particularly to the several letters from the British Library's Cotton MSS, which have been severely cropped by fire.

Wherever the bracketing indicates that only a part of a word can now be read, the arrangement can often be only approximate because of the modernization of the spelling. Dots not within brackets indicate editorial omissions. MS deletions and insertions are indicated only where the changes are substantive.

A Key to Documents (Appendix I) gives the MS and other bibliographical references. The List of Persons (Appendix II) provides biographical notes for many of the individuals mentioned; briefer identifications are given in the Index. The Glossary (Appendix III) explains technical terms.

1

THE BUILDING AND EQUIPPING OF
THE SHIP (1510–14)

COMMENTARY

It is not known exactly when, where, or by whom, the *Mary Rose* was built. There is a reference to four unnamed 'new ships' being fitted out at Southampton in December 1509, and if the *Mary Rose* was one of them, then she must have been laid down before April 1509; in other words the decision to build her must have been taken by Henry VII rather than Henry VIII. However, it is probable that these were much smaller vessels, and that the true date of the laying down of the *Mary Rose* and her sister ship the *Peter Pomegranate* was January 1510, represented by the warrant of the 29th (**1**). Neither ship is named, for the simple reason that names would not have been given at this early stage. Nor do the tonnages match those ultimately achieved; as they were eventually launched the *Mary* was about 600 tons and the *Peter* about 450, but tonnage measurement was notoriously inaccurate at that date, and if the ships were still in building the displacement was probably mere guesswork. The warrant, of course, does not represent more than a small fraction of the cost, and the reference to rigging suggests that the building was already well advanced. Ships of this size cost in the region of £3,000 at this time, a figure which should be multiplied by 1,000 to get an approximate modern equivalent. At a time when the King's ordinary annual revenue was about £100,000 a year, they represented a substantial investment. This cost would have been met by a series of warrants of this kind, drawn on a variety of different revenue

1

sources. This one is an assignment on the customs revenues of the port of Southampton, but others would been assigned on London, or drawn directly from the Exchequer or the Duchy of Lancaster.

Southampton was convenient, because honouring the assignment would have meant transporting cash in the shape of gold or silver coin, and it is almost certain from later references that the ships were built at Portsmouth. Robert Brigandine had been Clerk of the King's Ships since 1495, and knew most of what there was to know about the business. He was not trained to the sea, but had begun his career as a minor officer of the royal household. Henry VII had relied on him for advice on all matters relating to the ships, and he was clearly responsible for the building of the *Mary* and the *Peter*, but exactly what that meant is more difficult to say. Brigandine paid the bills, but he was not a master shipwright. Whether he was responsible for the design, and the shipwrights worked to his instructions, or he was merely the site manager and the shipwrights themselves were responsible for the design, we do not know. The latter is more likely, because they would have lacked the status to claim the credit – and as far as we are aware, no one ever did. Brigandine divided his time between Portsmouth and Woolwich, but was increasingly located at the former, and seems to have been working there throughout the time when these ships were being built.

It is reasonable to deduce that Portsmouth was the principal royal dockyard at this time, because work on the *Regent* and the *Sovereign*, both large warships and about twenty years old at this point, was being carried out at the same time, and also under Brigandine's supervision. The indenture, or contract, over which the Clerk was concerned in June 1511 (**2**) probably marks the end of the construction process. The sum of £1,075 14s 2d may well represent the whole cost of renovating the older ships, but £1,016 13s 4d would have been only the last instalment for the new constructions (**3**). The warrants for the balance do not appear to have survived. When the *Peter* was first launched, she seems to have been very similar to the *Sovereign*, and designed in the same way to carry a substantial number of small guns. It was only later that she was rebuilt to carry heavier weapons. The *Mary*, however, carried heavy guns from the start; not many, probably six or eight, but they necessitated a design feature which was new to the point of being revolutionary – the gunport. Whether she was actually the first warship to be built in this way, is not known; nor who was responsible for the idea. Ports had been used for loading purposes before, and seem to have originated in Brittany. It has been suggested that the King himself insisted on the *Mary* being built in this way, and his known interest in both ships and guns

The Tudor rose, surrounded by the Garter and topped by the closed imperial crown; with, below the King's monogram 'HR' (*'Henricus Rex'*). This mark of royal ownership appears on this demi-cannon recovered from the *Mary Rose*. (*Mary Rose Trust*)

makes that plausible; but Henry is not known for being inventive, and it seems likely that he got the idea from somewhere else, most likely France, although it is possible that he was already emulating his brother-in-law James IV of Scotland, as he was to do in 1514 with the *Henry Grace à Dieu*.

Although there is no record of the launch, it clearly occurred in the summer of 1511. The ships would have been named at that time; by 9 June they are known as the *Mary Rose* and the *Peter Pomegranate*. It was quite usual to give ships the names of saints, and in this case such names seem to have been combined with two well-known Tudor badges, the rose for the King and the pomegranate for the Queen. It is also possible that the former name was a recognition of the fact that the Virgin was traditionally known as the 'mystic rose'. It is often said that the ship was named after, if not actually by, the King's sister, but there is no evidence for this.

By the beginning of July the two new warships were afloat in Portsmouth harbour, awaiting a move to the Thames, where the guns would be loaded and the final fitting-out would take place. It seems from the accounts of Sir John Daunce that the *Mary*, at least, proceeded under her own sails, rather than being towed (**4**). Brigandine would have recruited the mariners, and it looks as though he paid them the bulk of their wages in advance, although that would have been unusual. The number of mariners is not mentioned, but the total cost was £170. A sailor was paid 5*s* a month, plus his victuals, and the officers significantly more, so if these crews were hired for a month, the number in the two ships would have been between 300 and 350, which would be about right at contemporary manning levels. It seems as though the journey from Portsmouth to the Thames also marked the commissioning, or handing over, of the ship to the King's agents, because from then on the bills were paid directly by the Exchequer. John Clerke appears to have been appointed master for the transit voyage only, because Thomas Sperte, who was the first regular master when the ship passed into service, had already taken over by the middle of October.

The last stages in the equipping of the *Mary Rose* can be roughly reconstructed from the same accounts. Stocks or carriages were most likely prepared specifically for the guns which each ship would carry, and therefore would remain on the ship when the guns were removed at the end of a period of service. What the 'stuff' may have been for the decking and rigging, can only be surmised. Most of both must have been already in place when the ship was sailed from Portsmouth, and it may have been the spare canvas, rope and timber necessary for running repairs in service which was acquired at this late stage. Last of all came the flags, both numerous and splendid, as can be seen from later inventories and from the illustrations in the Anthony Roll. The great streamer, which was flown from the mainmast on special occasions, was 51 yards long, in the Tudor colours of green and white. John Browne painted and stained flags of St George, and of the King's arms, flags blazoned with the King and Queen's various badges, and possibly some depicting the Virgin and the various devices associated with her. In November 1511 Henry joined the

Holy League of Pope Julius II and Ferdinand of Aragon, against France, and on the 24th Thomas Sperte rendered his last account for equipping his ship. She was now ready for action in the forthcoming war.

DOCUMENTS

1. *Privy seal warrant to the Exchequer for reimbursement of payments from John Dawtrey, customer of Southampton, to Robert Brigandine, Clerk of the King's Ships, 29 January 1510.*
  The 'two new ships', as yet unnamed, will be the Mary Rose *and her sister the* Peter Pomegranate. *The whole sum is assigned on the customs revenues of the port of Southampton.*

Henry, by the grace of God, King of England and of France and Lord of Ireland, to the Treasurer and Chamberlains of our Exchequer, greeting. Whereas our wellbeloved servant John Dawtrey, one of our customers of our port of Southampton, hath delivered and paid by our commandment to our servant Robert Brigandine, Clerk of our Ships, for the reapparelling of our ship called the *Regent* £180 4s 5d; also the said John Dawtrey by our like commandment hath delivered and paid unto the said Robert Brigandine, Clerk of our Ships, for the repairing and new making of our ship called the *Sovereign* £1,175 14s 2d; also the said John Dawtrey by our like commandment hath delivered and paid unto the said Robert Brigandine, Clerk of our said Ships, for timber, ironwork, and workmanship of two new ships to be made for us £700, and the one ship to be of the burthen of 400 tons and the other ship to be of the burthen of 300 tons; and also the said John Dawtrey by our like commandment hath delivered and paid unto the said Robert Brigandine, Clerk of our said Ships three hundred and sixteen pounds thirteen shillings and four pence for all manner of implements and necessaries to the same two ships belonging as particularly hereafter ensueth, first for sails, twine, marline, ropes, cables, cablets, shrouds, hawsers, buoy ropes, stays, sheets, buoy lines, tacks, lifts, top armours, streamers, standards, compasses, running glasses, tankards, bowls, dishes, lanterns, shivers of brass and pulleys for the said two new ships, victuals and wages of men for setting up of their masts, shrouds and all other tacklings for the said two new ships, which said several sums will extend in the whole to the sum of two thousand three hundred threescore and twelve pounds eleven shillings and eleven pence, for the which sum our said servant John Dawtrey as yet hath not had of us any manner of discharge by reason whereof

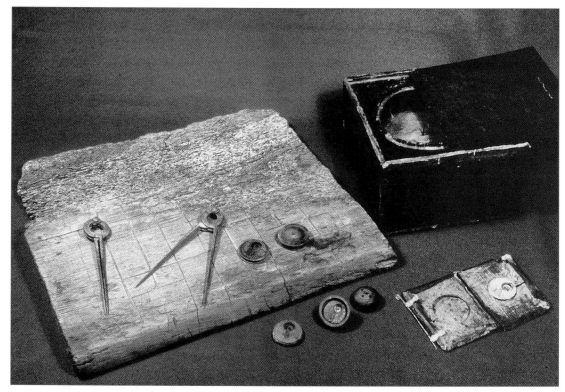

Two pairs of dividers, a compass and three sundials. The wooden board may also be a navigational aid, or simply used for gaming. (*Mary Rose Trust*)

he may proceed unto his accounts which he is in yielding before the Barons of our Exchequer; we, willing him to be sufficiently discharged of the said sum of two thousand three hundred threescore and 12 pounds eleven shillings and eleven pence as right and conscience re[*quir*]eth, wherefore we will and command you our said Treasurer and Chamberlains that you in due form do [*cause*] to be levied one tally or tallies containing the said sum of £2,372 11*s* 11*d* upon the said John Dawtrey and Thomas Wodeshawe as late customers in our said port of Southampton of the customs and subsidies grown within the same port to us due at Michaelmas last past; and the said tally or tallies in due and sufficient form levied, we will that you deliver unto the said John Dawtrey in discharging of his said accounts without prest or any other charge to be set upon the said John Dawtrey and Thomas Wodeshawe for the same. And for your indemnity herein, we will that you make issue of the said sum of £2,372 11*s* 11*d* as money paid by the said John Dawtrey unto the said Robert Brigandine, Clerk of our said Ships, by our said commandment for the causes above expressed. And these our letters shall be your sufficient warrant and discharge in that behalf. Given under our privy seal at our palace of Westminster the 29 day of January the first year of our reign.

Authorized by the King's Sign Manual initial: H.
Counter-signed by the duty Clerk of the Privy Seal: [William] Purde.

2. *Robert Brigandine to Richard Palshide, customer (customs officer) of Southampton, 9 June [1511].*
   This letter contains the earliest extant reference to the Mary Rose *by name. Although undated as to year, it is evidently answered by the indenture of 30 June 1511 which follows.*

Right worshipful sir, I heartily recommend me unto you, daily desiring to hear of your good welfare, furthermore desiring your mastership that for the indenture of parchment that I delivered unto you there may be made another new, extending to the whole sum of money as it specifieth of bearing the date and time according; but whereas it specifieth several sums of money, so much to the *Sovereign* spent and so much to the *Mary Rose* and *Peter Pomegranate*, I would not have it so, but the said whole sum of the indenture delivered by Master Dawtrey and by you unto me in general, as well for the repairing of the *Sovereign* as for the new making of the *Mary Rose* and *Peter Pomegranate* jointly together, and moreover that it will please you I may be recommended unto Master Dawtrey, desiring his mastership and you both that I may have the copy of the warrant whereby I received money of you for the keeping and for certain reparations done on the *Regent* in Ludovico de La Fava his time, and in as goodly haste as may be possible you would vouchsafe that the said indenture, and also copy of the warrant may be delivered unto the bringer hereof [or to my wife or John Peryn (I) pray you *inserted*] for the expedition of my account, as my very especial trust is in your mastership, as knoweth God, whom I beseech preserve you and all yours. Amen. Written at Woolwich, the 9th day of the month of June.
   By your own Robert Brigandine, Clerk of the Ships.
   Minuted: Master Brigandine, the indenture you write for is in my coffer of iron at London, where no man can see it till my coming thither by no means, but I shall be always ready to follow and to fulfil your desire therein as for it is all one to me.

Yours, J. Dawtrey.

3. *Indenture witnessing receipt by Brigandine from Dawtrey, 30 June 1511.*

This indenture made the last day of June in the third year of the reign of our sovereign lord King Harry the VIIIth betwixt John Dawtrey, one of the customers of our said sovereign lord the King of the port of Southampton on that one part and Robert Brigandine, Clerk of the King's Ships, on that other part, witnesseth that I the said John Dawtrey have delivered to the said Robert Brigandine at divers times for the new making of the King's ship called the *Sovereign* a thousand a hundred threescore and fifteen pounds fourteen shillings and two pence, and also for the new making of two other new ships for the King's grace, one of 300 tons and the other of 400 tons – a thousand sixteen pounds thirteen shillings and four pence. Sum of all – £2,192 7s 6d. In witness whereof the parties abovesaid to these present indentures interchangeable have set their seals the day and year aforesaid.

John Dawtrey.

4. *Extracts from the accounts of Sir John Daunce, a teller of the Exchequer, July–December 1511.*

    These include the first references to the Mary Rose *at sea.*

29th day of July. Also paid by our commandment to Robert Brigandine, Clerk of our Ships, towards the charges of the conveyance of our two new ships from Portsmouth unto the River of Thames, the one of them called the *Mary Rose* and the other called the *Peter Pomegranate* – £120.

    20th day of September. Also paid by our commandment to Robert Brigandine, Clerk of our Ships, towards the charges of [the King's *deleted*] our two new ships, the one of them called the *Mary Rose* and the other the *Peter Pomegranate* now lying upon Thames – £50.

    24th day of September. Also paid by our commandment to Richard Palshide, one of our customers in our port of Southampton, these parcels ensuing: first, for 24 coats of white and green for 24 soldiers for the sure conducting of our ship called the *Mary Rose* from Portsmouth to the Thames of London, and 6 coats of white and green for the master, 4 quartermasters and the boatswain, at 6s 10d the coat – £10 5s. Item for the wages of the said 24 soldiers by the space of one month and a half, at 5s a man by the month – £9. Item for the reward of the said Richard Palshide for his attendance upon the said ship – 40s. Item for the reward of John Clerke, master of our said ship – 20s. In all – £22 5s.

1st day of October. Also paid by our commandment to Cornelis Johnson, gunmaker, towards the new stocking and repairing of divers pieces of [our *inserted*] ordnance of [the King's *deleted*] four of our ships now being in Thames, the one called the *Mary and John*, the other the *Anne of London*, the other the *Mary Rose* and another the *Peter Pomegranate* – £20. Item for 8 loads of elm for stocking of the said ordnance, at 4s the load – 32s. In all – £21 12s.

18th day of October. Also paid by our commandment to Thomas Sperte, master of our ship called the *Mary Rose*, and David Boner, purser of the same ship, by indenture for all manner of stuff needful to be had for the decking and rigging of the same ship – £66 13s 4d.

17th day of December. Also paid by our commandment to William Botrys of London, mercer, upon a bill signed with the hand of Sir Edward Howard, knight, for certain tukes, buckrams, Brussels cloths and camlets of the said William bought for to make streamers and banners for the use of our ships called the *Mary Rose* and *Peter Pomegranate* – £50 19s 2d.

Also paid by our commandment to John Browne of London, painter, upon a book of parcels signed with the hand of Sir Edward Howard, knight, for painting and staining of certain banners and streamers for the use of our ships called the *Mary Rose* and *Peter Pomegranate* – £142 4s 6d [½d *deleted*].

18th day of December. Also paid by our commandment to Thomas Sperte, master of our ship called the *Mary Rose*, upon his account made and determined before Sir Edward Howard, knight, the [29 *deleted*] 24 day of November the third year of our reign, for all manner of charges concerning our said ship due upon the said account – 29s 1¼d.

[*To several of the pages of this book of accounts the King has added his Sign Manual: Henry R.*]

2

THE WAR WITH FRANCE TO THE DEATH OF SIR EDWARD HOWARD (APRIL 1512–APRIL 1513)

COMMENTARY

Henry's desire for war in 1511 was personal rather than political. He had no particular grievance against Louis XII, but he did have a strong desire to emulate his illustrious predecessor, Henry V, and to re-establish English control over at least a part of France. This was mainly because he was nineteen years old, and full of physical vigour and ambition; but it was also partly because he wanted to emancipate himself from his father's old councillors, most of whom opposed the idea. Henry wanted glory, and trophies to lay at the feet of his new bride, Catherine of Aragon. He may also have been aware that a new generation of nobles had grown up in England, who shared his aspirations. War was what noblemen did, and for a whole generation their ambitions had been thwarted, and their finances pressurized, by the pacific and suspicious policies of the old King. So Henry's intention was not entirely quixotic; he was also about to 'busy giddy minds with foreign wars', in case some of the same 'giddy minds' might be tempted to work out their frustrations on him.

The King mobilized his fleet between January and April (**5**). Altogether he prepared seventeen ships for action, but only three of them were his own: the *Regent*, the *Mary Rose* and the *Peter Pomegranate*. He had taken a small Scottish prize, the *Lion*, in 1511, and later in 1512 he was to buy two large Genoese carracks, the *Gabriel Royal* and the *Katherine Fortileza*, but none of these was included in this fleet, which mainly consisted of armed merchantmen varying from 70 to 400 tons burthen. Sir Edward Howard was appointed Admiral of the fleet on 7 April and given detailed instructions; and although the *Regent* was the largest ship available to him, he chose the brand new *Mary Rose* as his flagship. The King took his oath on 16 April, and dispatched £6,000 to John Dawtrey at Southampton to cover the expenses of the fleet in the forthcoming campaign. For a couple of weeks Howard did little but terrorize French fishing boats and Flemish merchants (who were supposed to be allies), but this was mainly because he held the initiative and no French warships had yet put to sea. In other words he had secured command of the English Channel without even the semblance of a fight.

One of the Flemings he appears to have terrorized was Jacques Berenghier of Lille. Margaret of Savoy, the Regent of the Netherlands, wrote a letter complaining that a grievous wrong had been done to her subject (**6**), while the articles against Berenghier accused him of an act of sabotage which endangered both his shipmates and his ship (**7**). In fact the two statements are not incompatible, as the articles do not explain how the Fleming came to be a gunner on the *Mary John*, and the Regent's letter does not even allude to the offences for which he had been punished. It is quite likely that he was press-ganged in the manner alleged, and endeavoured to get his own back by sabotaging the guns entrusted to his care. The relevance of the case in this context is that Berenghier was tried by Howard on board the *Mary Rose*, using his ex officio jurisdiction as Admiral. It seems very unlikely that he would have been pressed into service, and given a responsible position, because he was mistaken for a Frenchman. The French were, after all, the enemy, and Lille was not, at that time, in France.

The actual service of the *Mary Rose* during the remainder of this eventful summer is only thinly reflected in these summary accounts. No doubt Howard wrote dispatches from his flagship, as he was to do in the following year, but they have not survived. Early in June he escorted the Marquess of Dorset's ill-fated expedition to Guyenne as far as Ushant, but saw no action in the process. Throughout July and early August he 'kept the seas', capturing merchant ships and filling in the time until the French King had got his sea power together. About 5 or 6 August word reached Howard at Portsmouth that the French had at last assembled at Brest, and he set off to give battle. This was not what René de Clermont, the French Admiral, was expecting, because the normal tactic in sea-fighting up to that point had been to manoeuvre to keep the weather gage of your enemy, hold your fleet together, and hope that your victuals and the health of your crews lasted better than his. Maintaining control of a fleet was so taxing in itself that battle was best avoided. However, Howard came looking for a fight, and caught the French unawares about 2 or 3 miles outside Brest harbour, on the morning of 10 August. A detailed description of the resulting action survives, but it is not a first hand account, and makes no mention of the *Mary Rose*. It is contained in a letter written a few days later by Thomas Wolsey, who must have obtained it from an eyewitness. The most spectacular outcome of a messy and otherwise inconclusive engagement was the mutual destruction of two of the largest ships, the *Regent* and the *Cordelière*, both of about 1,000 tons, when the latter's magazine exploded as they grappled together. Over 1,000 men perished in this disaster, which made a huge impression on everyone.

Thereafter, the French retreated into Brest, and Howard signalled a somewhat equivocal victory by scouring the coast of Brittany, until shortage of victuals compelled him to retreat at the end of August. The French fleet disbanded in early September, having accomplished precisely nothing for a huge expenditure of money and effort. The English campaign account was wound up at the end of September, when it appears that Howard was allowed for 400 men on the *Mary Rose* (**8**). As this figure included about 35 'deadpays', in accordance with established custom, the actual complement of soldiers, seamen and gunners would have been 365. However, there were also 47 men present who were not allowed for in the official calculations: 31 servants of the Admiral, and 16 of the captain of the ship, Sir Thomas Wyndham. It was proper and normal for an aristocratic officer to take his own servants to sea, but presumably they had not been declared in advance. They were paid like the rest. The ship was then brought round to the Thames estuary and, having unloaded her ordnance at Blackwall, was laid up 'aflote' in the new dock at Erith, where some minor repairs seem to have been undertaken. She was then left in the care of her master, Thomas Sperte, and nine other mariners as shipkeepers. This account runs only from 28 October to 25 November, but she was actually there until 11 February, when John Hopton's maintenance records come to an end, and preparations for the new campaigning season began (**9**). Hopton was a Gentleman Usher of the Chamber who had been involved with the King's ships for more than a decade. At some point earlier in 1512 he had been appointed to the newly created office of Clerk Comptroller. The intention appears to have been to confine Brigandine to Portsmouth, and to make Hopton responsible for the operations in the Thames and Medway.

In 1513 Louis XII was determined not to be taken by surprise. During the winter he had introduced a new element into his armoury by bringing six war galleys from the Mediterranean under the veteran commander Prégent de Bidoux. On 13 March Prégent set out to raid the English coast, but was frustrated by bad weather. Apart from the galleys, there was at this time little to choose between the mobilization times of the two fleets. The new French Admiral, du Chillou, left Honfleur in Normandy at almost exactly the same time as Howard left the Thames, on about 20 March. On this occasion the English had the advantage of numbers. Henry had strained every nerve to acquire more ships of his own, and the fleet of 28 which Howard commanded included only 5 armed merchantmen. Du Chillou had 16, plus Prégent's 6 galleys. In spite of their light construction, and lack of seaworthiness, the latter posed a serious threat to sailing warships, even large ones, because they were armed with heavy forward-firing guns, known as basilisks. Early in March the Lord Admiral of England, the Earl of Oxford, died, and on the 19th Sir Edward Howard was appointed in his place; so it was with greatly enhanced status (if not much more actual power) that he set off on this new campaign. The English ships were well manned and armed, but the victualling was less organized, as Howard's letter, assumed to be of 19 March, makes clear (**12**). Wolsey was in charge of the logistics, and he was normally efficient, but in this respect he was struggling and the fleet set out inadequately provisioned, with serious consequences later on. Resupplying at sea, using small victuallers, was a bold and innovative solution, but only partially successful.

Howard's first shipboard dispatch to the King, dated 22 March, describes the fleet's progress from the Thames estuary to the Downs, off the Kentish coast (**13**). It is racy and circumstantial, but in this context mainly notable for its praise of the sailing qualities of the *Mary Rose*, 'the noblest ship of sail . . . at this hour that I trow be in Christendom'. This was no doubt why he continued to use her as his flagship; but the comment may also have been intended to please Henry, who seems to have been fond of this ship from the beginning. Perhaps he had had some say in her design (as he did later for the *Great Galley*), and such remarks were a subtle compliment to his skill. By 5 April Howard had reached Plymouth, and was itching for a fight (**14**). The 100 sail with which he was allegedly confronted was almost certainly a wild exaggeration, even if the smallest support ships were included, and did not dent his confidence at all. Victuals, however, continued to be a nagging problem, and were the main theme of this last dispatch before he engaged with the enemy. He sailed on 10 April, and any French ships at sea retreated into Brest as he advanced, a tactic which he typically attributed to cowardice, but which was in fact no more than traditional caution. By the 12th the whole French fleet, now numbered at fifty sail, had adopted a strong defensive position under the guns of the fortifications of Brest (**15**); the galleys, however, were separated, a little further down the coast. The Admiral continued to fret about his supplies, and about the 'Spanish ships', which were actually under command of English captains and because of various delays, never joined him at all. On the 13th he landed an amphibious force near Crozon, partly to threaten Brest from the landward side, and partly to forage for victuals, but it achieved little, and by this time the French fleet, apart from the galleys, was firmly blockaded in Brest (**16**). Howard appeared to make light of the threat from Prégent de Bidoux, and in that, as events were to show, he was seriously mistaken.

A probing attack on the harbour resulted in the loss of one ship, the *Nicholas of Hampton*, commanded by Arthur Plantagenet (Edward IV's base-born son), which struck a concealed rock. Realizing the hazards of operating without local knowledge, the English retreated to Bertheaume Bay, and Howard was now confronted with a critical dilemma. His supplies were almost exhausted, and he could not keep his fleet on station much longer to blockade the port. On the other hand, to retreat with nothing accomplished would have been an unspeakable dishonour, as well as (probably) costing him the King's favour. On the 22nd Prégent made up the Admiral's mind for him: his galleys attacked, sinking one English ship and badly damaging another. Howard decided to take out the galleys; then he could at least retreat with honour. They were backed into a strong anchorage, and Howard decided to attempt an outflanking movement ashore, and a frontal attack from the sea. Unfortunately he lacked the necessary shallow-draught ships for the latter operation, having only a couple of rowbarges and a number of ships' boats. With more valour than discretion, on the morning of 25 April he attacked, leading his insufficient force in person. His panache allowed him to come within an ace of success, but having boarded Prégent's own galley, he was inadequately supported, and was cut off and killed. Whether he died fighting, or was thrust overboard and drowned by his armour is not clear. His force fled in disarray, and the English fleet abandoned its campaign, retreating to Dartmouth, hungry and demoralized.

DOCUMENTS

5. *Extract from an account for charges for the first three months' service, 17 April–8 July 1512.*

Charges of the army and navy for the first 3 months beginning on Saturday the 17 day of April the third year of our sovereign lord King Henry the VIIIth and ending the 8th day of July the 4th year of his reign, as in victual, wages, deadshares and tonnage, as well of these 17 ships as other victuallers, crayers and other ships ensuing, some for less time as ensueth.

The *Mary Rose*. First to Sir Edward Howard, knight, chief captain and Admiral of the fleet, for his wages and victual at 10*s* a day, by the said 3 months amounting to – £42.

Also to Sir Thomas Wyndham, knight, for his victual and wages at 18*d* by the day, by the said 3 months – £6 6*s*.

Also for the wages [diet *deleted*] and victual of 2 lodesmen alias pilots, each of them at 20*s* a month, by the said 3 months – £6.

Also for victual of 411 [*men*], soldiers (251), mariners (120), gunners (20) and servitors (20) in the same ship, every man at 5*s* a month, by the said time – £308 5*s*.

Also for wages of the same 411 persons, every man at 5*s* a month, by the said time – £308 5*s*.

Also for 34 deadshares [*and*] half, at 5*s* a share, by the said time – £25 17*s* 6*d*.

Also for tonnage after 3*d* a ton a week, by the said time, 500 tons – nil, because the King's ship.

Sum – £696 13*s* 6*d*.

6. *Margaret of Savoy, Regent of the Netherlands, to Henry VIII, 15 September 1512. Summary.*

Jacques Berenghier of Lille, who went to England last Lent to trade, was seized on his return by Master Christopher, master of one of the King's ships, compelled to serve as a gunner, plundered of all his goods, taken for a Frenchman because he spoke the language, was racked by the captain Master Griffendon, and so lost a foot. Afterwards he was delivered to the Admiral and was long kept prisoner at Southampton, had his ears slit, and was threatened with hanging. The King will perceive by a certificate from the town of Lille that he is a native of that place, and of good repute. She desires reparation be made to him, and that such barbarities be not repeated. Antwerp, 15 September 1512.

7. *Articles against Jacques Berenghier, gunner in the* Mary John, *1512.*
An enquiry before the Admiralty Court, prompted by the Regent's complaint, established that the man had been found guilty by due process of an act of sabotage.

In the name of God Amen. All and singular the below-written articles, and each particular of them, the counsel of Sir Griffith Don, knight, gives, presents and instances against Jacques Berenghier.

First, that the said Sir Griffith Don, knight, in the months of April, May, June, July, August, September, October in the year of Our Lord one thousand

A bone carving of an angel, one of the few purely decorative objects recovered from the wreck. (*Mary Rose Trust*)

five hundred and twelve, and each of the said months, was captain of a ship called the *Mary John*, which was then with the fleet of the most excellent prince and lord, the most illustrious lord Henry, by the grace of God, King of England and France and Lord of Ireland, under the noble Sir Edward Howard, Admiral of the said fleet. Item that the said Jacques Berenghier was taken into the said ship by the said Sir Griffith in the place and duty of a gunner, and for the faithful exercising of his office in that part he received wages of the said most high prince, under the principal master gunner of the said ship, with obedience to the said Sir Griffith the captain of the same. Item that the said Jacques undertook the keeping of certain guns assigned to him in the said ship. Item that the said Jacques, the year and months aforesaid or one or other of them, falsely, wickedly, maliciously and fraudulently placed in certain of the said guns then in his custody two stones wrapped in thick cord, where it was not necessary or suitable to place more than one, so that many guns of these gunners in the said ship called the *Mary John*, being in battle with the enemies, were broken and fractured in such way that they could not harm the said enemies, and even some guns not committed to the said Jacques were charged with similar stones, to their destruction, by wicked deed of the said Jacques. Item that he had in his shoes certain gunpowder, very fine and light, with a certain little stone and an iron for striking light, notwithstanding the powder which he had in a horn hung from his neck, as the habit of gunners is. Item that because of the transgressions of the said John in the said office and duty committed to him, and further as a result of vehement accusations and enquiries, the said

16

A selection of items associated with a gunner including shot, shot gauge, powder scoop, ram, knife handle, together with a replica of his sleeveless jerkin. (*Mary Rose Trust*)

Jacques was arrested by Christopher Gybson, principal master gunner of the said ship, and by him and the said Sir Griffith the captain was sent to the said lord Admiral in the ship called the *Mary Rose*. Item that the said Admiral, having first examined the said Jacques on the foregoing, returned the said Jacques to the said Sir Griffith, so that he should strictly examine and detain him, and furthermore enquire by torture or otherwise if he had any companions or followers in the said transgression, or otherwise concerning the business of these guns. In certain of which guns the said Jacques was found to have placed two stones wrapped in thick cord where it was not necessary, as beforesaid, to place more than one stone, to the extent that by the operation of the said guns in battle with the enemies, many of the guns in the said ship were broken and fractured in such way that they could not, as aforesaid, harm the enemies. And likewise other guns not committed to him were charged and broken with similar stones, by the deed as aforesaid of the said Jacques. Item that the said Jacques was found to have in his shoes certain gunpowder, very fine and light, with a certain little stone and an iron for striking light, notwithstanding the powder which he had in a horn hung from his neck, as the habit of gunners is. Because of all which, not only on vehement accusation made, but by enquiries taken in law, he was put to torture and punished. Item that the said Jacques was returned by the said Sir Griffith to the said lord Admiral, who punished him by the authority lawfully given to him in that part, having had the opinion and advice of the officers of the said ship, who condemned him to have both his ears cut off, and to be wholly removed from the ship's company. Item that he who is detected in a similar transgression and is condemned for the same shall lose all his goods which he has with him, which being taken shall be applied to the chest. Item that the foregoing matters were all and singular true, notorious, manifest and well known throughout the whole said fleet and in other places.

8. *Extract from an estimate of charges for the second three months' service, 9 July–30 September 1512.*

A rate for wages, victual, tonnage, deadshares and other charges of [the King's] navy of 17 ships and the army of 3,000 men in them upon the sea etc. for 3 months as ensueth.

Also for the overcharges and excess of wages and victual of 31 men charged and being on Mr Howard's ship the *Mary Rose* over his first muster, with 16 of Thomas Wyndham's servants not roomed in his muster, with 5 trumpets and certain mariners and gunners, forasmuch as he is allowed for 400 men and hath 431 men, so in excess for 3 months past – £46 10s, and 3 months next to come – £46 10s, after 10s a man for wages and victual by the month of the said 31 men for 6 months – £93.

9. *Extract from an account of charges for four weeks, 28 October–25 November 1512.*

Here ensueth the expenses, costs and charges had and made by the King's great commandment for the King's ship named the *Mary Rose*, paid by the hands of John Hopton, as well the mariners that keepeth the said ship as of all manner of workmanship, provision of stuff, tackle and apparel with all other and sundry necessaries for the use and behoof of the said ship, from the 28 day of October unto the 25 day of November the year of the reign of our sovereign lord King Henry the VIIIth the next ensuing, by the space of 4 weeks, that is to say:

Wages of shipkeepers
Thomas Sperte, master mariner, taking for his wages 3s 4d the week, by the
    time of 4 weeks – 13s 4d.
Jeffray Hickes, taking for his wages 2s 3d the week, by the time of 4 weeks – 9s.
Thomas Colte, taking for his wages 15d the week, by the time of 4 weeks – 5s.
John Preston, taking for his wages 15d the week, by the time of 4 weeks – 5s.
Rallyn Cotte, taking for his wages 15d the week, by the time of 4 weeks – 5s.
Edmund Juller, taking for his wages 15d the week, by the time of 4 weeks – 5s.
Richard Farmer, taking for his wages 15d the week, by the time of 4 weeks – 5s.
Robert Colte, taking for his wages 15d the week, by the time of 4 weeks – 5s.
John Tomlyn, taking for his wages 15d the week, by the time of 4 weeks – 5s.
William Schipard, taking for his wages 15d the week, by the time of 4 weeks – 5s.
                    [Sum] – £3 2s 4d.

Lighterage. Also the said John Hopton hath paid unto John Dyer for lighterage of the ship's ordnance when that she lay in grounding at Blackwall by the space of 4 days – 6s 8d. So paid for the said [ship *deleted*] lighterage in time of this account in all, amounting to – 6s 8d.
Flags with St George's cross. Also there is paid by the said John Hopton unto John Browne, painter of London, for flags with St George's cross at 3s the piece, for 14 of them – 42s. So paid and delivered the same flags to the use and behoof of the said ship in time of this account in all amounting to – 42s.

10. *Warrant from Admiral Sir Edward Howard. Undated, but before 25 April 1513.*

Master Treasurer, deliver the master of the *Mary Rose* 27 deadshares and half, which John Daunce left unpaid for the first month. And this bill shall be your discharge. By me Edward Howard.

  £6 17s 6d.

11. *Extract from an account of expenses, February–April 1513.*

Mary Rose. Gunstones. Also the said John Hopton hath paid unto Nicholas Sesse for gunstones of iron with crossbars of iron in them at £19 the ton tight, one ton tight – £9. For one ton tight half of round gunstones of iron – £10. And in like wise to a man of Maidstone for gunstones of hewed stone at 13s 4d the 100, for 2,700 of them – £18. So by him paid and delivered the foresaid gunstones to the *Mary Rose* in time of this account, in all [*repetition*] amounting to – £37.

12. *Sir Edward Howard, Lord Admiral, to Thomas Wolsey, King's Almoner,*
[*19 March 1513*].
  The first of the letters written aboard the Mary Rose. *The Saturday on which it is dated is likely to be 19 March, the first after the patent by which Howard was confirmed as Admiral and leader of the ships in the army 'for the defence of the Roman see' (16 March). Cf. the chronology established in the next dispatch. Coincidentally, Howard's patent as Lord Admiral of England was issued on 19 March. The 'guest' he mentions was, of course, a prisoner; by 'well twitched', he was recommending stiff interrogation.*

Master Almoner, in my heartiest wise I can recommend me unto you. And I have received your letter, whereby I perceive that you have sent my fellow [*William*] Keby with a clerk with him to take a view how much victual we have here. Sir, without I should lose a tide, it cannot be. And you shall have as good a certainty there at London of the deliveries of the victual which have delivered the pursers upon their bills to them made as much victual as is come to our ships. And the most part of our pursers we have left them behind for hasting of the rest of our victual, by whom you shall be in a certainty. I have caused Keby to come to you again with all haste. And I have sent a guest up to the King that was taken in the *Maria de Loretta*. I pray you let him be well twitched, for I [*think*] well he can speak news. Sir, I have received the satin of Bruges. I shall order it as I shall think best to the King's honour and profit, and certify you by

Thomas Wolsey. This figure from the 'Judgement of Solomon' window in Fairford church, Gloucestershire (attributed to Barnard Flower), has been identified as Thomas Wolsey, the future Cardinal Archbishop of York, whose great career in church and state was founded on competence as a military and naval organizer. (*Dr H.G. Wayment*)

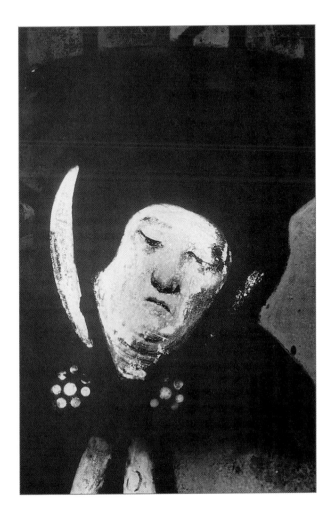

the next post when I am come to the Downs, and if you will anything with me, send it to the Downs.

Written in the *Mary Rose*, this Saturday by yours to my little power.

Edward Howard.

Endorsed: To Master Almoner be this delivered in haste.

13. *Sir Edward Howard to the King, 22 March 1513.*

This report, unfortunately now much damaged, presents a vivid image of Henry VIII's fleet at sea, and notably commends the sailing qualities of the Mary Rose. *By contrast the* Christ *is dangerously overloaded with ordnance. The Bristol ships mentioned were the* Trinity, Christopher Davy *and* Matthew Craddock. *The* Baptist of Harwich *was assigned as victualling tender to the* Mary Rose.

Pleaseth your grace to understand that the Saturday in the morning [*19 March*], after your grace departed from your fleet, we went down to have gone into the Deeps, but, or [*before*] we came at the danger of entering into the Deeps, called 'Gyrdelar' Head, the wind veered out of the West-North-West into the East-North-East, wherefore [we were] fain to go to an anchor for that day, And the same morning that I came toward the Deeps, I commanded [*some*] of the small ships as would go the next way to the Downs to get them over the land's end, and [there] went that way both the new barks, the *Lizard*, the *Swallow*, and eight more of the small ships. [The] residue kept with us through the Deeps. And, Sir, all Palm Sunday we stirred not, for the wind was [. . .] here with us at East and by South, which was the right course that we should draw to e [. . .]. On Monday the wind came West-South-West, which was very good for us, and [. . .] we slept it not, for at the beginning of the flood we were all under sail. And [. . .]. And from our first setting of sail [. . .] slacking where the *Katherine*

That literacy was evident aboard the *Mary Rose* is shown by this pen and inkpot, and other objects seen above as well as from the letters presented here. The stamped leather cover came from what must have been a prized book, its contents lost. The flagon and bowl are also inscribed. (*Mary Rose Trust*)

Fortileza sailed very well and [. . .]. All such ships as made sail even together with her once a quarter of a [. . .] three mile sailing your good ship, the flower, I trow, of all ships that ever sailed, reckoning [. . .] every ship, and came within three spear length of the *Katherine* and spake to John Fle[myng], Peter Seaman, and to Freman, master, to bear record that the *Mary Rose* did fetch her at the [. . .] best way and the *Mary*'s worst way. And so, Sir, within a mile sailing left her in flight [. . .] at the stern, and she all the other, saving five or six small ships which cut [. . .] the Foreland the next way. And, Sir, then our course changed and went hard upon a bowline [. . .] the Foreland, where the *Mary Rose*, your noble ship, set the *Mary George*, the *Katherine* prow, a bark Lord Ferrers hired, the *Leonard of Dartmouth*, and some of them were a long mile afore me, or ever I came to the Foreland. The next ship that was to me but [*except*] the *Sovereign* was 3 mile behind, but the *Sovereign* passed not half mile behind me. Sir, she is the noblest ship of sail [and] great ship at this hour that I trow be in Christendom. A ship of 100 ton will not be sooner at her [. . .] about than she. When I came to an anchor, I called for pen and ink to mark what ships [*came*] to me, for they came all by me to an anchor. The first next the *Mary Rose* was the *So*[*vereign, then the*] *Nicholas*, then the *Leonard of Dartmouth*, then the *Mary George*, then the *Henry of Hampton*, then the *Anne* [. . .] then the *Nicholas Montrygo* called the *Sancheo de Garra*, then the *Katherine*, then the *Mary J*[*ames*] – Sir, one after another. There was a foul tail between the *Mary Rose*, and the aftermost was the *Maria de Loretta*. And the *Christ* was one of the worst that day, she may be [. . .] sail, no more may the *Katherine*. I trust we shall remedy her well enough that she shall follow with the best; Sir, she is overladen with ordnance, beside her heavy tops, which are big enough for a ship of 8 or 900 [*tons*].

Sir, we had not been at anchor at the Foreland but the wind [*turned*] up at the Northerboard so strainably that we could ride no longer there without great danger, [*so*] we weighed to get us into the Downs through the 'Gowles' [*Gull Stream*]. And when we were in the midst, between the 'Brakkes' and the Goodwin, the wind veered out again to the West-South-West, where we were fain to make with your great ships three or four turns, and God knoweth [. . .] row channel at low water. As we took it, the *Sovereign* and the *Mary* stayed [. . .] a quarter of a mile off the Goodwin Sands, and the *Maria de Loretta* offered her [. . .] would none of it, and was fain to go about with a forewind back [. . .] where that she lyeth [. . .] I fetched the Downs with many turns, and thanked be to God I [. . .] Downs at an anchor in fast. And I pray God that he send our victual sh[ortly . . .] for in Christendom out of one realm was never seen such a fleet as [*this. I assure you that*] with our barketts come to us, that the first fair wind that cometh, we might be doing [*service, for you*] saw never poor men so in courage to be doing as your men be.

I beseech your g[*race not to be*] miscontent that I make so long a matter in writing to you, and of no matter of substance, but that you commanded me to send your grace word how every ship did sail, and this same was the best trial that could be, for we went both slacking and by a bowline, and a 'cool[. . .]', a course and a bonnet, in such wise that few ships lacked no water in over the lee wales.

Sir, the ships of Bristol be here with me, I assure your grace, gorgeous ships for their burthen; one that Anthony Pointz is in upon a 180 [*tons*], and another of 160, and another of 140, I had not spoken [*of*] when I wrote this letter. I understand they lack victual. I have written to Master Almoner for it and for their mariners. Your grace must command Master Almoner to make a warrant to ble[. . .] to deliver to Hopton 200 harness for them, which shall send it down in the victuallers.

[*I have*] no more news to write to your grace as at this time, but that the next fair weather [. . .] lie here in the Downs, I will send forth your two new barks, the *Lizard*, [*the two row*] barges, the *Baptist of Harwich*, to play up and down between Dover and Calais [. . .] perchance will fall in their hands that we might have some news thereby out of [*France*].

Sir, for God's sake, haste your Council to send us down our victual, for if we shall lie long [here], the common voice will run that we lie and keep in the Downs and do no good but spend money and victual, and so the noise will run to our shames, though your grace know well that we can no otherwise do without we should leave our victual and fellows behind us. I r[emit] all this to the order of your noble grace, whom I pray God preserve from all adversity, and send you as much victory of your enemies as ever had any of your noble ancestry.

Written in the *Mary Rose*, by your most bounden subject and poor Admiral,
Edward Howard.

14. *Sir Edward Howard to Wolsey, 5 April 1513.*

In marked contrast to the flowery report he had sent to the King on 22 March, the Admiral addresses the Almoner on prosaic issues of meat and drink. Despite shortages, he exudes optimism, and manages a side-swipe at a negligent carpenter.

Master Almoner, in my heartiest wise I can I recommend me unto you, certifying to you that I am now at the writing of this my letter in Plymouth road with all the King's fleet saving the ships that be at Hampton, which I look for this night. For when I came open of the Wight I would not go in, but sent a ship of [*William*] Compton's to cause them to come in all haste. And the wind hath been ever since as good as was possible. And as for our Spaniards that should come out of Thames, I hear no word of them; God send us good tidings of them. Sir, I think our business will be tried within 5 or 6 days at the furthest, for an hulk that came straight from Brest showeth for a certainty that there be ready coming forward a 100 ships of war besides the galleys, and be prest [*ready*] upon the first wind, and says that they be very well trimmed and will not fail to come out and fight with us. Sir, these be the gladdest tidings to me and all my captains and all the residue of the army that ever came to us, and I trust in God and St George that we shall have a fair day on them; and I pray God that we linger no longer, for I assure you was never army so falsely victualled. They that received their proportion for 2 months' flesh cannot bring about for 5 weeks, for the barrels be full of salt; and when the pieces keepeth the number, where they should be penny pieces they be scant halfpenny pieces, and where 2 pieces should make a mess, 3 will do but serve. Also, many came out of Thames but with a month's beer, trusting that the victuallers should bring the rest, and here cometh none. I send you word for a surety, here is not in this army one with another past 15 days.

Two pots found in the hold. The one on the left was used to heat tar, the other, a cooking vessel. (*Mary Rose Trust*)

Sir, the *Katherine Fortileza* hath troubled me beyond reason; she brought out of Thames but for 14 days' victual, and no victualler is come to help her. And so have I victualled her with [beef *deleted*] beer ever since, and so brings my victualling back, for it is no small thing that 500 men spendeth daily, and no provision here for her. I have sent to Plymouth on mine own head to get some victual, if it be possible. I trust you will allow for it. I would I had never a groat in England that I might keep these west parts till they and I meet.

Sir, [you *otiose*] my lords of the King's most honourable Council wrote to me of a proportion that should be already delivered. Sir, if some be well victualled, the most part be not; and you know well, if half should lack, it were as good in a manner that all lacked, in consideration to keep the army together. Sir, for God's sake send by post all along the coast that they brew beer and make biscuit, that we may have some refreshing to keep us together upon this coast, or else we shall be driven to come again into the Downs and let the Frenchmen take their pleasure; and God knoweth when we shall get us up so high westward again. I had liefer [*rather*] then that we should be driven to that issue to be put all the days of my life in the painfullest prison that is in Christendom.

Sir, the *Katherine Fortileza* has so many leaks by reason of Bedell the carpenter that worked in her at Woolwich that we have had much to do to keep her above water. He hath bored an 100 auger holes in her and left it unstopped, that the water came in as it were in a sieve. Sir, this day I have all the caulkers of the army on her. I trust by tomorrow she shall be more staunch.

Sir, where you write to me that you send hoys to take our pipes: Sir, they are such men that they would throw them that you sent with the victual over [the *deleted*] board, and when the pipes hath been brought, and they gone from us, they throw them over board and goeth into Flanders. Sir, I know no man's proportion but mine own, nor one captain knoweth what his purser hath received, for we left all our pursers at London to haste forth our victual, and neither hear we of our pursers nor our victuals. And well I wot [*know*] that I have given such order in dispending of our victual that there was never army so straited, not by one drinking in a day, which I know well hath been a great sparing; but for all this we be at the issue that I showed you before. And whereas you write that it were no reason that the King should pay for his own goods: sir, I am of the same opinion; but, sir, or ever I had knowledge of any man, the deliverers of victual [that *deleted*] had received divers foists of divers ships, and given the stewards 4*d* for every tun drawing, which I thought a perilous example. Howbeit, one that [*William*] Atclif sent for the sealing of certain commissions for the taking and preserving of the foists showed me that

Master Atclif had commanded them to pay every man 4*d* for the drawing of a tun. And, sir, if that had not been, I should have seen all delivered without any penny taking. But, sir, never man complained to me of any such things. Sir, all the victual that shall come to us, let it come to Dartmouth, for there it may lie ready for us. And sure enough, sir, there is much victual at Sandwich, and they have no vessels to bring it to us. Fill some of your Spaniards ships their bellies full: 3 or 4 of them will carry much. And spare not to spend victual upon us this year, for with God's grace the fleet of France shall never do us hurt after this year. And if they be so ready as the hulk hath showed us for a certainty, I trust to God and St George that you shall shortly hear good tidings. And howsoever the matter goeth, I will make a fray with them if wind and weather will serve or 10 days to an end.

Therefore I pray you recommend me to the King's noble grace, and show him that he trust no tidings till [*he*] hear word from me, for I shall be the first that shall know it if I leave, and I shall be the first that shall send him word. Sir, I pray you recommend me to the Queen's noble grace, and I know well I need not to pray her to pray for our good speed; and to all good ladies and gentlewomen, and to my fellows Sir Charles [*Brandon*] and Sir Henry Guildford. And, sir, specially recommend me to my lord my father, beseeching him of his blessing. And, sir, I pray you to knit up all which have me most humbly recommended to the King's noble grace as his most bounden servant, as knoweth Our Lord, who evermore send him victory of his enemies, and you, my special friend, your most heart's desire. Written in the *Mary Rose* the 5th day of April, by your to my little power,

Edward Howard.

Sir, I need not to write unto you what storms we had, for you know it well enough. Sir, I saw never worse; but thanked be to God all is well, saving the loss of one of our galleys; all ill go with her. Sir, I send you in this packet a letter to my wife; I pray you deliver it to her.

15. *Sir Edward Howard to the King, 12 April* [*1513*].

Reporting the first encounters with the enemy. The signature to this letter has been lost, but there is no doubt as to its provenance.

[Pleaseth your grace] to understand that on Sunday last, was the 10 [day of April, we adv]anced out of Plymouth with your noble army, and we [. . .] night.

[The Monday last *inserted*] the wind rose so sore at North-North-East that we were fain [to] set us in with the Trade, and went in at the broad sound, where [w]hen we came afore St Matthew's [*Pointe St Matthieu*] there lay at road a

Henry VIII's arms, as borne by all English monarchs from Henry IV to Elizabeth I. The fleurs-de-lis in the first and third quarters were a continuing reminder of their ancient claim to the throne of France. This example comes from a bronze demi-cannon. (*Mary Rose Trust*)

15 sail of men-of-war, which, as soon as they spied us, they like cowards fled to the Brest water, so that they were got in or [*before*] we could get as far as St Matthew's. And the wind shot out to East-North-East, and the e[bb c]ame, that with all the turning we could make, we could get no further than the mouth of the entry of Brest water, where we saw rid[ing al]l the fleet of France to the number of 50 sail, which we should [not] have missed if the wind and the ebb had not come. And so we [weighed] an anchor in their sight, determining that the next morning, [if] we could have wind to lay it on a-board, that we would have [. . .] them there [*sic*] they lie. For, Sir, this ship cannot get in by [the cas]tle but at an high water and a drawing wind. Sir, the wi[nd has] blown so at East-North-East that we cannot as yet come n[earer sti]ll, we have them at them at the greatest advantage that ever men had. [God] worketh in your cause and right, for upon a 5 or 6 days [afore we came to] the Trade, Peryjohn [*Prégent*] with his galleys and foists, for skant [of wind went] to St Malo's, and a

5 or 6 small barks [. . .]le between the fleet. And all their trust [. . .] there shall never come together with God's [. . .] them to leave them [. . .] his issue. Sir, the first wind that ever cometh [. . .] have broken heads, that all the world shall speak of it.

Sir [. . .] ships resort with our victuals into the Trade, setting their course on f[ast] along the coast of England or they hale over. And if they hear ne[ws of] us there, then let them come over, on God's name, 'commyn at the broode', for they be enough to beat Peryjohn and all his fleet, I warrant your grace, having them a-seaboard.

Sir, this Tuesday at night I heard as I lay at anchor that a ship of 80 lying in Crozon bay, and 4 small men, had run themselves aground, so I sent out the *Lizard*, the *Jenet*, the *Baptist of Harwich* and my ship boat well trimmed, and commanded them to bring them away if they could, or else to burn [them]. And so, Sir, the ship of 80 was run so far aground that they could not [get] him off, and my boat set him on a fair fire, and made a goodly [. . .], and the residue of the small men were brought to me, whereof [one] was laden with salt, which I have sent to bring this letter to [. . .] that he could come to of England.

And, Sir, I have sent a letter [to the captains of the s]hips of Spain and victuallers, if so be they be come on the coast [. . .] to your grace that they shall resort hither with all diligence.

Sir, if [God is] so good to send us any wind, not having no part of the e[. . . the army] of France shall do your grace little hurt. At the [. . .] shall not tarry long here for it, for Sir, that we w[. . .] in 2 days, with God's grace. And it pleased God, I w[ould . . . that] we had done our business with the army t[. . .] also with all Brittany, for here is [. . .] that is fell little, and [. . .] a land [. . .] eth at all.

Sir, there was never such a sort of captains that the [. . .] the sea, nor such a sort of soldiers and mariners so well willing to do [. . .]. And to be doing with your enemies, Sir, we lose no time, I warrant you, for [we] think upon none other thing but how we may best grieve our enemies. [And] if victual serve us, as your men and ships are determined, we shall this year [make] a bare coast all the realm of France that boundeth on the sea coast, [which] shall never recover it in our days. Therefore, for no cost sparing, let pro[vision] be made, for it is a well spent penny that saveth the pound, for [. . .] was wont to be spent in 3 or 4 year on the sea with one expense now, we shall do more good than in 4 year by driblet. Sir, I remit all the further order of this great matter to your noble [wisdo]m and discreet order of your wise councillors, and I pray God send us [bette]r wind, that we may do your grace that service that our heart desireth [. . . I pray] this the blessed Trinity send your grace victory of your enemies.

[When] I was writing of the latter of this letter, the *Lizard*, the [. . .] row-galleys and rowbarges went in to them with the flood rowing [. . .] them and caused them to come to their sails, and so came large [. . .] we come and fought with us, and so I weighed and came to sail [. . .] made to them-ward with the skant wind that we had that [. . . lac]ked but wind. God if we had it come it on th[. . .]ll is one to us. Sir, St George to 'borowgh[. . . ']] he yet for 10 days here and [. . .] have our victual.

16. *Sir Edward Howard to the King, 17 April [1513].*

The immediate interest of this letter is its account of the accident which befell Arthur Plantagenet, the future Lord Lisle, commanding the Nicholas of Hampton. *But it is also the last letter from Sir Edward Howard, who was to be killed in the assault on the galleys eight days later.*

[Pleaseth] your grace to understand that the next day after [I had writt]en to your grace, I caused all my boats of the army with the [. . .] head to make a countenance of landing on the side that Brest [. . .] one, for to make the country to resort down to the waterside [. . .]d the victual of the country, and to weary of them. And I am [sure there] was within an hour above 10,000 men. Such as they be, Sir, my [men wo]uld have landed to have fought with them, and I dare say we [had no]t in all the boats past 1,500 men. Sir, for to content somewhat the [me]n's minds, which are hardly handled in the distributing of [da]ily victualling by reason that as yet our victualling is not come to us, a[nd to] keep them out of murmuring, which is hard to do without [th]ey be set a-work with somewhat, I skirmished there the past [tw]o hours with our ordnance. And when I spied the country sore moved and [. . . to] the waterside, for fear of our landing I went over to the other [si]de of Brest, that new Crozon stood on, and landed all our boats, and made two battles, and so went over all the neck of land in [the ba]y, and made our muster so straight afore the castle that they might see that we were not afeared to land our men afore their sight, to proc[eed] to come forth, yea, and to anger them were burned up all the ho[uses that] stood in their sight on the waterside, to their great displeasure and the [pleasure] of our men.

Sir, there I viewed how the ships lay. Sir, they be run underneath the castle, and they have by, as far as we can spy [. . .] all the hulks afore the mouth of the haven, for because we should [do] them no hurt. By reason of, for no otherwise, Sir, we dare not put [. . .] because of lack of victual. Sir, and we be

This display of personal items reflects hygiene (a comb) and private devotion (a rosary). (*Mary Rose Trust*)

able to land [. . . as] many horse as will carry two pieces of good ordnance, with the carts, [with wh]ich these ships shall be sunk where they lie. Sir, it were too great a p[eril they] should ever escape, seeing that we have them in this danger. I remit this to your great wisdom,

Sir, as for the galleys, we make great w[ay with] them, as Master Arthur [*Plantagenet*] can show your grace. And, Sir, if there come any other by day or by night, the boats and small vessels and row[barges and] row-galleys shall lay them sharply aboard, and rather than they [*should*] escape us, I have assigned [*William*] Harper, the *Thomas of Hull*, my bark, [*Sir William*] [Trevy]nyan's bark and two or three small ships [not to *inserted*] spare to give t[. . .]stand [*even*] though they should run them aground for to make them [sink]. And, Sir, if they came amongst us, they shall not escape clean with good.

Sir, we marvel sore that we hear no word of our three Spaniards [that] should come out of Thames. We fear that they have been in some danger, [which] God defend, in the Deeps, for they have had as fair winds to c[ome unt]o us as can be wished, and our victuallers too. I shall think long [to] have word from your grace of all your further pleasure how you will ha[ve all] further ordered. Sir, and our victual come not to us by tomorrow, we be in [great] despair to have any remedy, for now these two days hath blown [the] fairest wind that could be devised. God send us comfort of them shortly. We can do no more than is possible, and that will we do to bid you [greate]st pain that ever did men, seeing that God hath sent us here in so great [advantage] of your enemies, as I am sure [*William*] Sabyne hath informed your grace.

Sir, [I have] taken all Master Arthur's folks and bestowed them in the army where I [lacked b]y reason of death, by casualty and otherwise; and, Sir, h[ave given him licen]ce to go home, for, Sir, when he was in the extreme danger [*and hope gone*] from him, he called upon Our Lady of Walsingham for help and comf[ort, and made] a vow that, and it pleased God and Her to deliver [him *inserted*] out of that pe[ril, he w]ould never eat flesh nor fish till he had seen Her. Sir, I a[ssure you] he was in marvellous danger, for it was marvel that the ship, be[ing with] all her sails striking full but a rock with her stem, that she br[oke] not on pieces at the first stroke. Sir, we shall have a great w[ant of] him out of your noble army, for I know no man dis[. . .] that, considering his power, should better have served you if the fortune had not been; for, Sir, he was well trimmed, and hath [. . .] he had in effect. And, Sir, he would not have departed but [for] that vow he should do here in a manner your grace but small service, [and to] himself great discomfort to see every man shipped, and to see h[is own] place and his men divided from him. Therefore, and because [. . .]th inform your grace what place we stand in, and to be set [. . .]d again if your grace will have to come to us, which will be as [. . .] thing as possible, wheresoever you will command him. I have sent [him to your] grace, beseeching your grace to be his good and gracious lord. [I assu]re you he shall do your grace good service wheresoever you [. . . at] both for his good order and hardiness. And, Sir, he is the sorriest man I ever saw, and no man here can comfort him. Therefore I beseech again your grace to give him comfortable words to be his good [lord].

I beseech your grace to send me word how you [do hear of] Scotland to s[end] a spial of his ships. And Our Lord send you victory ever of your enemies. Written to [*towards*] St Matthew's, the 17th day of April.

Your bounden servant, Edw[ard Howard].

Endorsed: To the King's grace, in all possible haste.

3

THE WAR WITH FRANCE AFTER SIR EDWARD HOWARD'S DEATH (APRIL 1513–MAY 1514)

COMMENTARY

Thomas, Lord Howard, Sir Edward's elder brother, succeeded him as Lord Admiral on 4 May 1513, and was immediately posted to Plymouth to take up his responsibilities. The weeks which followed are the most intensely documented of the whole war, and since Howard also established his flag in the *Mary Rose*, are the most heavily represented here. The fleet had actually returned on 30 April, and a letter expressing the King's acute displeasure had preceded the Admiral to Dartmouth, making his task infinitely more difficult. Morale was at rock bottom; there was no food; many soldiers and seamen had deserted, and the discipline of those who remained had disintegrated, so that they were plundering and terrorizing the country round about. Howard set about his task with energy and good sense. He appointed a new captain for his flagship, Edward Bray (**19**), mobilized the local magistrates to round up his deserters, and erected a pair of gallows on the dockside, although it is not recorded that he executed anyone. More important, he summoned the officers to a council aboard the *Mary Rose*, and listened to what they had to say. They were, of course, full of excuses and good reasons for their precipitate flight. Their supplies were exhausted, the weather was threatening, the galleys had proved far more dangerous than they had supposed, and so on. In the process they provided the Admiral with a blow-by-blow account of his brother's last fight, but because their main objective was to demonstrate their own impeccable behaviour, this is probably less useful than it might have been (**17**). When writing to Wolsey on the same day that he reported these things to the King (his normal practice), he indicated that he might have found two scapegoats for his brother's death (**18**). Two men who were sufficiently humble to be vulnerable 'did their part very ill' that day, and he proposed to punish them if the accusation was upheld. We do not know what happened.

Henry's first instruction was that his fleet should return to the Trade (off Brittany) as soon as it could be revictualled, but fortunately Howard was spared the need to carry out such an unpopular (and unreasonable) order. Instead, the King instructed him to stay where he was, revictual, and await reinforcements. This was better, but not much, as Plymouth harbour was too cramped for so large a fleet, and too difficult to get in and out of. On 13 May he announced his intention to move to Southampton Water, which would be more convenient, both as an anchorage and as a departure point (**21**). Meanwhile, the revictualling was, at last, proceeding satisfactorily. For about ten days Howard struggled to carry out this decision, but was constantly blown back by adverse winds (**22–5**). On the 20th he was still desperately trying to warp his way out of the Cattewater into Plymouth Sound (**26**), and it seems to have been about the 23rd before he finally made it to the Solent. For the moment Howard was doing his best to monitor the activities of the French, using both his own scouts and whatever casual information came his way. He concluded that if they heard about Henry's intention to return to the charge, they would take countermeasures, particularly to safeguard the coast south of Ushant, but otherwise they were not likely to do anything. In the meantime the reinforcements did not arrive, and on 4 June the King countermanded his orders for a fresh assault on Brittany (**28**).

The reason for this was that he had changed his strategic priority and decided to put his main effort into a campaign in Picardy. By 8 June the *Mary Rose* was at Portsmouth (**30**), and by the 22nd at Sandwich, preparing with the rest of the fleet, to escort the King's 'Army Royal' across to Calais (**33**). This was accomplished by 30 June, but the fleet seems to have remained at Sandwich. On 4 July the *Mary Rose* was revictualled until 28 August, but it is not clear what she was doing by the latter date. Most of the soldiers and some of the ships intended for the Brittany campaign seem to have been paid off, but the King's own ships remained on active service. This may have been partly because there were persistent rumours that

Scottish and Danish ships were about to join the French fleet (**27–31**). There was some truth in this. Scottish ships left Leith on 25 July, and joined forces with the French in early September. A few days later (9 September) James IV was killed at Flodden and Scotland effectively dropped out of the war, but the ships remained under the command of Louis de Rouville, who was appointed on 17 September. The Breton and Norman ships were revictualled for two months in early August, and Prégent's galleys were refurbished and re-equipped. At the same time, running repairs were also being carried out to the English warships. All this action seems to have been focused on Henry's anticipated return from Picardy, but when the time came in early October the Franco-Scottish fleet was scattered by a storm, and Henry returned in triumph without the slightest impediment. The *Mary Rose* seems to have been brought specially from Harwich to form part of the escorting fleet, which presumably survived the gale (**38**). With the exception of three which remained in Louis's pay, the Scottish ships returned to Edinburgh early in November; and on the 7th Hopton noted that the *Mary Rose*, and other ships, had been laid up for the winter, but he did not say where. It was probably at Woolwich or Erith.

By the beginning of 1514 the war cries were diminishing on both sides. Louis had kept some warships in service through the winter, as though he intended to steal a march on his rival, and French privateers were active in the Channel. There were also persistent rumours that Louis would send a large force to Scotland, but the Scots had no stomach to continue the fight under their new (and very young) King. Mobilization seems to have begun as usual, and the *Mary Rose* was moved to Blackwall (presumably to load ordnance), and then to Portsmouth. At some point, probably at the beginning of March, she was at Newcastle; a move obviously related to the Scottish rumours (**37**). On the 2nd of that month John Browne took over the duties of master from Thomas Sperte. Shortly afterwards a truce was signed, and although it was not very strictly observed on either side, there seems to have been no appetite for large-scale campaigning. At the end of May the Lord Admiral, who had become Earl of Surrey on 1 February when his father was created Duke of Norfolk, was on his flagship the *Mary Rose* at Dover, apparently expecting action against Prégent and his galleys (**39–40**). Instead, on 14 June he was able to report a successful raid on the French coast, but it was the last fighting of the war (**41–2**). Within a few days Henry ordered a ceasefire, and in July the fleet began to be demobilized. Peace was finally concluded in early August.

Documents

17. *Thomas, Lord Howard, Lord Admiral, to the King, 7 May 1513.*

Howard's patent of office, in place of his younger brother, had passed the Great Seal three days before. This letter was written as soon as he had arrived to take up his command.

Please it your most noble grace to understand, yesternight I came unto Dartmouth at 9 of the clock, and this day at one of the clock I came hither, as weary a man of riding as ever was any. At which time I assembled in the *Mary Rose* my Lord Ferrers and all other noblemen and captains and most expert masters of your army, and there rehearsed unto them your commandment given unto me, and after that I enquired of them the cause of their coming from the parts of Brittany without your commandment. Unto which they answered with

Thomas Howard, Earl of Surrey and later 3rd Duke of Norfolk. As Lord Admiral he flew his flag in the *Mary Rose*. This portrait by Holbein shows him in later life, carrying the white wand as Lord Treasurer. (*The Royal Collection © 2002, Her Majesty Queen Elizabeth II*)

one whole voice and in one tale they did it upon divers and reasonable grounds. One was they had great default of victual, and had not in their board for 3 days, notwithstanding that Sabyne brought with him nine crayers laden with victual. And such victuallers as were appointed for them came from London hither and to Dartmouth, and here remained till the coming hither of your army, without coming to them. One other cause was all your captains and masters generally say that, and [*if*] they had continued there and one day of calm had come, if the galleys being within 3 mile of them would have done their worst unto them, as it is to suppose they would have done, they should not a-failed to have sunk such of your ships as they list to have shot their ordnance unto; which ordnance, if it be such as they report, is a thing marvellous. Without that your said army could in any wise have annoyed them, Whereupon [I] reasoned with your masters, saying if the galleys had come forth and that your two galleys and two rowbarges, with the help of the boats, had set on them, what they thought they had been able to have done to the said galleys. And with one accord they answered me that one of the galleys in a calm would distress your two galleys and rowbarges, and to drown with their oars as many boats as came within the reach of them. And also all the masters say that if the wind had blown strainably at South-West or West-South-West, or West and by South, there had been no remedy [and by] force they must have run into Crozon bay, where they should have lye [. . .] near, the shores of both sides being already sore bulwarked, that without [they] had been able to have beaten the Frenchmen from the land, the said French [men with] their ordnance might have destroyed all your fleet lying there. And as [according] to the actual feats of all such noblemen and gentlemen as were pr[esent], my brother the Admiral was drowned (whom Jesus pardon). I assure your [grace] hereforth as I can by any wise understand, they handled themselves as [well as ever] men did to obtain their master's pleasure and favour.

Sir, there w[ere with my brother] 175 men, of whom were left on life but 56, and of those [being] my Lord Ferrers' men, 25 slain and 20 hurt; and may [. . .] my galley had not fallen on ground, being near the shore, then the ot[her in like] wise boarded as the other did, and of likelihood few had escaped. [Sir Henry] Sherborne and Sir William Sidney boarded a galley, they being in a sma[ll crayer], and yet by fortune had but three men slain and seven hurt. [. . .] [*Thomas*] Cheyne and [*John*] Wallop, being in a little crayer, boarded in like wise, and yet [they] had no man slain nor hurt. William Tolly and his brother Sir Robert, b[est] of all men, and had 12 men slain and above 20 hurt. [*Edmund*] Wiseman m[. . .] boarded not, but he had all his men slain or hurt. Sir Wystan

Bro[wne had] three men slain, and divers other boats had many men slain and hurt. [Please] your grace that, as far as I can understand by any man's report, [it was] the most dangerful enterprise that ever I heard of, and the most manly handled of the setters on, insomuch that I see no likelihoood [nor] possibility to bring the mariners to row the galleys or boats to s[hore without] other bargain. Sir, I had forgotten two men that did as well as was possible: [one] was [*Thomas*] Gurney, being in the *Jenet Purwyn* and good Lewes [*Southern*] with the one [. . .] in the *Elizabeth of Newcastle*, as well appeared by the slaughter of [. . .] and bouging of their ships. And all other gentlemen which had [part] of the enterprise are the most angry men in the world, that they ha[ve . . .] thereof.

Also, Sir, please your grace to understand I have declared [. . .] unto all the captains and masters how your grace would I should w[ith the] army return unto the Trade, demanding of them what service t[here] shall be possible for us to do your grace there. And as well the captains [as the] masters have answered me that, considering the great fortification out [. . .] the great danger of the galleys if a calm come, the great danger of [the] winds afore rehearsed, if they fortune to blow strainably, they all be[ing of one] mind say precisely they see no likelihood nor possibility but that o[ur return] there shall rather turn to our great reproach, loss of ships and [men than] otherwise. And also they all think it not possible, the premises consi[dered], anything that may redound to the honour of your grace, your re[alm and] our poor honesties, unless that your grace would so furnish us with[al, that] we might be able both to keep our ships and also to defend th[em against] your enemies for five or six days; which done, all the expert cap[tains and] masters think verily your grace shall not only cause us to d[estroy the ships] of France with the galleys, but also put your enemies to the [. . .] that ever they had in Brittany.

Sir, I have not written unto [your grace] the premises but that the noblemen and captains of [*the army*] signed with their hands the copy of the same. And now, Sir, in my most humble w[ise], I beseech your grace that with all possible diligence I may know how your pleasure shall be that I shall order myself, and that I may have answer from your grace by Wednesday at night, before which time it shall not be possible for me to depart hence, considering that your army would not have their victual in before that time, and also a great part of your army is sparkled abroad on the land, and slain, and departed from the army I am not sure so few as 500. At which time, if I he[ar] no word from your grace, the wind serving with God's grace, I shall see the Trade. And if I can perceive any thing that may be done, I shall accomplish the same to the best of my power; and if it may stand with your pleasure that I shall seek alo[ng] the coast of Brittany beyond the Trade how I may most annoy your enemies, I beseech your grace I may be advertised thereof. For, Sir, if your pleasure shall be to send us no greater number of men, as far as I can perceive by all your masters, the greater displeasures that we may do your enemies shall be beyond the Trade to Rochelle-ward, where if your grace will that we shall meddle with the isles 'patessed', as they have done with yours, I doubt not to do them great hurt. And as touching the fleet that lieth at Brest, they dare not come forth toward the west parts of your realm for, and they did, that wind that should serve them should serve me to clap between them and home, which I pray God to give me grace once to see. And as for victual, your servants from Hampton being come to me, I doubt not to be well furnished [for] two months. And if they would go to Normandy-ward, then I would trust your grace should shortly have your pleasure of them. Sir, I can say no more unto your grace. Mine poor advice shall be, hearing so much as I have heard, that either your grace shall send us a sufficient company to land, or else to let us seek our best ad[vantage], for in the Trade, if your masters may be trusted, is nothing to be done; and in [the] letter which I send Master Almoner, your grace shall understand m[ore]. And thus Our Lord preserve your most noble grace.

Written in the *M[ary] Rose* in Plymouth haven, the 7 day of May, at 11 a'clock at night.

Your most [bounden servant, Thomas Howard].

Endorsed: To the King's grace. Delivered the post at midnight. My lord Admiral.

18. *Thomas, Lord Howard, to Wolsey, 7 May 1513.*

Written immediately after the previous letter (which took half an hour to write). It gives a more detailed account of his brother's last action: the term 'ferse' is obscure, but might be 'farce[d]', meaning tightly closed, and therefore explaining that Sir Edward's ship was too close to the enemy to risk an incendiary attack.

My own good Master Almoner, all such matters as I have written to the King's grace of, I will leave unwritten to you, assuring you that I have here found the worst ordered army and furthest out of rule that ever I saw. This day, when I came hither, I am sure there were more than half the army on land, and I fear me, by hearing say, there is a great number stolen away. At my coming to Exeter I heard of their departing, and so have sent through all the country to bring them again. Never man saw men in greater fear than all the masters and mariners be of the galleys, in so much that in a manner they had as lief [*rather*] go into Purgatory as to the Trade. But that notwithstanding, if the King's grace send me not contrary commandment, I trust to be there by Friday [*13 May*] at the furthest. Also, the King's letter sent unto the captains hath greatly troubled and discouraged them, for they had trusted to have had great thanks, and undoubted, as many gentlemen as were warned thereof did as valiantly as was possible. And as for the galleys might have been burnt, but my brother (whom God pardon) was so 'ferse' that he would suffer no man to cast in wildfire, and the said galleys did our men but little hurt. But both the shores were so well bulwarked, and so innumerable ordnance therein, that it is too wonderful to hear the report of them that saw it.

Good Master Almoner, cause the King's grace to write unto the captains some favourable letter, for I assure you it is needful, and if any of them would make labour to await on his grace when her goeth over sea, for God's sake stop it, for and [*if*] one should go, all the residue would desire the same.

Here is two men that, as I hear say, did their part very ill that day my brother was lost; the one was [*William*] Coke, the Queen's servant, in a rowbarge, and the other Freman, my said brother's household servant. If it be of truth, I shall punish them that all other shall take example, I assuring you that I see very few or none, great nor small, that with their wills would go again to the Trade; what the cause is, as yet I cannot say, but shortly I trust to see if the danger be so great as I am informed of. Beseeching you that the King's grace take no displeasure with me that I tarry here so long, for I assure you no man is so weary thereof as I, and before Thursday it shall not be possible for us to depart, what for taking in of victual, whereof a great part as yet is uncome, and also I fear we shall much ado to get our soldiers aboard, but and they come not, you shall hear of sharp justice. Also the *Anne Gallant* is in such case that she shall not be able to go to the sea this year; she lieth here on dry ground, and in her stead I have taken another.

I would write to you of many other causes, but that I will not tarry the post no longer; and if the King's letters come to Plymouth when I am gone, I shall leave one to bring them after, with God's grace, who keep you. Scribbled in great haste in the *Mary Rose* at Plymouth, half hour after 11 at night, the 7 day of May.

Your own, Thomas Howard.

19. *Lord Admiral's warrant for payment of wages to the newly appointed captain of the* Mary Rose, *with effect from 9 May 1513.*

Cousin Wyndham, whereas I have appointed Edward Bray to be captain in the *Mary Rose*, I will that you pay him for 2 months' wages after the rate of 18*d* the day, the first month beginning the 9th day of May, and the other the 6th day of June then next after, in the 5th year of King Henry VIII. And this my writing signed with my hand the 18 of June the year aforesaid shall be your warrant for payment of the same.

Thomas Howard.

20. *Lord Admiral's warrant for wages of soldiers aboard the* Mary Rose, *with effect from 9 May 1513.*

Cousin Wyndham, whereas I was commanded by the King's grace to bring down to the sea 200 soldiers to serve his grace in his wars there, whereof 111 could not conveniently be put nor bestowed in the *Mary Rose* nor elsewhere until such time as a great part of the retinue of my brother Sir Edward Howard, late Admiral, were despatched, which was by the space of one month beginning the 9th day of May in the 5th year of King Henry VIII, for the wages of which month I will that you pay to every of the said 111 soldiers 5s, which amounted to – £27 15s. And this my writing signed with my hand the 18 day of June the year abovesaid shall be your warrant for payment of the same.

Thomas Howard.

21. *Thomas, Lord Howard, to the King, 13 May 1513.*
   There was as yet no naval establishment at Plymouth, and Howard's disparagement of the anchorage (repeated in the two following letters) should not be interpreted as lacking in foresight.

Pleaseth it your most noble grace to understand this day at 11 before noon I received your most gracious letters, with undeserved thanks on my behalf, but only of your great goodness, beseeching Almighty Jesus that I may once do your grace's service worthy thanks. And whereas I understand by your said letters bearing date the 12 day of May that your grace intendeth with all haste to send my cousin Sir Charles with many other noble men to us; Sir, I doubt not, God and the wind serving, your grace shall obtain your desire touching the destruction of the French navy, and beside that to the destruction of a great part of Brittany about the sea coast. And where your grace willeth me to remain here till my said cousin Sir Charles' coming hither; Sir, under your correction, it is not to be done, for divers causes. One is we lie here in the most dangerous haven of England for so many ships, and lie moored together in strait room, and divers of your ships hath been in great danger, and nightly fall together; howbeit, God be thanked, there is no hurt done. Also, the wind blowing any part off the South, it is unpossible to get hence. Whereupon I have called to me the

41

Plymouth harbour. Part of a panoramic map of the south coast of Cornwall and Devon, made in about 1540. Cattewater appears in the centre of this detail, and St Nicholas Island centre left. From British Library Cotton MS Augustus I, i, 35, 36, 38, 39. (*British Library*)

most expert masters of your army and have asked their opinions; and they all say that, considering your grace will send a more company from Hampton, it should be most convenient for us to draw thither and so to come all whole together, for that wind that will bear us in here will bring us from Hampton to Brittany.

Also Sir, under your correction, methink of our lying here can ensue no good; and seeing your grace will not that I shall draw to the parts of Brittany till my cousin Sir Charles' coming, I being in Hampton Water shall be as ready to depart thence as he with his company. And for him being at Hampton, this is clean out of his course to come hither; and in his coming hither, if the wind blew anything off the South, he should be forced to draw in to harbour, where he might fortune remain till his victual were spent, which might be occasion of breaking of your noble pretended enterprise. And therefore, Sir, the premises considered, if wind will serve, I intend to draw to the Isle of Wight, there to ride beside Portsmouth, and doubt not your grace that my being there shall be any ways but profitable and setting forward of your enterprise. Beseeching your highness to call unto you some expert men, and I doubt not they will say the same.

And where I understand your pleasure is that my Lord Broke and Sir Piers Edgecombe shall come in this company with my said cousin; Sir, in eschewing of the charges that your grace should bear in their going unto Hampton, and also the wearying of the men, I have taken on me to cause them to take shipping here, and shall provide victuals and ships for them, and shall leave sufficient wafters [*escorts*] for them. And also, Sir, if your said company that cometh with my said cousin should have too skant shipping for their men, we will make shift to take some good number of them into our ships for the season; and at our coming to Hampton, I undertake that none of our company shall come on land.

Also, Sir, considering the unlikelihood of the coming forth of the French army, as I wrote to your grace yesterday, I see not in [more *deleted*] my poor reason what good might ensue of our remaining here, but rather many hurts; and therefore, unless that I have contrary commandment from your grace before the wind serve me to go hence, with God's grace I will not fail to draw to Hampton-ward. Also, pleaseth it your noble grace to understand your gracious letters directed to my Lord Ferrers and other your servants and captains here hath marvellously rejoiced them, and they all most humbly thank your grace for the same, trusting shortly to show what mind they be of to serve your grace. Also, according to your commandment, I have sent [*William*] Fitzwilliam, which is right sore against his mind to have departed till he had done you some other service; and, Sir, most humbly I beseech your grace to be good lord unto him. And, Sir, I am sure at all times when your grace shall command him he shall do you hardy service. Also, Sir, while I was writing this letter, I had word that 20 sail of Spaniards with 6,000 men should be come to Falmouth, but I know it not for a truth; and if it be so, your grace shall know it shortly. And thus Our Lord send your highness the accomplishment of your most noble heart's desires. Scribbled in the *Mary Rose* at Plymouth, the 13 day of May at noon.

Your most humble subject and Admiral, Thomas Howard.

22. *Thomas, Lord Howard, to Wolsey, 14 May 1513.*

Master Awmner I hertly recommande me unto you. And wher I wrote
yesterday to the Kynges grace that as sone as the wynd wold serve
me I wold come with all the navie men off war and vitellers
God and the wynd serving [to Hampton] I entend kepe the same purpose
onles that I have contrarie commandment. Assewryng you
that we ly here in the worst havyn in Inglond to gett out off
for our armye lieth in iij parties and all within Plymmouth Sownd
so that no wynd save onely north can bryng us all forth
without warpyng. I pray God bryng the wynd
out off the south or els none of us can get forth. Here we
ly vitellers and men off war I am sewer above C sayle, and
Gonstone is yet at Dertmouth, and yet he went hens before
my commyng, and in no wise can get to Hampton. Sir the
cause of my wryting to you is to advertise you that none of the
shippes ye named in Dalaber is bill, nor none of the vitellers ar
departed yet hens. And yet they and we be redy to depart as
sone as God shall send wynd. And therfor consideryng it woll
aske a tract off tyme after the seid vitellers be come to Hampton
and after their commyng or their vitell can be shipped me thynk
it wer [well] done ye shuld cause all souldiors that shall come with
Sir charles to tary aboute Salysbury Wynchester and other places
without commyng to Hampton tyll the shippes be come and their
vitelles in, for in my mynd their abode there shuld be the cause
of wastyng of suche provysion as shuld serve the armye, and
doute ye not I shall not lose one oure off tyme when the wynd
shalbe possible to serve. And thus Our Lord kepe you and send
me onys hens. Scrybled in the Mary Rose at Plymmouth the
xiiij day of May.

Assewredy yours
Thomas Howard.

Lord Admiral Howard to Thomas Wolsey, 14 May 1513. The original spelling is transcribed opposite. (*Public Record Office*)

Master Almoner, I heartily recommend me unto you. And where I wrote yesterday to the King's grace that as soon as the wind would serve me I would come with all the navy, men-of-war and victuallers, God and the wind serving, [to Hampton *inserted*], I intend to keep the same purpose unless that I have contrary commandment, assuring you that we lie here in the worst haven in England to get out of, for our army lieth in three parts, and all within Plymouth Sound, so that no wind save only North can bring us all forth without warping. I pray God bring the wind out of the South, or else none of us can get forth. Here we lie, victuallers and men-of-war, I am sure above 100 sail, and [*William*] Gonson is yet at Dartmouth; and yet he went hence before my coming, and in no wise can get to Hampton. Sir, the cause of my writing to you is to advertise you that none of the ships you named in [*James*] Delabere's bill, nor none of the victuallers, are departed yet hence; and yet they and we be ready to depart as soon as God shall send wind. And therefore, considering it will ask a tract of time after the said victuallers be come to Hampton, and after their coming or [*before*] their victual can be shipped, me think it were well done you should cause all soldiers that shall come with Sir Charles to tarry about Salisbury, Winchester and other places, without coming to Hampton till the ships be come and their victuals in. For in my mind their abode there should be the cause of wasting of such provision as should serve the army. And doubt you not I shall not lose one hour of time when the wind shall be possible to serve. And thus Our Lord keep you, and send me once hence. Scribbled in the *Mary Rose* at Plymouth, the 14 day of May.

Assuredly yours, Thomas Howard.

23. *Thomas, Lord Howard, to Wolsey, 15 May 1513.*

Master Almoner, I heartily recommend me unto you. And, thanked be God, the wind is where I would wish it, howbeit it bloweth so sore that I with the *Peter* and divers great ships cannot get out of this water called Cattewater; also, here be many small men of victuallers that cannot get out, the wind blowing thus strainable. But I trust against night this West-North-West wind will lie, and then we will forth with warping, and otherwise we cannot, for till we be past the point [of the castle *inserted*], the wind is full in our way, as every shipman can show you. Wherefore I heartily desire you to call unto you some mariner that knoweth this coast, and then I doubt not you shall know there is nothing undone that may be done here.

In following the King's pleasure, also the *Sovereign* and all the carracks and all the great ships ride under St Nicholas' Island, and with this wind may go where they will; and so I have commanded them to go forth and ride in the Sound, and as soon as this letter is written I shall go myself into Ash water and send all the victuallers there forth to Hampton [water *deleted*]-ward, and with them Anthony Pointz, Wiseman and Draper, for wafters. And if it be possible that the wind be anything peaceable, this night with all the residue of men-of-war and victuallers, I will to Hampton[-war]d. At which time I require you I may have a [strait *inserted*] letter directed to m[e comma]nding me to suffer no man, captain nor other, to go on [land, al]so another to the captains not to go on land without [licence]. Sir, I am loath to complain, and also it is no ti[me with]al, howbeit I assure you I am deceived [. . .] wind came westerly and I had [. . .] to bring them to their ships, which be sparkled 12 [miles] abroad in the country, I have given no longer day but to [. . .] to be aboard, and I have made a pair of gallows at [the] waterside, where I fear some will totter tomorrow, [for I would] rather hang half a dozen knaves than any oftener to [. . .] this displeasure, all [men *deleted*] captains do not amiss, but I assure you [. . .] most part in this behalf. Wherefore I require you to cause these sharp [letters] to be directed, and make your ground that the King is [infor]med that the soldiers be abroad in the country and rob [and] steal and do much hurt. Touching this matter I say [no] more: *sapienti pauca*.

Also I send you a writing of [. . .] Spanish which a merchant of [Bristol *inserted*] gave me this day and [came] hither this night, and was at Cadiz [in Spain *inserted*] 10 days past, and [heard] the same proclaimed, and for his safeguard if he h[ad] to meet with Frenchmen brought the same with him. I [think] the King shall speed the better if [the King *inserted*] trust his own [*people*].

Also, Sir, I am surely informed by Sabyne that at the [same] time Brest castle was won by Mons. de Rohan and M[ons.] de Shamperons, the French King's lieutenant, then [. . .] obtained it by these ways. There was many Bretons [in] the castle which had their lands lying in the country adjoining, and the said French captains gave warning that, unless they yielded them, the[y would] burn and destroy the whole country and [cut] their timber trees by the midst. W[. . .] especial felling of their trees [. . .] they yielded the keys with [. . .] send us 2 or 300 axes.

Also I beseech you that, at my coming and Sir Charles to Hampton, we may find there my lord of Winchester, to debate with him such enterprises as we have to do; and I trust to rip him well in every cause, for, when I am not occupied, it is my most business to be instructed of them that can skill, most heartily desiring you to beseech the King's grace not to think no laxness in me for our long abode here with the victuallers, for I assure you the fault is in the wind and not in me, as I am sure every skilled man can show you. And whereas I write unto you often, and peradventure every cause I write of be not of great gravity, yet I require you ascribe not the same to my default, for I assure you I had rather the posts took pain in sparing their horses than I should be found too slow in writing or working when time shall require; and till I see you I shall not forget your words *ad captandam benevolentiam* [*of timely goodwill*]. And Our Lord hold the wind where he is, and on Tuesday at night you shall not fail then to have the victuallers [there deleted] at Hampton, and the men-of-war about the Row and the Wight. And thus Our Lord keep you. Scribbled [in] haste in the *Mary Rose* at one at after [noon], when the w[ind . . .] too sore if God would otherwise.

[I have] appointed ships here for [my Lord] Broke and Sir Piers Edgecombe [. . .] for a month of provision [. . .]tre and wafters for [. . . Lord] Broke will keep his [. . .] not, he is to blame.

Yours assuredly, Thomas Howard.

Endorsed: To Master Almoner with the King's grace. Delivered at Plymouth, this Whitsunday before 2 at afternoon.

24. *Thomas, Lord Howard, to Wolsey, 16 May 1513.*

Master Almoner, I heartily recommend me unto you. And whereas I wrote to you yesterday of our departure hence to Hampton, this day at 10 a'clock, when all men were ready to depart and the most part of the ships ready in the Sound to weigh their anchors, the wind, being at West, shot southerly and blew so rudely that all the ships, victuallers and other, were forced to come in again; and so God knoweth it is unpossible for any ship to depart hence till God send fair weather. And because you should not look for us at Hampton so shortly as I had trusted to have be there, I write to you to certify you how misfortunately the wind serveth us, not doubting but you will look wisely on the matter of the wasting of victual that Sir Charles's company should do if they came to Hampton before the ships were ready for them. Also I send you now the Spanish letter which I wrote to you of, which my servant that closed your letter forgot. Sir, this day be come hither two ships of Flanders from the Rochelle, saying that they hear the peace proclaimed between France and Spain, and that five ships of Spain be lading wines at Rochelle toward Flanders, and nine other at Bordeaux. I require you to send me word, if any of this navy meet with them or with any Flemings laden with wine, whether you think I should send them to London, Hampton, or elsewhere into England, or else let them freely go; and if I shall make a price thereof or not, and what price I should set, as well Gascony as Rochelle. At this time I write no more unto you, fearing you be weary of my often writing; but I had rather to be judged too quick than too slow. And thus Our Lord send you that your heart most desireth. In haste, at 2 a'clock, in the *Mary Rose* the 16 day of May.

Yours assuredly, Thomas Howard.

25. *Thomas, Lord Howard, to the King, 18 May 1513.*

Pleaseth it your most noble grace to understand the 17 day at 10 a'clock before noon, I received your letters of the 15 day, by the which I perceive your pleasure is to have certain ships to come into the Narrow Sea. And according to your highness's commandment I have sufficiently victualled them as much as they can bestow. And beside that, I have appointed the *Peter of Fowey*, which hath a great substance of victual in her, to go with them in the *Mary of Brixham*'s stead, for she is as good with a sail as the other, and in her I have put 40 tall men and two gentlemen of mine for captains. Beseeching your grace to take no displeasure that they, the victuallers, nor the residue of your army, departeth not hence, for I assure your grace, as yet it is not possible. We be all ready, and have been these six days; and now these two or three days past, the wind blowing at West-South-West, which is the best wind possible to bring us to Hampton, hath and yet doth blow so strainable that we have been forced every man to lay out shot, anchors and all, and have broken many anchors and cables. Assuring your grace that whosoever bought your new cables hath done you shrewd service, for they be made of the worst stuff that ever man saw, as at my coming to Hampton your grace shall well perceive by an example I shall send you of the same. Sir, your grace may make a sure reckoning, God willing, within one day and a night after this great tempest is done, to have all your victuallers at Hampton, and the ships by your grace appointed shall come into the Narrow Sea as shortly as shall be possible. And I with the whole army will come along the coast of Normandy, which me think shall cause them to think that we intend no more to come in Brittany, they seeing us draw from thenceward toward England. And, Sir, at our coming again thither, I trust it shall cause them to be the more unprovided. Sir, I beseech God that your pretended enterprise be not known by your enemies, for and it be, I fear they shall draw all their ships from Brest unto Rochelle or Bordeaux. For, Sir, I assure your grace I have so debated here with them that knoweth Brest everything what we may do, as well by land as water, and what resistance your enemies may make, that I think, God willing, it shall not be possible for them to save their ships nor galleys if we find them at Brest. And thus I beseech Almighty God to send your grace the accomplishment of all your most noble heart's desires. Scribbled in the *Mary Rose* the 18 day of May, at Plymouth, where I pray God defend me for ever coming again with such a small army.

Your most humble subject and Admiral, Thomas Howard.

26. *Thomas, Lord Howard, to Wolsey, 20 May 1513.*

Master Almoner, with all mine heart I recommend me unto you. I send here enclosed a letter which was sent me yesterday, and I have examined him that brought it, who was in Guernsey this day seven-night. He saith that there came from Brittany-ward and went toward Normandy the 11 day of May 60 sails and above, and also there came in like wise [18 *then* 13 sail *deleted*] 18 sails from Brittany to Normandy-ward the 13 day. Also he saith that there is divers ships of Brittany laden with wine and linen cloth come into Guernsey, and the Bretons of the said ships say that they have taken their ordnance out of their ships and had it into the castle, and will no more meddle on the sea this year, but will defend the land; for on the sea they be not able to compare with the King's army, but against the next year they will make ships enough to defend the sea. Also he saith that the Bretons say that Frere Barnardyne is looked for in Brittany with 10 galleys, which I believe not to be true, for I never heard he had more than one galley and one foist. Also he saith that the Normans bring their goods fast into Guernsey for fear of the King's landing there, and the said Normans say that, and the Englishmen come thither and burn not, the country will yield to them. In base Normandy here be all the sayings of this man. Also I have a Breton here which came [thence *deleted*] with English prisoners the [17 *corrected to*] 7 day of May from St Pol de Leon. And I have straitly examined him; who saith that the mariners that came from Brest by stealth, having no will now longer to serve in the ships of war, say that the ships of war were come forth from the castle and would return to their countries; and that the hulks that were at Brest said they would go homeward and convey the Admiral to Honfleur, where he intended to lay up his ship for this year. I asked him further and if the French King's mind were to have his army come forth, and for how long he thought it would be or they might be victualled; and he said it was not possible for them to be victualled in two months. Also he saith that the ships of Brittany that be at home be haled up into creeks and digged in pits, not thinking to come to the sea this year. Also he hath showed many other things which be of no great weight. Master Almoner, I write unto you the premises because, you being informed thereof, may debate among my lords of the Council what is to be done every way. I mean thus, if it so be that the navy of France be sparkled every ship to his port, and few or none left at Brest, methink the enterprise pretended there should be greatly chargeable to the King, and small profit should ensue thereof; the certainty whereof I doubt not to certify you as shortly as wind and weather will serve, for I have appointed three good barks to go along the coast of Brittany only to take me some fisherman or other that may ascertain me of the truth of the premises. And if they can take none such, yet shall they go to Guernsey where [*Sir Richard*] Weston shall certify me if any of the men-of-war be gone to Normandy-ward, which he knoweth as well by report of Bretons that daily resort thither, as also in seeing them that do pass by the isles; not doubting by this means at my coming to Hampton to have perfect knowledge of all their doing. Desiring you most humbly to have me recommended to the King's grace and the Queen's, to my lord my father and all such as you know my friends; beseeching his grace to think no default in me of our long abode here, which is to me the most sorrow that might have come to my heart. But against the wind I cannot make ships sail, and if I might, I had been hence nine days past, as God knoweth, who have you in his tuition.

Scribbled at Plymouth, the 20 day of May, warping with much pain from Cattewater to the Sound.

Yours assuredly, Thomas Howard.

27. *Thomas, Lord Howard, to the King, 28 May* [*1513*].

Pleaseth your most noble grace to understand this morning at 5 a'clock came unto me Sabyne, whom with two other ships I had sent to the coast of Brittany. Sir, they have taken 13 sails laden with salt, and are in the Needles. Sir, [the *otiose*] Sabyne saith that Weston sent one out of Alderney to Normandy to know tidings, and he saith that on Thursday last he left the *Lewis*, the ship of La Bouille and the ship of Dieppe, and divers others ships without Honfleur in the road, and Sir, I think it shall not be possible for them to get in these neap tides. Wherefore, with God's grace, I will forth this day so that I may be with them in the morning by day. I pray God I may find them there; and then I trust to do your grace some service. Also, Sir, the prisoners taken say that all the men-of-war were coming to Normandy to revictual, and at [*St*] Brieuc took their counsel, and so [the galleys with *deleted*] the ship of Bordeaux, the ship of Rochelle, the ship of Rouen with 12 sails returned to Brest and the rest went

51

toward Normandy. Also they say that the Queen is come to Nantes and hath sent money to pay wages for three months, and also a ship of 60 laden with powder and ordnance to Brest. Also they say that the French King hath sent Mons. de la Motte into Scotland with money to pay the wages of five Scottish ships and 18 of Denmark, and with him two ships laden with flour, and be gone by the west parts of Ireland. Sir, other news here be none, but shortly I trust your grace shall have others. With God's grace, who send the accomplishment of your most heart's desires. Scribbled in great haste, the 28 day of May at 6 a'clock in the morning.

Your most humble subject and Admiral, Thomas Howard.

Endorsed: To the King's most noble grace, and in his absence to my lords of his most honourable Council. Haste, post. On thy life.

28. *Thomas, Lord Howard, to Wolsey, 5 June [1513].*

The King had been at Southampton, but was now on his way back to London. No text survives of instructions cancelling a further assault on Brittany; the order seems to have been given verbally to the Admiral on 4 June, as explained here.

Master Almoner, with all my heart I recommend me unto you. Good Master Almoner, I have found you so kind unto me that methink I can do no less than to write unto you from time to time of all my causes. So it is, though I be unable therefor, it hath pleased the King's grace to give this great room and authority more meet for a wise, expert man than me. But since it hath pleased his grace to admit me thereunto, as far as my poor wit can extend, I shall endeavour myself from time to time to do all manner of service where I shall think to deserve his most desired favour. And, good Master Almoner, as my most singular trust is in you, send me both now and at all other times your good advice and counsel, assuring you that never poor gentleman was in greater fear to take rebuke and ill report than I am of such as knoweth not what may be done, which generally be the greatest number, and for many causes, of which I shall rehearse a part.

First, I well perceive what reports both this year and the last was made of my brother (whom Jesus pardon) because there was none other service done, considering what great charges the King was at in keeping so great a navy on the sea. And I well know that I nor no man hath better will nor more hardly durst serve his master than he, as the proof hath showed; and as for experience, I am yet far from that he had, [which *deleted*] and yet his fortune was not to have at all times the best report, many men putting fear what he durst do, which opinions the day of his death he well proved untrue. Alas, Master Almoner, I see not now how I shall escape such reports, for I cannot see how I may do any pleasant service to my master, for I see no ways but one of the two.

The one is that, at my going to Brittany, my fortune might have been so good that, either I might have burned the ships at Brest castle, or else to have destroyed the haven there with drowning of ships, as I have before written unto you. Which enterprises being debated before his grace, and such dangers as I thought might thereof ensue by me declared before his grace, I showed his grace I durst not enterprise the said feats unless that his grace would discharge me if any misfortune fell by the same. And then his grace bade me not spare to adventure the same, and to go with his army into the great water of Brest. And now, since his departure hence, my lord of Winchester and my Lord Lisle have devised upon the said enterprises, and yesterday called me unto them and commanded me in the King's name not to enter the water of Brest till I knew further of the King's pleasure, for great causes which they would advertise the King and his Council of.

And so, this matter taking none effect, I see no way how I shall deserve thank unless the Scots and Danes join with the Frenchmen, without whom I never think we shall find the Frenchmen abroad. And therefore I beseech God that shortly they may join, which only may be the safeguard of my good name. And, good Master Almoner, if you see surely that the Scots and Danes come not, let me have licence to discharge all this army, save only the King's ships, with whom the navy of France will not fight this year. And as for the Spaniards here, I assure you [*they*] would fain be at home ever since they heard of the truce.

And thus most heartily I beseech you, if my misfortune shall be to do no acceptable service, to be means for me to the King and his Council to consider that never man endured more pain than I shall do to see all other where they may do good service if they will, and I can do none but his enemies will adventure as well as I. And, for God's sake, let his grace and his Council command me to some hard enterprise to see if I will follow the same, being in despair save only of the Scots and Danes coming.

Master Almoner, all the premises and all other my causes I remit to your wisdom, fully trusting that you will not only from time to time give me your good advice and counsel, but also with your friendly words withstand all ill reports undeserved made [of me *inserted*], as my singular trust is in you. And thus Our Lord have you in his tuition. Scribbled at Hampton, the 5 day of June.

Yours assuredly, Thomas Howard.

29. *Thomas, Lord Howard, to Wolsey, 6 June 1513.*

Master Almoner, with all my heart I recommend me unto you. This morning at 8 a'clock came to me [*Richard*] Calthrop and Harper, whom I had sent to the Normandy coast to know some tidings, and they have taken a fisherman with seven men and brought unto me the master, whom I have straitly examined; and he saith that there came 15 or 16 days past 18 ships out of Brittany to Honfleur, and be all laid up under the town, and all the mariners and soldiers returned to their houses, saying they will no more go to the sea this year without the Scots and Danes come, whom they look daily for. I asked him if they made any preparation for new revictualling, and he saith nay, save that Hob a Barton hath already mustered men to furnish a new ship that he hath made and a bark that shall go with her, with whom he will go toward the north parts. Also, he saith that it was said that a great power of Englishmen would land in Normandy, and that all the country was in great fear, and if any such came, would gladly yield themselves English, so that their country were not robbed nor burned. The French King had so pilled them with more larger *tailles* by the third part than ever he had done, that they would gladly be English and to be out of his thraldom, saying that, and [*if*] the war continue one year, Normandy shall be utterly destroyed. Also, Wiseman being in company with Calthrop and Harper, hath brought with him a hulk which came laden long ago with wines from Bordeaux, and she was attached and brought unto Dieppe, and her wines taken from her. Because an Englishman of long time dwelling in Flanders was master of her, who now of late was suffered to depart with the ship and is come with Wiseman, and as yet is not come to me; but Calthrop and Harper saith that he saith in everything as the other Frenchman doth, saving he saith Hob a Barton is already departed northward with 12 sails of small ships, intending to seek his profit northward. I pray God he meet not with the Iceland fleet. Also the Englishman saith that a ship of more than 200 of those that came out of Brittany fell on a leak and was brought to Harfleur; and in bringing her on ground watered on the one side and is perished. Which premises heard, I took horses and rode to my lord of Winchester and to my Lord Lisle hither, to show them the premises, and forthwith will return to the ships. As for news out of Brittany, yet I have none, but I look hourly to hear, for I have three ships on that coast. And when my departure shall be I cannot yet certify you, for there is slow lading of beer at Portsmouth, and tomorrow I will take the musters, and with as much haste as may be possible I will depart to Brittany-ward, with God's grace, who have you in his tuition. Scribbled at Winchester, the 6 day of June at one at afternoon.

[*Postscript*]: Sir, as yet I hear no word of anchors nor cables from you.

Yours assuredly, Thomas Howard,

Endorsed: To Master Almoner with the King's grace. Delivered at one at Winchester the 6 day of June.

30. *Thomas, Lord Howard, to the Council, 8 June 1513.*

Pleaseth it your good lordships to understand the 7 day of June I received your letters at midnight of the 6 day, and where it pleased you in your first article to answer that I wrote to you touching my return to Brest; my lords, I assure you there can no man be more joyful than I am to go thither, for no creature alive would more gladly do some acceptable service than I. And without it be done there, I see not where I shall do it, unless the Scots and Danes come, and you may be sure I shall do the best I can to do the pretended enterprises with as good policy as I can use to save the King's navy. But without some adventure none exploit of war will be achieved, trusting your good lordships shall well perceive there shall lack no good will in me.

And as touching the receiving of bows and arrows, I shall see them as little wasted as shall be possible. And where your lordships write that it is great marvelled where so great a number of bows and arrows be brought to so small a number, I have enquired the causes thereof; and as far as I can see, the greatest number were witch bows, of whom few would abide the bending. But as for that was done before my time, I cannot call again, but from henceforth, if I do not the best I can to keep everything from waste, I am worthy blame, which I trust I shall not deserve.

And as touching the safe keeping of foists, assuredly, before my coming was great waste, and since my coming I trust few or never one hath been wasted, nor shall be.

And where your lordships write for the discharging of victuallers not necessary, my lord of Winchester and my Lord Lisle can inform you how I have ordered that, for of 140 and more I have taken under 30, and would not have had more than 14 save only to bring the foists again hither as they be emptied.

And as touching divers other causes which your lordships hath made me now answer of, I shall not need to touch the same, but other causes requisite here.

Yesterday I began to take the musters, and this day and tomorrow by noon I trust to make an end. I fear there is a great number gone without licence. My Lord Ferrers' men mustered yesterday, and were but 300 and 11. He saith he is sure he wanteth above 100, and is as angry therewith as ever was man, and

A reconstruction of the aiming of a longbow through one of the removable blinds on the museum reconstruction of the upper deck. (*Mary Rose Trust*)

hath delivered me two that were going away; whom, if I can prove that they were departed, I shall not fail to cause to be hanged tomorrow. Also he showeth me that the gaol of Hereford is full of his men that be run away. Wherefore methink it were well done that the King's grace should command some of them to be put to execution, which shall put others in fear; and if some might be brought hither against my return, to be put to execution here, methink it should be well done.

And as touching my departure hence, I assure your lordships I tarry for nothing save only for lading of beer, which is the slowest work that ever man saw. There is but two cranes, and the crayers that shall be laden with them must come in at a full sea, and at a full sea go out. Wherefore, if your lordships see not another provision for lading of beer against the next revictualling, I fear me we shall spend half or we get hence. Wherein I have communed with William Pawne and Palshide, and we see no remedy so good as to do it with lighters, as we do in the Thames, and in this country is none. Wherefore, if it would please your lordships to send hither out of the Thames two or three of the greatest, and to be towed hither with crayers, we think it should be the most profitable way for the King's grace. And with making them higher with a strake of board, we doubt not they shall come safe hither. [Hither *corrected to*] Here is the goodliest sort of [bows *deleted*] brewhouses that ever I saw, and already do brew 100 ton a day, and great pity it were that there should not provision be made shortly to ship the same. Also, when the beer is put in the vessels, there is no houses to lay it in, but are fain to lay it abroad in the streets, where now the hot weather coming on, it shall shortly be destroyed. Wherefore I have commanded William Pawne to cause great trenches to be digged and to be

Christopher Dobbs holds one of the 137 complete yew longbows recovered. (*Mary Rose Trust*)

covered with some boards, turves, sedges, and such stuff as may be gotten, to keep the heat therefrom. Also, the beer that came hither for my Lord Lisle is such as no man may drink for the most part. I have assayed the most part of it, and the Treasurer and the Clerk Comptroller the rest, and as much as may be drunk is delivered to the ships; and the rest I shall send again to London, for Heron's servants that hath the delivery of it here saith that the brewers be bound to take as much as is unable stuff. I know not what the King payeth, but I assure your lordships, much of it is as small as penny ale, and as sour as a crab. I doubt not your lordships will see the brewers punished.

Also I send your lordships a charter party which I have received of a master of an hulk laden with woad. I have put him under arrest till I know your pleasure. If it be a prize it is worth £3,000 or better, and if the truth be well tried, I think it will prove Frenchmen's goods. I beseech your lordships I may know your pleasures therein, and whether you will I shall deliver the goods to Dawtrey or no till the trial be made. If it be laid on land, at the least the King shall have the custom.

Also, the King's grace promised me to send me certain hackbuts in exchange for such as I shall send his grace. I beseech your lordships they may be shortly sent hither by land. And with all possible haste I shall depart forward, with God's grace, who have you in his blessed tuition. Scribbled at Portsmouth, the 8 day of June.

Thomas Howard.

Endorsed: To my lords of the King's most honourable Council. Delivered at Portsmouth at 11 before noon. Haste, post, haste, haste.

31. *Thomas, Lord Howard, to the Bishop of Winchester, the Earl of Surrey, and Wolsey, 13 June 1513.*

Pleaseth it your lordships to understand this day at 3 after noon I received your letters of the 12 day of June, and by the same I perceive your pleasures touching the wages of the ships in the Narrow Seas, and so shall follow your pleasures therein; but before your letters came, the *Carrack of Savona* [alias *Santa Maria de Loretto*], the *Katherine Fortileza*, and the *Mary George* were gone out of sight toward the Narrow Seas, and with them many small men, some with the King's mounts of the New Forest, and some with other necessaries sent from Hampton which I know not what they carry, and many to convey the King's army over, and I doubt not will be in the Downs or [*before*] you shall have this letter. And where your lordships write to me of the being of the ship of Denmark in

Flanders, and also of the galleys in Dieppe, I have sent three small ships after the said carracks with a letter to advertise them thereof, and also if the galleys come forth, to meet with them; without which small ships, if the galleys meet with our ships, little good would be done, and peradventure if a calm came, much danger might ensue. And therefore, to provide for the worst, I have sent them; and yet, thanked be God and the King's grace, we be strong enough here to encounter with the whole fleet of France. And if the wind had served, I had been well onward toward Brest or now, as knoweth Our Lord, who have your good lordships in his tuition. Scribbled in the *Mary Rose* before Quarr Abbey, abiding to know the King's pleasure; beseeching your good lordships to command me shortly what shall be your pleasures.

Yours assuredly, Thomas Howard.

Endorsed: Delivered at Portsmouth at 4 at afternoon the 13 day of June.

32. *Lord Admiral's warrant for oars, 18 June 1513.*

Cousin Wyndham, I will that you pay to the purser of the *Mary Rose* 20s for 2 dozen oars. And this my writing signed with my hand the 18 day of June in the 5th year of King Henry VIIIth shall be your warrant for payment of the same.

Thomas Howard.

33. *Miscellaneous expenses of the ship, 14 March–16 July 1513.*

The charges of the good ship called the *Mary Rose* from the 14 day of March unto the 16 day of July.

[*Jesus at the head of each page*]

Item paid for a lighter the 18 day of March for carrying of 2 great curtals to Woolwich – sum 2s 6d.

Item paid to Hoberd dwelling at the Queenhithe the 21 day of March for a small rope weighing 82 lb, the lb at 1½d – sum 10s 3d.

Item paid for an axe and 2 great garnets the 21 day of March – 2s 8d.

Item paid for 10 ells of fine Normandy canvas, the ell 7½d – 6s 3d.

Item paid the 25 day of March to William Hallyngberry dwelling in Sandwich for 2 small ropes weighing 272 lb the 100 [cwt] at 13s 4d – 36s 1d.

Item paid for 2 small lines – 16d.

Item paid at Sandwich 26 day of March for 12 lb of sail twine, the lb at 6d – 6s.

Item paid at Dartmouth for a 100 spikings – 2s 6d.

Item paid at Plymouth for making of the cat [hook *deleted*] – 2s 8d.

Item paid for 2 gallons of vinegar for Nicholas Kyng to make fine powder for hand guns – 8*d.*

Item paid the 20 day of April for mending of the standard and the flags and streamers – 8*d.*

Item paid for thread for the foresaid business – 3*d.*

Item paid the 10 day of May at Plymouth to William Randdale for a small rope weighing 36 lb, the lb ½*d* – 4*s* 6*d.*

Item paid the 10 day of May at Plymouth to John Pounde for 2 small lines – 2*s.*

Item paid the 11 day of May at Plymouth to John Pounde for half a 1,000 of 10-penny nail, the 100, 10*d* – 4*s* 3*d.*

Paid for half a 1,000 of 5-penny nail, the 100 at 6*d* – 2*s* 1*d.*

Item paid the 11 day of May at Plymouth to John Boene for a great elm for the stock of a brazen piece – 3*s* 4*d.*

Paid to the said man for 6 small elms, 4 of them to make axle-trees for falcons and the other two for the bumkin – 3*s* 4*d.*

Item paid the 12 day of May at Plymouth to Richard Koke for 2 boat hooks – 13*d.*

Item paid to William Edzskome at Plymouth the 12 day of May for ironwork that went to the stocking of the brazen pieces, weighing net 120 lb, the lb 1½*d* – sum 14*s* 7*d.*

Item paid at Plymouth the 19 day of May to Nicholas Elles of Topsham for 3 small hawsers weighing 300 quarters, price the 100 [*cwt*] 12*s* 4*d* – sum 40*s* 1*d.*

Item paid at Plymouth the 23 day of May to the vicar for a piece of timber for the cock's wale – 16*d.*

Item paid to Richard Chalfer of Plymouth the 23 day of May for a 100 rough and clench nail – 16*d.*

Paid to the same man for making of a chief of iron for the cock's head – 10*d.*

Paid to the same man for half a 100 of spikings, weighing 14 lb – 2*s* 4*d.*

Item paid the 4 day of June to Robert Myle of Southampton for 4 lb and a half of marline – 12*d.*

Item paid the 8 day of June at Plymouth to John Johnson for 2 bands and 2 bolts of iron for a great piece of brass, the which weighed net 34 lb, the lb at 2*d* – sum 5*s* 8*d.*

Item paid to the same man for 2 boat hooks – 12*d.*

Item paid to John Byrd the 18 day of June for 2 lb of sail twine, the lb at 6*d* – 12*d.*

Item paid at Sandwich the 22 day of June for ironwork for the boat's rudder and the cock's rudder, weighing 14 lb, the lb at 2*d* – 2*s* 4*d.*

Item paid at Sandwich the 10 day of July to Thomas Balze for 300 6-penny nails – 18*d*.

Item paid at Sandwich the 12 day of July to John Messyng for a hook to fetch the anchor with, weighing 32 lb – 5*s* 4*d*.

Item paid to the same man for 2 boat hooks – 12*d*.

Item paid at Sandwich the 15 day of July for 2 small masts for the making of the deck, to France Sketto – 5*s* 4*d*.

Item paid the 15 day of July at Sandwich to William Hallyngberry for 6 small ropes weighing 88 lb, the which ropes shall be occupied for the net in their upper deck – sum 11*s* 9*d*.

Sum total – £9 8*s* 10*d*

Received by a warrant of my lord Admiral of Master Treasurer – £8.

So rest unto me – 28*s* 10*d*.

Minuted by the lord Admiral: Cousin Wyndham, I pray you pay him the said 28*s* 10*d*.

Thomas Howard.

34. *Ordnance charges authorized by the Lord Admiral aboard the* Mary Rose, *12 July 1513.*

These be the parcels which I Sir William Sidney have laid out in making ports and other things necessary in the *Great Carrack* in time of the King's going over.

Item, for boards and planks which was [?] fetched from Rye to the Downs – 30*s*.

Item for a crayer hired to bring the same stuff – 10*s*.

Item for 4 great trees and 8 spars which was bought at Deal – 14*s* 6*d*.

Item for iron and coal to make joints, spikes, clenches for making of the ports, to smiths working upon the same – £3 5*s*.

Item for nails great and small – 8*s*

Item for tallow to tallow the ship with – 20*s*.

Item for reed and broom – 5*s*.

Item paid to 6 carpenters for working upon the said ship – 20*s*.

Item for a new stock to the great gun – 8*s*.

Item for the hire of a gear to wind up the piece – 12*d*.

Item in meat and drink for the carpenters working upon the same gun – 4*s* 10*d*.

Item for iron and the workmanship thereof upon great bolts and breeches to the said gun – 12*s*.

Item to the carpenters working upon the same gun – 6*s* 8*d*.

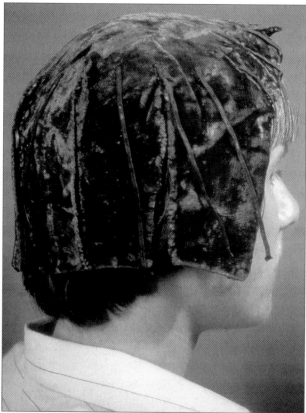

Cap of silk velvet, found in the barber surgeon's cabin. Similar coifs are seen in a contemporary painting of the Barber Surgeons' Company. This one was probably worn by Robert Symson's successor in 1545. (*Mary Rose Trust*)

Items recovered from the barber surgeon's cabin which reflect his multiple functions: razors, whetstones, bowls for shaving, medicine bottles and a pewter bleeding bowl. (*C.T.C. Dobbs/Mary Rose Trust*)

Item for ironwork and plate for 2 serpentines – 4s 4d.
Item for a man that rode in post from Flushing to Calais – 20s.
Sum – £11 9s 4d.

Minuted by the lord Admiral: Cousin Wyndham, I pray you allow these parcels above written, and this shall be your discharge. Written in the *Mary Rose* the 12 day of July.
Thomas Howard.

35. *Lord Admiral's warrant for payment of wages to the master surgeon and his assistant, 20 May 1513; with entry in the accounts of Sir Thomas Wyndham, treasurer of the army, for payments made by authority of the King's letters missive for the month beginning 13 July following.*

Cousin Wyndham, where Robert Symson was appointed by my brother Sir Edward Howard, whom God pardon, to be the master surgeon within the *Mary Rose*, and is not expressed within your letter missive to you directed from the King's grace to receive the wages of a master surgeon, that notwithstanding, my said brother's promise considered, I will you pay him the wages of a master surgeon every month from the 14th day of March during the time that he shall continue in the said *Mary Rose*, and his servant's wages after the rate of another surgeon, being no master, for the said time. And this my writing shall be your discharge in this behalf. Written at Plymouth the 20th day of May in the 5th year of the reign of our sovereign lord King Henry the VIIIth.
Thomas Howard.

[*The warrant attached to the following entry in the account.*]

To the *Mary Rose*. To Robert Symson, [master *inserted*] surgeon assigned and appointed to the *Mary Rose*, for his wages at [10s *deleted*] 13s 4d by the month, by my Lord Admiral's warrant hereunto annexed, which surgeon remaineth unpaid for 5 months as in the said warrant appeareth, which amounteth to – 66s 8d.

To Henry Yonge his servant, surgeon assigned and appointed to the *Mary Rose*, for his wages at 10s a month, being unpaid for the foresaid 5 months as in the said warrant doth appear, which amounteth to – [20 *deleted*] 50s.

36. *Lord Admiral's warrant for compensation to a wounded gunner [after 1 February 1514, when Howard was created Earl of Surrey].*

Cousin Wyndham, I will that you pay to Andrew Fysch, one of the gunners of the *Mary Rose*, by the way of reward to heal him of his hurts – 13*s* 4*d*. And this my warrant shall be your discharge.

T. Surrey.

37. *Lord Admiral's disbursements for a fortnight at sea, 1514.*

Money that I Thomas, Earl of Surrey, Admiral of England, doth ask allowance of for such charges as I [*replacing* he] and my [*replacing* his] company were at from the time we [*replacing* he] landed at Newcastle into the time we [*replacing* he] took the sea again, [by the space of 16 days *inserted*].

The *Mary Rose*. First for the wages of the footmen at 6*d* a day a man, by the space of 16 days, of which number the captains and every captain's number hereafter ensueth.

Item Edward Bray, Captain of the *Mary Rose*, for his wages for the said 16 days, at 4*s* a day – 64*s*.

Item for 201 soldiers and mariners brought with the said Edward Bray out of the *Mary Rose* for the said 16 days, after 6*d* a day a man – £80 8*s*.

Item for 12 gunners of Danzig taken out of an hull to serve for the said journey by land, for their wages and in reward to 7 of them that were hurt – £13 6*s* 8*d*.

38. *Petition from John Wodlas, pilot, to the Council, received 2 May 1514.*

Asking for his expenses in conducting the Mary Rose *through the North Sea, and on another occasion attending the* Salvator of Lübeck (*alias* Great Elizabeth).

Pleaseth it your good lordships to understand that I, John Wodlas of Harwich, have given his attendance upon the conveying of the King's ships as hereafter ensueth.

First the said John conveyed the *Mary Rose* out of Harwich haven over a danger in the sea called the Naze, and incontinent after, continued to conduct and bring the same ship over again into Harwich haven; and within five days was commanded to conduct and convey the said ship out of the said haven through a place in the sea called the Slade to meet with the King's grace coming from Calais-ward, and so did. And then incontinent after, conveyed her out of the Downs through the Black Deeps into Thames, which was in the whole by the space of three weeks, and three men at his charges, with his boat by the same space.

64

Item the said John Wodlas received the said *Mary Rose* now last at Blackwall, and conducted and brought the same within the haven of Portsmouth, and then returned himself to London by land.

Item then incontinent was commanded by your lordships to go unto the North Foreland to give attendance upon the King's ship called the *Lübeck*, and so [to *otiose*] conveyed the same unto [Portsmouth *deleted*] London, and by force of weather a storm 'but' [? brought] her to the Camber, and there she came to an anchor; and as soon as I heard thereof took my boat and went thither, and before my coming she made sail and went to Portsmouth. Which attendance given unto these said last journeys hath been since the first beginning of Lent past [*1 March*].

In consideration whereof, it may please your same good lordships to allow unto him his reasonable costs and allowances for the same. And besides all this I have lost in 'bewyons' in the Black Deeps and iron chains which were not possible to be lost by tempest of weather, which amounted to the sum of £4.

Minuted by Wolsey [*now bishop of Lincoln*]: Fellow Daunce, you must pay to Woodeles for conveyance of the King's ships as is before expressed through the Black Deeps and other places, twenty marks. T. Lincoln.

Endorsed: Received by me John Woodeles of Sir John Daunce, knight, by the King's commandment, twenty marks sterling, for the conveyance of the King's ships through the Black Deeps as within expressed, the second day of May in the 6th year of King Henry VIIIth.

Per me John Wodlas.

39. *The Earl of Surrey, Lord Admiral, to the Council, 27 May* [*1514*].

[Pleaseth it] your lordships to understand I came yesterday unto Sandwich, [suppo]sing to have found the ships in the Downs, but they were [not] there. And so by 7 a'clock I came unto Dover; and before my coming, about noon, the Vice-Admiral, by the advice of the most expert captains and masters on the coast of Boulogne, sent over Sir Henry Sherborne and Sir Stephen Bull with 10 sails of small men and the rowbarges, galleys and other, well manned, and this was their order, which was as good in my mind as was possible. The wind was at North-North-East, and was so great an haze that skant o[ne] might see a mile; and so upon the flood they drew over with Escalles cliffs, and then with the ebb they came with a good blower towards St John's road, and sent before them 4 or 5 miles [Sir] Stephen Bull, Thomas Vaughan and three other small men, to the in[tent] to have gotten between the galleys and Boulogne haven, and the r[est] of our ships kept them out of sight; and so our five sail made as much as they might toward the haven. And Prior John [*Prégent de Bidoux*] with five galleys, three foists and two barks road at the point of St John's road toward Calais, 5 miles from Boulogne, and as [soon] as our men were in sight, which were but five sail, away went all the Frenchmen with sails and oars all that they might, and won the point of the haven under the bulwark. Which our men perceiving, and that it was unpossible to come unto [them] there without utter confusion, shot at them their ordnance and [. . .] at them. And then our men, perceiving the wind drew northward, they haled out into the road and came to [. . .] anchor before the galleys, without that the said galleys saw [no] more of our ships but those five, and would never weigh to come [with] them. And then about midnight the wind was so [. . .] our men might no longer abide there, but came their w[ay . . .] and none of them but two might recover Dover road, but w[ent] as far as Camber. And my cousin Wyndham in like [. . .] 20 sails with him, and at this hour I see him with them [. . .] coming again unto us.

My lords, I have written at [length] unto you hereof, because I would you should perceive as well [the] good handling of our men, as also to consider what Pri[or John] intendeth, which after my mind is to make a train [. . .] within the danger of their bulwarks, supposing t[hey *might do what*] they did the last year, or else to watch for a ca[lm . . .] to do some displeasure to some passenger if he can [. . .] for the best I can, and have written unto Master [. . .] he shall suffer no passenger to come over in no calm w[. . .] them to go over seaboard Goodwin, which is as short way [. . .] within 4 miles and out of danger.

My lords, all this day h[as been] as calm as was possible, so that I might send no ship [over]. This night before midnight, if there blow any wind, I [have] appointed Sir Henry Sherborne with 10 sails, and Wiseman [and] Wallop with other 10 sails, to go over. Sir Henry shall dra[w] by West Boulogne, and if the wind will serve him to get between Boulogne and the galleys, if they be abroad in the [sea] as they were yesterday, and Wiseman shall come from Cal[ais]-ward along that shore to essay what he can do in like [wise].

And if this way will not serve, I can see no ways how t[o get] unto them without likelihood of extreme danger and peril, [unless] that I might have 2 or 3,000 of such soldiers as be now [in] Calais shipped in the haven there and so sent unto me, and to set other 3,000 on land within 2 miles of Boulogne. With which company I think without danger the said galleys would [be] put in great danger to be had. Which I remit to be deb[ated] and ordered after your wisdoms, beseeching you to advertise [me] of your further minds in the premises and I shall gladly follow the same.

Also Sir Thomas West is as Sandwich w[. . .] and I have commanded him to remain there till he k[nows your] further pleasures. May it therefore please you to certify him how he shall be ordered. Also I have sent two good ships [unto] Zeeland to waft the fleet there. I have also appointed and [ordered] to depart, when wind shall serve, nine good ships to go n[orthward], which be sufficient if the Frenchmen b[. . .] sails. With God's grace, who keep you. Written in the *Ma*[*ry Rose*] in Dover road, the 27ty day of May at 7 at night.

Yours, T. Surrey.

40. *Lord Admiral Surrey to the Duke of Norfolk (his father), Wolsey, and Richard Fox, Bishop of Winchester, Councillors.*

The 'bill' said to be enclosed does not survive. The words here printed in bold are at the foot of the recto in the MS; the secret part of the dispatch can be read by simply turning the page.

My lords, pleaseth it you to understand, whereas I wrote unto you yesterday how I had appointed certain ships to have essayed an enterprise against the galleys [**39**], this morning the wind came unto North-West, so that we dare not adventure within St John's road, for it were not possible to come out of that road, the wind being there. And because I would be assured that nothing should be omitted that may be feasible, with God's grace with the next fair wind that may possibly serve to go and come, I will go over in the King's *Less Bark* with such company with me of small ships as with God's grace shall do that is possible to be done. And if they abide without the bulwark, I doubt not to displease them without great loss; and if they go within the bulwark, as far as I can understand it is as dangerous as it were to enter within Rysbank tower, which is not to be adventured with none but with them that will cast themselves away wilfully. And my lords, if this enterprise will not take effect, under your corrections, methink it were not honourable that all the army should remain here for fear of the said galleys. And notwithstanding that I know well your lordships can more substantially determine this matter than I can advise you, yet I shall be so bold to advertise you of my poor advice; which is, first considering that it should not be honourable for so royal an army as this to lie here for fear of the said galleys, and also that they cannot long abide here, but must draw to the Wight for their victualling, methink that such ships as be named in a bill here enclosed should suffice to defend the passage, and also sufficient to encounter with the said galleys if they would come abroad. And that Sir Wystan Browne should be most meet man to have the conduct of the said ships; and that the rest of the army should draw Westward to do the most annoyance to the Frenchmen they can.

This side of the leaf the most part of the captains have seen, and desired me so to write. But none is privy to the other side.

My lords, one other matter is, I shall be bold to put you in mind of. If this Frenchman that now is come should conclude a peace with the King's grace shortly, and then the great ships should be gone westward, the wind might come so that it should cost his grace £2,000 more to bring them into Thames from thence than it should do, they being now here. Wherefore of the premises I beseech you to advertise me of your pleasures, not doubting but you will, as you shall see the case require, either shortly stop or else haste forward as well the King's great ship with her victuals, as also such victuals as John Dawtrey shall prepare more for this army. In looking whereupon shortly, much money may be saved if the peace conclude. And after my mind, if you think the matter will be concluded within a fortnight, it were better the great ships abode here than to go any further West, [considering the King will have them in to Thames *inserted*], and small ships may be sent thither. And the ships here be now sufficiently victualled for a fortnight and more, and those that go northward for a month. And of the premises I beseech your lordships to advertise me by post, and also how long you would I should remain here, to the intent that, and [*if*] I should tarry here, I might send for more of my servants, for I have not here passing 18 with me, which is too few. And thus Our Lord have you in his assured tuition. Scribbled in the *Mary Rose* in Dover road.

[*Postscript*]: My lords, yesterday in the calm, Preer John with his galleys and foists chased a small balinger of ours, but he would never come 2 mile from the shore.

Yours, T. Surrey.

4

LAYING UP AND OUT
OF SERVICE (1514–22)

COMMENTARY

Surrey's last dispatch of the war was written on the *Mary Rose* as the returning fleet entered Poole harbour (**42**). The two small-scale raids he reported were specifically in reprisal for a French raid on Brighton, which had taken place a few weeks before, when peace negotiations were already in hand. Surrey (clearly) and Henry (probably) thought that had been a blow below the belt, hence the satisfaction which is clear from this letter.

At some point during July most of the ships engaged on active service, including the *Mary Rose*, were brought round to Deptford and decommissioned. This was a fairly comprehensive business, and was carried out under the supervision of a royal commission appointed for the purpose, in this case headed by Sir Henry Wyatt, the Master of the Jewel House (**43**). The rigging was dismantled, and the masts unshipped and handed over to John Hopton the Clerk Comptroller, for storage (presumably, although this is not stated) in the new storehouses recently built at Erith. Anchors, pulleys, and all the rest of the sailing equipment was similarly disposed of, including the contents of the galley. The 'munitions and habiliments of war', that is to say the hackbuts, bows, arrows, bills and body armour, were handed over to John Millet and Thomas Elderton, financial officials acting for the Ordnance Office, presumably for return to the Tower of London. Rather strangely, however, the guns were left on board, and were placed in the care of John Browne, at this point the master of the ship, and the purser, John Bryarley.

The guns were normally the first pieces of equipment to be unloaded, so this provision is somewhat mysterious. It seems unlikely that such valuable pieces would have been left for any length of time on board a ship which in other respects had been stripped bare. It may have been a transitional arrangement, because the appropriate officer was not available to receive them, or it may have meant that Browne and Bryarley were simply made responsible for the unloading and storage. What it also means, though, is that the master and purser remained on the payroll, and continued to be in some sense responsible for the ship, which would have been provided with a skeleton crew of 'shipkeepers', to guard against accident or misdemeanour while she was laid up.

A wrist guard (bracer) worn by an archer. This drawing shows more clearly than a photograph how this simple object was embellished with the royal arms and emblems. (*Mary Rose Trust*)

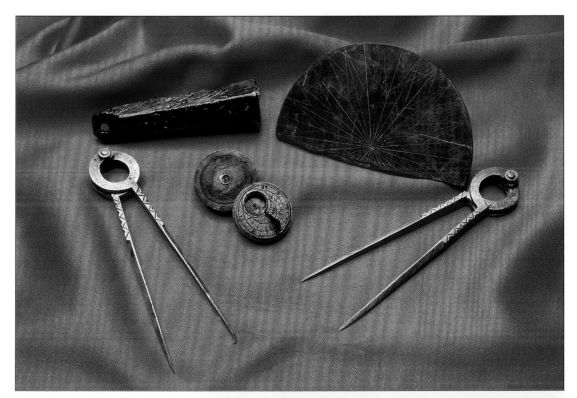

The discovery of a protractor and two pairs of dividers in the ship shows that the ship's course was plotted on charts. (*Mary Rose Trust*)

A wooden lantern. Any naked light was a potential hazard aboard a wooden ship and the protective housing had to be solid. The horn inserts between the wooden staves have not survived. (*Mary Rose Trust*)

The ship's watch bell was among the last of the finds recovered from the site. It carries the inscription 'IC BEN GHEGOTEN INT YAER MCCCCCX' ('I was cast in the year 1510'), so was presumably brought from the Netherlands as the *Mary Rose* was being built. (*Mary Rose Trust*)

A pocket sundial, held easily in the palm of the hand. (*Mary Rose Trust*)

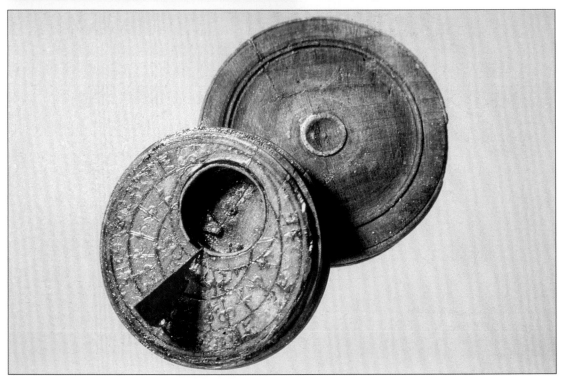

Domestic and personal items including combs, wooden plates and dishes, pewter and wooden spoons and flagons. (*Mary Rose Trust*)

Some of the many styles of leather shoe recovered. (*Mary Rose Trust*)

hije

Gonnepowder Shotte of yron

Serpentyn   for Cannon
                        for D Cannon

The *Mary Rose* in the Anthony Roll. Anthony Anthony, a clerk of the Ordnance Office, completed his illuminated munitions inventory of Henry VIII's 58 ships in 1546, by which time the *Mary Rose* was at the bottom of the Solent. This is the only contemporary image of the ship, distinguished by the rose emblem at the bow. The MS was given by Charles II to Samuel Pepys, in whose library at Magdalene College, Cambridge, it is preserved. This illustration accompanies document **58.** (*The Master and Fellows of Magdalene College, Cambridge*)

A backgammon board, of oak inlaid with yew and spruce, was found together with its counters in the carpenter's cabin. It is the finest of several gaming pieces recovered. (*Mary Rose Trust*)

Several musical instruments were recovered, some of them from the crew's quarters. Those seen here are a shawm (right, partly fragmented), predecessor of the oboe, and a tabor pipe. (*Mary Rose Trust*)

These silver clothing fasteners, found in a small circular box, probably belonged to an officer. (*Mary Rose Trust*)

Gold angels of 23 carats. This design, produced between 1542 and 1545 and worth 8s, depicted a ship on the reverse. Each was worth much the same as an ordinary seaman's monthly pay, and the relatively few that were found must have belonged to the officers. (*Mary Rose Trust*)

The hull on display in Portsmouth during the conservation process, before the deck timbers were replaced. *Inset*: the immense rising knees on the main deck. (*Mary Rose Trust*)

The commissioners began their work on 27 July, but it was presumably 9 August by the time that they got around to the *Mary Rose*, which is listed eighth of the thirteen ships being decommissioned. The document reproduced here is the rigging inventory, which may be interpreted by consulting the Glossary (Appendix III). Accounts surviving from the period October 1517 to December 1521 suggest that for most of her time out of service, the ship was cared for by no more than five shipkeepers, exclusive of the master and purser. Wherever the anchorage was located, it appears not to have been satisfactory, because in June 1517 Hopton was contracted to excavate a new 'wet dock', or pond, at Deptford, at a cost of 600 marks (£466 13s 4d) (**44**). The intention was that five Great Ships, among which the *Mary Rose* is named, were to be kept afloat in that dock, rather than in an open roadstead. It was suggested a little later that ships anchored in the Thames or the Medway were liable to suffer damage from drifting ice during the winter, but whether this was the consideration behind this move or not, is not known. It appears that the project, like so much construction work, ran over budget, and Hopton probably considered himself very fortunate to be able to extract a further £400 from the Treasury in payment of a debt for which he was in theory liable himself. At first the pond clearly served its intended purpose, for the *Mary Rose* was there when she was pumped and caulked in October 1520 (**45**). Thereafter, however, it seems not to have been thought a success, and was later used not for anchoring ships but to store mast timber, which seems to have been kept wet in order to preserve it.

The *Mary Rose* was briefly back in commission when Henry mobilized nearly all his 'prestige' ships to escort him to his meeting with Francis I at the Field of the Cloth of Gold in June 1520. By the end of 1521 Henry was committed to a return to war against France in the summer of 1522, and the end of Hopton's care and maintenance account in December of that year probably marks the point at which the *Mary Rose* began to be prepared once more for a full campaign.

DOCUMENTS

41. *Lord Admiral Surrey to the Council, 14 June 1514.*

My lords, pleaseth it you to understand that yesterday I la[nded] in Normandy 3 miles by West from Cherbourg, and so have burnt [4] miles West of my landing and 3 miles East hard to [the] walls of Cherbourg town and castle, and also more than [2] miles in to the land as far as any house might be seen fo[r] great woods, without leaving any [thing *deleted*] house unburnt that wa[s in] sight, abbeys and churches only reserved, whereby the country m[en] hath not only taken great hurt, but divers gentlemen [of] the country which hath their houses clean burnt, that were rig[ht] goodly houses well builded and stuffed with hangings and be[ds] of silk, of which neither they nor our men have little pr[ofit], for all or the more part was burnt. And when all was burnt that was in sight, we shipped all without loss of any one man. Also, pleaseth it your lordships to understand, because I would th[at] the burning of Preer John [*Prégent de Bidoux*] should be surely acquitted, the night before I landed I sent Wallop, Gonson, Sabyne and di[vers] other to the number of 700 men to land 30 miles by West [of] where I landed [which to land *deleted*], and as yet they be not returned, for they were so far on our lee that they shall not recover this place till night. And therefore I cannot certify your lordships as yet what they have done, but we might well see that t[hey bur]nt sore, for the smoke rose so sore in all that country that [we] lost sight of the high hills of the Hague, and my trust is [th]at they have done no less displeasure to the Frenchmen than we [wer]e done. And, my lords, I beseech you to help that the King's grace [mi]ght

This walnut chest, recovered from the barber surgeon's cabin, contains many of the items illustrated on p. 62. (*Mary Rose Trust*)

write a thankful letter to the Vice-Admiral and all [the] captains of the army for their good demeanour in every c[ase. By] my faith, I never saw men of better will to serve their ma[ster. My] lords, I send unto you my servant Edward Bray, who can inf[orm more] of the matter of the towns, villages and houses [*as h*]e was one of them that had the order of burning. [My] lords, me think it were well done you sent unto Dover [and t]o Hastings to fortify themselves and to make good watch, [for if] and Prégent [intend to *inserted*] make any new business, in my mind he would [med]dle with one of those two places, for they be meet for his purpose; [an]d if he will give the adventure, I think he may sure[ly bur]n any of them without danger. And as shortly as any wi[nd wi]ll serve possible, I shall send six ships more into those parts to encounter with him. And thus Our Lord have you in his tuition. Scri[bbled in] the *Mary Rose* before Portland, the 14 day of June.

Yours, T. Surrey.

42. *Surrey to the King,* [*14 June 1514*].

Almost identical to the dispatch to the Council; written on the same day, but a few hours later as the returning fleet proceeded Eastward along the South Coast. In writing to the King, the Admiral refers specifically to the French raid on Brighton as the attack he had revenged.

Sir, pleaseth it your grace to understand that whereas I have [been] delayed for the accomplishing of your commandment to land and [. . .] burn in France, as well some time with calm weather as a[t other] with contrarious winds and lack of victual, yet yesterday it [pleased] God to send such wind that I landed in Normandy three m[iles] from the castle of Cherbourg by West the same, and so have [I] burnt all the country 4 miles Westward from where I landed and 3 miles Eastward to the town walls of Cherbourg, and more than 2 miles in to the land, which is as goodly a cou[ntry] and as well builded for small towns and villages as I have seen in any country, and no [thing *deleted*] house left unburnt that mig[ht] be looked on save only Cherbourg, which is a marvellous strong town and castle. Also pleaseth it your grace to understand at the same time I landed I [sent *deleted*] caused Wallop, Gonson, Sa[byne] and divers others to the number of 700 men to land by [the] West of me 30 miles, which be not yet returned, and ther[efore I] can not certify your grace what they have done, but well we mig[ht s]ee they made such smoke in the country that within a while we lost sight of land by reason of the said smoke. And, Sir, I trust they have done no less hurt for their part than we have f[. . .] ours, and thus, Sir, I trust your grace be not in the French m[en's deb]t for burning of late of Brighton. And because your grace should understand anything of this matter that it shall [. . .] you to enquire of, I send to your grace my servant Edward [Bray], who was one of those that had the order of the burning, [who] can show your grace more than I can. Beseeching your grace [to wr]ite letters of thanks for their toward minds unto the best [so]rt of gentlemen that I have here the rule of, that [. . .] my life to do your grace some service. And the Blessed Trinity send your [grace that your m]ost noble heart desireth. Scribbed before Poole, the [. . .] hand of [. . .].

Your most humble subject, [T. Surrey].

43. *Rigging indenture, 9 August 1514.*

This indenture made the 9th day of August the 6th year of the reign of our sovereign lord King Henry the VIIIth between Henry Wyatt, Andrew Windsor, knights, George Dalison and Thomas Chaworth, commissioners by our sovereign lord's appointment to take the view of all such stuff, tackle and apparel as remained in our said sovereign lord's ships the day above written on the one party, and John Hopton, overseer of the King's ships on the other party, witnesseth that the said commissioners hath delivered to the said John Hopton the day of making hereof in the name of our said sovereign lord and to his use these parcels of stuff ensuing out of the *Mary Rose*. That is to say, first a mainmast, a main yard, 2 courses to the main sail, 2 bonnets to the same, 2 tacks, 2 sheets, 2 bowlines, a parrel, 2 trusses, 2 thrings, 2 brasses and a pair of ties, a winding halyard, 2 lifts, a gear, a stay, a 'schyrwyn', 26 shrouds, 26 iron chains with bolts pertaining to them, 8 swifting tackles, 8 polancres, 3 garlands. Item the main top, a topmast and a maintop yard, the parrel, a maintopsail, 2 bowlines, 2 sheets, 2 lifts, 2 brasses, a tie, a halyard and a stay, with 10 shrouds and a truss. Item the topgallant, a mast, a sail, a yard with the parrel, 2 bowlines, 2 sheets, 2 brasses, 2 lifts and a stay with 6 shrouds. Item the foremast, a yard, the parrel, a course with 3 bonnets, 2 tacks, 2 sheets, 2 bowlines, 2 lifts, 2 brasses, 2 trusses, 16 shrouds, 16 iron chains with their bolts, 4 pulleys, a stay, 2 ties, a halyard. Item the foretop, the topmast, a yard, a sail, 2 bowlines, 2 sheets, 2 lifts, 2 brasses, a tie, a halyard, a stay and a parrel. Item the bowsprit, a yard, a spritsail and a bonnet, a truss and a pair of lifts. The main mizzenmast and his yard, a parrel, the sail, a tie and a halyard, a truss, a sheet, 2 brasses, a lift, a stay, 12 shrouds and 12 iron chains with their bolts. Item the main mizzentopmast, a yard and parrel, his

A compass found in the Pilot's cabin. One of three recovered from the wreck, which are the oldest gimballed compasses from European sites. The bronze gimbal counteracts the motion of the ship. (*Mary Rose Trust*)

0   20cm

sail and truss, a lift and 8 shrouds. Item a bonaventure mast with the yard, his parrel, 2 sails, a tie, a halyard, a truss, a sheet, a stay, 8 shrouds. Item 4 shivers of brass to the halyard of the bonaventure mast, 4 shivers of brass to the main mizzen halyard, 4 shivers of brass in the tackle of starboard side, one shiver of brass for a garnet of the same side, 13 shivers of brass in the tackles of larboard side, 4 shivers of brass in the garnets of the same side, 3 shivers of brass for the lift pulley of the same side, one shiver of brass for the topsail sheet of the same, 2 shivers of brass in the knight, one shiver of brass in the

Log reel found on the upper deck. This was used with a chip and line to measure the distance a ship sailed within a certain time span. (*Mary Rose Trust*)

ramshead, 3 shivers of brass in the lifts a-starboard side, one shiver of brass for the topsail sheet of the same side, 3 shivers of brass in the gear, 4 shivers of brass in the halyards of the foremast, one shiver of brass in the tackle of starboard side, 3 shivers of brass in the tackle of larboard side, 2 shivers of brass for the sheets of the sail, one shiver of brass for the tie of the spritsail, 2 shivers of brass for the main bowline pulley, 2 shivers of brass in the davit in the forecastle, one shiver of brass in the davit of the 'destrelles', one shiver of brass in the cat, 2 shivers of iron, one in the cat and another in the boat davit, 2 great shivers of brass, one small shiver of brass, 3 compasses, 3 running glasses, 2 sounding leads and 1 sounding lead of 40 fathom, 7 anchors, that is to say 2 sheet anchors, one starboard bower and a larboard bower [broken *inserted*], 2 'dystrelles', a cagger, a new sheet of cables to the sheet anchor, a new sheet to the starboard bower, a new sheet to the larboard bower, 3 worn cables and 4 old junks, 2 lagging cables, 2 cat hooks, 2 fish hooks, 2 luff hooks and a leech hook, 6 warping halyards. Item a boat, a mast and sail and 20 oars. Item a cock, a mast and a sail and 6 oars.

In witness whereof the parties abovesaid to these indentures have set their seals interchangeably the day and year abovesaid.

Andrew Windsor. Thomas Wyndham.

44. *Agreement for construction of a dock at Deptford, 9 June 1517.*

This indenture made the 9th day of June in the 9th year of the reign of our most dread sovereign lord King Henry the VIIIth between Thomas, Earl of Surrey, great Admiral of England, and John Heron, Treasurer of our said sovereign lord the King's most honourable Chamber, for and in the name and by the commandment of our said sovereign lord the King on the one party, and John Hopton, Clerk Comptroller of the Ships of our said sovereign lord the King on the other party, witnesseth that it is covenanted, condescended and agreed between the said parties the day and year abovesaid of and for the making of a pond wherein certain ships of the same our sovereign lord hereafter expressed shall ride afloat. The same John Hopton knowledgeth and confesseth himself by these presents to have received and had of our said sovereign lord the King by the hands of the said Earl and John Heron the sum of six hundred marks sterlings in ready money of and for the full contentation and payment of the same pond, the which pond the foresaid John Hopton covenanteth, promiseth and granteth and him and his executors by these presents bindeth that he, his executors or assigns, at their own proper costs and expenses, before the feast of Christmas next coming after the date of these indentures, shall well, surely, sufficiently and substantially cause to be made and cast in a meadow next adjoining unto the storehouse of our said sovereign lord at Deptford Strond, at the West end of the said storehouse, a good and able pond, wherein shall ride at all times on-float these ships ensuing, that is to say the *Great Galley*, the *Mary Rose*, the *Peter Pomegranate*, the *Great Bark* and the *Lesser Bark*. And also the said John Hopton covenanteth and granteth by these presents that he, his executors or assigns, at their like costs and charges before the same feast, shall well and substantially make or cause to be made a good, able and sufficient head for the same pond, and also certain able sluices through the which the water may have entry and course into the foresaid pond, as well at spring tides as at neap tides. Moreover the foresaid John Hopton covenanteth and granteth by these presents that he, his executors or assigns, at their own proper costs and expenses before the foresaid feast, shall well and sufficiently enclose all the same pond with good, able and sufficient pale of timber of oak, of the scantillon in thickness of one inch of assize every board thereof, and that the same pale shall contain in height seven foot of assize. Provided alway that if the said five ships cannot be conveyed and brought into the same pond and there to ride on-float as is aforesaid, then the foresaid John Hopton covenanteth, promiseth and granteth and him and his executors by these presents bindeth well and truly to restore and repay or do to be restored and repaid unto the said Earl and John Heron, their executors or assigns, the foresaid sum of six hundred marks sterlings unto the use of our said sovereign lord the King, without any delay in any wise. In witness whereof the parties aforesaid to these indentures sunderly have set their seals, given the day and year abovesaid.

Signed: John Hopton.

Endorsed: Delivered to John Hopton by the hands of his servant Saward the 3rd day of August in the 9th year of Henry VIII for the causes within written, four hundred pounds: £400. Per me Thomas Saward.

45. *From expenses of shipping for and after the Field of the Cloth of Gold, 1520.*

The Mary Rose *had led a detachment of five ships to 'scour the seas' before taking part in the King's crossing to Calais on 31 May. This extract from one of many accounts finds her later in the year back in the dock at Deptford, built three years before.*

The book of the accounts of costs and charges done and made on the King's ships for the transporting of the King and the Queen to Calais to the meeting of the French King, and from thence into England again, in the 12th year of Henry VIII.

Paid also by the said John Hopton the second day of October in the said 12th year to certain caulkers that wrought and caulked on the *Mary Rose* within the pond at Deptford, that is to say first paid to Rawlyn Talkyn for 3 days [*and*] half, at 6*d* the day – [18*d deleted*] 21*d*, and to John Colyns for 2 days – 12*d*. And to further of Deptford for 2 days – 8*d*. Paid also to 7 men that helped to pump the Mary Rose by the time of one day and a night – 2*s* 8*d*.

5

THE WAR OF 1522–5

The peace between England and France which had been signed in 1514 lasted precariously for nearly eight years. It had been sealed by a marriage between Henry's younger sister, Mary, and Louis XII. But Louis died in December of the same year, worn out, it was said, by his energetic young wife. The new King was Francis I; he was much the same age as Henry, and shared many of the same tastes and characteristics. However, he sought his military reputation in Italy, and did not break the peace in the north. Henry toyed with the idea of a new French war in both 1516 and 1517, but drew back on each occasion. Meanwhile, his chief minister and Lord Chancellor, Thomas Wolsey, was trying to shape an Anglo-French entente as part of a general European peace settlement. In 1518 he succeeded, and Tournai (Henry's conquest from the war of 1512–14) was returned to France under the terms of the Treaty of London. This ambitious treaty, which temporarily raised the reputations of both Henry and Wolsey to dizzy heights, was intended to be permanent, but lasted in fact only some three years. Ferdinand of Aragon (de facto King of all Spain), Henry's father-in-law, had died in 1516 and had been succeeded by his grandson, Charles of Ghent. Charles was also the grandson of the Emperor Maximilian, and in 1519 Maximilian died in turn. His son Philip having died in 1506, Charles was elected to succeed him, thus creating an empire of unprecedented dimensions. Charles now ruled, under various titles, the Holy Roman Empire (including most of northern Italy), Spain (including most of southern Italy) and the Low Countries. These domains virtually surrounded France, and a renewal of a Franco-Imperial war was therefore only a matter of time. For obvious reasons, both sides wanted Henry's support, and it was with that in mind that Henry and Francis staged their famous 'summit conference' at the Field of the Cloth of Gold in 1520, an exercise in competitive display which caused Henry to parade his full credentials as a 'sea king'.

The meeting failed, largely because the competitive display strained goodwill to breaking point, and in September 1521 Henry entered into an agreement with the new Emperor, for a joint attack on France in the following year. When Charles visited England to confirm their treaty, Henry met him at Dover, where the two monarchs inspected the fleet and went aboard the *Henry Grace à Dieu* and the *Mary Rose* (**46**). By the terms of the agreement, however, although England was bound to declare war on France in May 1522, Henry was not pledged to a major land campaign until the following year. The first campaign in the summer of 1522 was therefore fought at sea. In spite of this, Henry made no attempt to augment his existing fleet, and this must raise some doubts about how seriously he was proposing to take his commitments. In 1512 there had been a considerable build-up, but between 1515 and 1522 only five ships were added to the fleet; two of them were small, and one was a gift from the Emperor. The only important new ship to be built was the *Great Galley*, launched in 1515. Mobilization of the existing fleet began in December 1521, and by May it was at sea, as had been agreed. The intention seems to have been to bring the ships round from the Thames estuary to Southampton, and there to embark an expeditionary force to attack Le Havre. The Earl of Surrey was in overall command, and in spite of the presence of the *Henry Grace à Dieu*, which from the comments made on her sailing qualities was clearly part of the force, he carried his flag in the *Mary Rose*. From the first letter (**47**) it is clear that the Vice-Admiral, Sir William Fitzwilliam, was in operational command of the fleet, and was probably not in the same ship; however, John Browne was still her master, and the veteran Clerk of the King's Ships, Robert Brigandine (who was to retire in the following year), was still active.

By 21 June the soldiers had been embarked, but Surrey felt unable to sail because of the usual difficulties over victualling (**48**). Most of his letter of that date is taken up with frantic pleas to get his supplies moving, because although he did not need to await their arrival, he did need to know that they would follow him. The trouble, clearly, was money. There were no funds to pay the brewers, and the ordnance at Portsmouth was falling apart for lack of maintenance. The King had spent his father's accumulated surplus during his first French war, and by this time was living from hand to mouth. Over the next few days Surrey, having presumably received some reassurance over the victualling problem, set out, first to St Helen's and then to Dartmouth, his movements largely dictated by the wind (**49–51**). Most of his letter of 30 June is an extended digression on the merits of Dartmouth as an advance wintering place for the ships (**52**). This advice fell on deaf ears, because in spite of the commodious anchorage and the availability of timber, it was too remote. Again, victualling was the snag. Not enough was available locally, and the place was inconveniently situated for supplies which came mainly from Kent and Essex, via London.

While all this was happening, the Emperor was continuing his visit to England. He had been lavishly entertained by the King, who could find money for that purpose, even if not to victual his Navy. While he was in England, Henry belatedly declared war on Francis, and the two monarchs agreed to a detailed plan for a joint attack on France in the following year. Charles embarked for Santander on 7 July, but whether the *Henry* escorted him as suggested is not apparent. By then Surrey had achieved such modest success as was within his reach. He had seized and partly destroyed the Breton port of Morlaix on 1 July, presumably because it was more accessible than Le Havre, and less strongly defended. However, the supplies for which he asked so urgently on 3 July seem never to have reached him, so that his proposal to 'draw beyond the Trade' – that is, to launch an attack on Brest – had no effect (**53**). Shortly after, Surrey and his fleet returned to Portsmouth, and the Lord Admiral was redeployed to lead an 'Army Royal' of 15,000 men out of Calais into France. That adventure also turned out to be a waste of money and effort, because the Emperor's forces were all tied up in Italy, and without Imperial support the English were not strong enough to achieve anything beyond the same kind of destruction which they had wrought at Morlaix. By 16 October Surrey was back at Calais, and his army was disbanded.

The navy, though, was redeployed, and in that respect Fitzwilliam's letter to Wolsey of 4 August is particularly interesting (**54**). It is not known which of the various options proposed was eventually adopted, but it seems clear that a significant proportion of the Great Ships available was to be kept in service. Some were to 'keep the Narrow Seas' (later called the 'Channel Guard'), some were to go westward, and some to the north. Of course, this was not winter provision. Two months victualling from early August would only last until early October, and what seems to have happened was that a reduced fleet under Fitzwilliam returned to the Brittany coast in mid-August. This was mainly a defensive measure, because Henry feared a counter-attack, or reprisals for the sacking of Morlaix. The *Henry* was probably taken out of service at this point, because although the *Mary Rose* was described as 'the second ship of the fleet', she was clearly used by Fitzwilliam as his flagship. The Channel fleet returned to Portsmouth at some time during October, and she may well then have been taken out of service, as there are no further references to her. By this time a Channel Guard was being maintained through the winter, but smaller ships would have been used for that purpose, as no major attack would have been expected.

The war resumed in 1523. English ships commanded by William Sabyne had already attacked France's ally, Scotland, in 1522, bombarding Leith and Kinghorn, and in 1523 there was actually some fighting in the North Sea. The Scots briefly blockaded the Humber, and an English North Sea fleet cruised off the east coast to prevent French troops from arriving in the north. On 11 June there was a skirmish in which the English commander, Sir Henry Sherborne, was killed. Under his successor, however, at least seven ships heading for Leith were taken. It was not until 21 September that the Duke of Albany with 3,000 men managed to get through, using the Irish Sea route. By then the Scots had concluded that it was too late in the year to launch a campaign, and nothing more happened. Normally in wartime the King's main battlefleet would have been in the Channel by the end of May, but there is very little evidence of what happened in 1523, and certainly no mention of the *Mary Rose*. Fitzwilliam seems to have been patrolling in June and July, but it is not known what ships he was using. Early in August he attacked and burned the small port of Tréport, but his main service was to escort the Duke of Suffolk's expeditionary force to Calais later in that month. As this was an Army Royal, it can be assumed that most of the capital ships available would have been deployed, but neither the accounts nor any relevant dispatches have survived. Suffolk's campaign is not relevant in this context. Henry expected great things of it, but foul weather and the failure (again) of Imperial support to materialize, meant that it achieved nothing at vast expense. Henry had now completely run out of money, and 1524 was largely taken up with diplomatic attempts to heal the rift with the Emperor, and to take advantage of the fact that the Constable of France, the Duke of Bourbon, had defected to the Habsburgs. There was no campaigning, and as far as is known, the fleet never left port. By November the *Mary Rose* was laid up at Portsmouth, and Wolsey was urging the King to make peace.

DOCUMENTS

46. *The Emperor Charles V goes aboard the* Mary Rose *at Dover when arriving for his meeting with Henry VIII, 30 May 1522.*

*From the chronicle of Anthony Anthony, who also compiled the illuminated roll of the King's ships (**58**).*

26 May 1522. The Emperor arrived at Dover and went to the Castle. 28 May. The King went down river and met the Emperor at Dovergate. 30 May 2 p.m. The Emperor and K. Henry went aboard the *Great Harry* and *Mary Rose*. After the fleet had discharged all their ordnance, they took horse and came to Canterbury 9 p.m.

47. *Sir William Fitzwilliam, Vice-Admiral, to the King, 4 June 1522.*

Please it your highness to understand that on Friday at night last past, which was the self same day your grace departed from Dover, the wind came to the West-South-West, and blew so strainably that we were constrained to forsake

William Fitzwilliam, Earl of Southampton, drawn by Holbein. As Vice-Admiral in 1525 he flew his flag in the *Mary Rose*, and his letters document the second French war in which she served. (*The Royal Collection © 2002, Her Majesty Queen Elizabeth II*)

that road and go into the Downs, where we were fain to abide that night and Saturday and Sunday all day, for because the wind abode there continually and blew exceeding strainably. And Monday the wind came to the West and by North, and so we made sail, purposing to have stopped at every flood, and so to have plied to Hampton with the tides. And when we were more near half seas over, the wind blew at South-West again so sore that we were forced to forsake the sea and come to the Downs again for harbour. And since that day hitherto the wind keepeth and hath kept in that quarter continually, insomuch that we cannot go to Hampton as yet. Howbeit, the next wind that is, there shall no slackness be found in us in that behalf, by God's grace. And to advertise your grace of the sailing of the *Henry Grace à Dieu*, the same day we made sail, she sailed as well as any ship that was in the fleet, and rather better, and weathered them all save the *Mary Rose*. And if she go by a wind, I assure your grace there will be hard choice between the *Mary Rose* and her, and next them the *Galley*. Howbeit and the said *Galley* may veer the sheet, she will go from us all. And yesterday the wind blew as sore and strainably as I have lightly [*commonly*] seen, and thanked be Our Lord, the *Henry* rode as still and as gently at an anchor as the least ship that is in the fleet did, whereof I and all the rest of [*the*] army be right glad.

Furthermore, the foresaid day your grace departed from Dover, I called to me according to your commandment Brigandine, my fellow Gonson, and all the wisest masters in the fleet, and examined them whether the Camber were a meet place to lay up the *Henry* this winter, in case your highness were minded she should be, or not. And they all agreed in one saying, and said they thought it not meet. Howbeit, for the trial of the premises, I sent John Browne, master of the *Mary Rose*, and John Clogge, master of the *Peter Pomegranate* thither, and they called to them one John Fletcher and John Swanne, which be two of the wisest masters within the town of Rye. And they all together went and sounded the said Camber, and every place therein, and can find no place there meet to lay her in safe, and so I am sure the said John Fletcher and John Swanne will affirm whensoever they shall be examined upon the same. And the said masters conclude all together and say that Portsmouth or Dartmouth be the meetest places to lay her in that be, and reckon that it is too great a danger to bring her into the Thames again. As the blessed Trinity knoweth who ever have your highness in his blessed tuition. Written in the Downs this Wednesday the 4th day of June. By your humble subject and most bound servant,

William Fitzwilliam.

48. *Lord Admiral Surrey to the King, 21 June 1522.*

Pleaseth it your most noble grace to be advertised that upon Thursday at noon I, with all your grace's army here, embarked, and only remain here for lack of wind, which I pray God shortly to send, for as yet it continueth at South-West and West, which is the way that we should go. And to advertise your highness how your grace is deceived for the furniture of victual for your army, where it was promised that by the last day of May we should have had the whole complement for 5,000 men from Portsmouth of beer, and from Hampton of all other victual, with much difficulty we be furnished now, which is the 20 day of June, from Hampton of flesh, fish and biscuit for the said two months, and from Portsmouth by no means we can have none than for one month of beer. And where the Vice-Admiral was promised before this day to have had his whole complement, none of his ships have full furniture of all victuals passing three weeks, and of those right few, and some but for 8 days, and the most part not passing for 14 days. And whereas of late is come from London 13 or 14 crayers with victual for the said Vice-Admiral, the victuallers there have caused the masters to indent with them for such proportions as they have received, not sending to me nor to the said Vice-Admiral any letter to advertise us what is sent nor when the rest shall come. And where all their doubts hitherto hath

Barrel end. The barrel was the basic storage component aboard ship; a vessel's capacity was originally reckoned by the number of barrels (or 'tuns') it could carry. This barrel is from the orlop deck and contained beef bones. (*Mary Rose Trust*)

The basic structure of the galley was a vast cauldron built into a brick firebox. Those who enjoyed the fruits of this reconstruction did not share Lord Admiral Howard's complaints about the quality. (*C.T.C. Dobbs*)

been ever for lack of casks for the beer, I cannot perceive but that they be as far or further behind them with flesh, biscuit and fish as with beer, wherein I think is some negligence. Most humbly beseeching your grace to consider that it shall not be possible for me and the company here to accomplish all that we be determined to attempt unless we be better furnished with victuals than we be yet, as well from London as Portsmouth, and great pity it were that your grace should spend thus much money without that some great displeasures might be done to the enemies, which we that be here, having well debated what we may do, see good likelihood to do that your highness shall be contented with if the wind and victuals serve us, doubting much more of the victual than wind. Beseeching your grace to cause some substantial man to go to London for the hasting forth of that is there, and the same to be shipped in the *Christopher Davy* and other good ships, and to be conducted within the Wight by Thomas Vaughan and his company. And also to send one other wise man to Portsmouth for to see diligence used for the beer there. And I have left William Symmond with 100 sailors to embark in such good ships as shall come from London to conduct all the victuals of London, Hampton and Portsmouth unto me. Also I, Sir [*Richard*] Wingfield and divers others have been at Portsmouth to see in what case the ordnance and bulwarks be there, and also to show our opinion for the fortification of the same, and undoubtedly we find all the ordnance there so far out of order that no piece can be shot, the most part of the stocks being rotten and all the woulding clearly consumed, and much of the ironwork failed. And Palshide, having no money to pay the brewers, as this day without which payment they will not labour, nor also no money being there for making of bulwarks nor repairing of ordnance, I, having a little money here of mine own, have delivered unto him two hundred marks. And, Sir, after my poor opinion, methinketh it were well done that William Pawne or some other expert man should be sent thither [to *otiose*] for the ordering of all business there. Also that it might please your grace to cause James Worsley to come home to the Wight to see that good watch be made to descry such ships as may come to do any displeasure, and to see beacons and fires made to give warning to Portsmouth, and also beacons to be made upon Portisdown, and the country to be warned with diligence to resort to Portsmouth when the beacons shall be on fire. Finally, Sir, your grace shall be tomorrow advertised by Mr [*John*] Jenyns of all the state of the affairs of your army here, beseeching your grace to examine him yourself of the same. Written in the *Mary Rose* within the Isle of Wight, the 21th day of June.

Your most humble subject, T. Surrey.

Ordnance equipment – shot, measuring ring, powder scoops, rams and buckets. (*Mary Rose Trust*)

49. *Surrey to Wolsey, 23 June 1522.*

Pleaseth it your grace to be advertised that at the writing hereof I was under sail near unto St Helen's, the wind being meetly good, but it bloweth very little. Most humbly beseeching your grace to command straitly the victuallers at Hampton, Portsmouth and London to make despatch with all diligence in sending after me all the rest of my victual, which if they do, I trust your grace shall be content with that shall be done, if God send us good wind. Also, I beseech your grace to send a strait letter to Christopher Coo to follow the advice of Harper, and in no wise to come within havens. Your grace shall know by the victuallers of London for how long he and Harper be victualled. Thomas Clere is victualled of beer but for one month, and for all other victuals for two months at Hampton. Also I beseech your grace to write straitly unto Thomas Vaughan to convey the victuallers of London within the Wight, and then to return, and that in any wise when he is in the Narrow Seas that he keep more the coasts of Calais than the Downs, and that he sail not nightly to lie near Calais, for by that way the Frenchmen do steal away in the night, both Northward and from by North. And thus Our Lord send your grace that your heart most desires. Scribbled in the *Mary Rose* the 23 of June.

Yours most bounden, T. Surrey.

Addressed: To my lord legate's good grace.

50. *Surrey to the King* [24 June 1522].
   The date is deduced from no. **51.**

Pleaseth it your most noble grace to be advertised that at the writing hereof I was under sail going forwards, the wind being at the North, which is good, but it is very little wind. Most humbly beseeching your grace to cause our victuals to be sent after us, as well from London as from Hampton and Portsmouth. It were pity that we should let to accomplish that we intend to attempt only for lack of victuals. Also I send your grace herewith a book of such cables as of very necessity must be with all diligence provided for your highness's ships, beseeching your grace to command some sure man to see for the provision of the same. And Our Lord send your highness the accomplishments of your most noble heart's desires, and me grace to do you such service as my poor heart desireth. Written in the *Mary Rose* near St Helen's, under sail.

Your most humble subject, T. Surrey.

51. *Surrey to the King, 27 June 1522.*

Pleaseth it your grace to be advertised that on Tuesday last [24 June] we departed from St Helen's, the wind being contrarious, and with force of the ebb stopping the floods, be this present hour come before Portland, and so from tide to tide intend to do unto the time we may get as far as Dartmouth, where we must of force abide unto the time God will send wind to serve us to run over with the coasts of your enemies. Sir, considering how little victual we have on board, contrary the minds of the masters of the army, we have thus plied the tide to the intent something might be done against your enemies before our victual be spent; most humbly beseeching your grace that the rest of our victual might be with haste sent after us, and with God's grace there shall be no time foreclosed by us your poor servants here to do that thing may be to your highness's contentation and pleasure. Written in the *Mary Rose*, the 27th day of June.

Your most humble subject, T. Surrey.

89

52. *Surrey to the King, 30 June 1522.*

Nothing came of this proposal to make Dartmouth a principal anchorage for the navy. The idea that security could be provided by big dogs was only one of the impracticalities.

Pleaseth it your grace to be advertised that yesternight I came to the road, and because of divers of my company were within sight and might not come so far forth unto this tide, and also for lack of fresh water, whereof we were all

Dartmouth harbour. Another section of the panoramic map of the south coast from about 1540. A ship is entering the mouth of the River Dart, and another lies at anchor within Dartmouth harbour (the town of Dartmouth with its square-towered church to the left). Above is the bridge at Totnes, and to the left, Dartington. From British Library Cotton MS Augustus I, i, 35, 36, 38, 39. (*British Library*)

destituted, [I] thought best to abide here this day. And so I, with Sir Richard Wingfield, Sir William Fitzwilliam, Sir Richard Jerningham, Hopton, Gonson, Sabyne, John Browne and divers others, took a boat and went into Dartmouth haven to view and see what places we might find to lay in your grace's great ships this winter, and to advertise your grace as we have seen. In my life I never saw a goodlier haven nor more sure lying, after all our opinions, for your said ships, than here. First, at the entry of the haven there is a blockhouse made of stone, and of the same side an old castle; on the other side there is another old castle, and besides that another blockhouse, and a chain ready to be laid over the haven and all thing ready for the same. The town is not two arrow shot from thence, and the ships may lie two miles further within the haven under John Gilbert's house, and at the best 5 fathom at a low water. The chain that is at Portsmouth may be laid within the other chain, so that we here think it shall not be possible for any ships to come within the haven. The most danger we see is that if the enemy would come with a great puissance and land at a place called Tor Bay, which is but two miles from the place where the ships shall ride, they might with casting fire into them do some hurt, or else some fellow might in the night steal into them [and throw wildfire into them *inserted*]. The remedy whereof, after our opinions, is this, that your grace should write unto the Bishop of Exeter and to all the best gentlemen of Devonshire, showing unto them that your grace is informed that they be now making a blockhouse a little beside Brixham within Tor Bay, and if they would make another at Churston within the said Tor Bay, your grace would help them with ordnance and powder. I perceive by divers gentlemen that have been aboard [this] day that they would make the same upon their own costs; [which] being made, as we here be informed, it shall be unpossible f[or an] army to land there to do any displeasure to your grace's said [ships]. And as for casting of wildfire into them by stealth, in the [. . .] if 3 or 4 acres of low wood be cut down that is gro[wing by] the shore where they shall ride, and a wall of stone made [not] passing 800 pace long, which will cost no great money [*there being*] so great plenty of stone there; and within the said wall [. . .] great bandogs to go loose a-nights, I think they should [be] good surety for taking any hurt by stealth, notwithstanding [it] might stand with your highness's pleasure to have them kept [under] your grace's correction. I think it were well done your grace should [appoint] two or three wise expert men, as well to see and view the said [. . .] also such places as shall be fortified within the haven and else[where] near where the ships shall be kept, where the enemies might [*land*] which I and the others here with me have had to leisure to [view]. Assuring your grace that, after my poor opinion, with the spending [of an] hundred pounds, such sure defences may be made for the s[urety] of your royal navy here that it shall be in manner not possible for [the] enemies to do any displeasure unto them, And within 4 m[iles of where] they shall lie your grace hath a park called Dartington, [wherein] is 2,000 goodly oaks, as I am informed, and may be br[ought by] water, which from time to time will serve for the reparations [. . .]. And undoubtedly they shall spend less in tackling here than [at] Portsmouth by as much as in one year as in all the charges of [new] making here shall extend unto. And if it shall be your gr[ace's pleasure] to have them kept here, then after my poor opinion, it sho[uld not be needed] to spend much for the reparations of Portsmouth, but wh[ile the Emperor] should pass into Spain, to cause the *Henry Grace à Dieu* to [keep him] company thus far, and then to be brought in hither, f[or as] I am informed, there will be gathered together here of your [grace's army] within 24 hours 9 or 10,000 men for their defence ag[ainst the *enemies*].

[*Concluding in Surrey's own handwriting*]: Finally, Sir, at the closing of this letter, all the ships were under sail, and if the wind hold, with God's grace tomorrow we shall land upon your enemies' ground; and because Nicholas Semer, mayor of this town, is a very wise man and can well inform your grace of this haven, I have sent him to your grace with this letter, to whom it may please your highness to see for his costs. I have also desired divers of those that were with me at the viewing of this haven to put their hands to this letter. Written in the *Mary Rose* in Dartmouth road, the last of June.

Your most humble subjects, T. Surrey,

R. Wingfield, John Hopton, W. Gonson.

53. *Surrey to Wolsey, 3 July 1522.*

Pleaseth it your grace to be advertised that at this time I have advertised the King's grace of the taking of Morlaix, with the circumstances of much part of that hath been done since my coming hither, whereof I do forbear to write to your grace because I know the same shall come to your hands. I trust of this time your grace hath caused more victuals to be sent after us, which shall be very welcome for we have need thereof. Sir William Fitzwilliam's company is now without flesh and fish in a great number of his ships, and so I am fain to lend him part of mine, and all my company have beer but for 12 days. Great pity it were to see this well-willed company, for lack of victual, to leave undone that we here be in mind to essay, and what danger it shall be, with so little victual, to put ourselves so far from the coasts of England upon the coasts of enemies I report me unto your grace, notwithstanding undoubtedly as soon as we shall have wind to depart hence and to draw beyond the Trade we shall not fail so to do, and shall not return as long as we have any beer left, though in our return we should drink water. I beseech your grace that letters of thanks might be sent to all the lords and gentlemen here which have deserved the same right highly, as more at length at my return I shall show unto your grace. And thus Our Lord send your grace that you most desire, and us the rest of our victual, with good winds to bring our intended enterprise to pass, which we be like to essay without the help of others that were promised. Scribbled in the *Mary Rose* within the haven of Morlaix, this Thursday the 3 day of July.

[*Postscript*]: Sir, this day our anchors were weighing to have gone about other enterprises, and then the wind turned and compelled us to abide.

Yours most bounden, T. Surrey.

54. *Fitzwilliam to Wolsey, 4 August 1522.*

Please it your grace to understand that this day about one of the clock at afternoon I received your letter dated at Westminster the 3rd day of this present month of August, the contents whereof I have well overseen, with a bill specifying the names of such captains and ships, with the number of men, as be appointed to keep the sea. Your grace shall understand that yesterday my lord Admiral departed towards Calais, and this day hath had the wind right fair, so as I trust, and the wind keep there where it is, he shall be there tomorrow. Afore whose departure he appointed as well the ships as the captains and number of men to keep the sea, whose names shall appear unto your grace by a book which I send unto you herewith, which is not possible now to change. For here is left no more ships save only they, and they have their whole proportion of victuals already delivered unto them for two months, of such victuals as was left that was provided for the army, and also their wages paid unto them for one month. Also, such ships as be appointed to go Northwards be not only despatched, but also such as be appointed to go Westwards shall be despatched tomorrow, all save only the *Gabriel of Topsham* and the *Trinity George*, who were appointed to be manned and victualled with the men and victuals of the *Mary Rose* at such time as she should be laid up. And as to the ships that shall keep the Narrow Seas, I shall send them forth incontinently, all save the *Mary Rose* and the *Great Bark*, which cannot be made ready as yet these three days. Beseeching your grace, considering that Mr Pointz is already departed with my lord Admiral to Calais, I may know your pleasure what you will I shall do. And if so be your grace be minded to have the *Mary Rose*, which now is in a-readyness, and the *Peter Pomegranate*, laid up, to keep the sea, you must then discharge the *Gabriel of Topsham* and the *Trinity George*, or else cause a new proportion of victuals to be provided for them, and also send money for their wages. Which, the appointing of the *Mary Rose* or the *Peter Pomegranate* to keep the sea (if it may stand with the King's grace's pleasure and yours) me seemeth should not need ne'r no more great ships save the *Great Bark*, the *Mary James* and the new Spaniard, unless it were advertised for a truth that the French King made forth an army; and that once known, any of the ships in Portsmouth might soon be made ready. And in mine opinion the *Gabriel of Topsham* and the *Trinity George* should do better service in the West Sea, as well for the coming home of the fishers from the Newfound Land as for the going of the Frenchmen into Scotland: then, either the *Mary Rose* or the *Peter Pomegranate* in the Narrow Seas for these two months (unless the French King made an army, as above).

And as touching my going to Calais, the King's highness can command me to go into no place in the world that I shall refuse. And in case his pleasure be that I shall go thither, I then beseech your grace I may not only be advertised thereof with diligence to the intent I may send my folks thither and provide myself of such things as I have need of, and when I have put everything in order, run in post thither; but also, that it will please your grace to write to my lord Admiral to keep me such tent or pavilion as was appointed for me.

And if the King's pleasure shall be that I shall go to Calais, that then I may know his grace's pleasure whether Gonson shall be Admiral, according to the book my lord Admiral brought from his grace, or not; seeing that Master Pointz is not here. Furthermore, as touching Mr Hert, he is not here; n'er here be no more gunners save 50; howbeit I shall speak to [*John*] Westowe to take up as many gunners as he can get, to the number of an hundred.

And as touching the *Maglory*, my lord Admiral hath taken her with him to Calais for the conveyance of my Lord Fitzwalter forth thither. And as soon as they be on land, the said ship is at her liberty. As the Blessed Trinity knoweth, who ever have your grace in his blessed tuition. Written in the *Mary Rose* the 4th day of August, by your servant to the best of his power,

William Fitzwilliam.

6

LAID UP AND (MAINLY) OUT
OF SERVICE (1525–42)

Henry's poverty finally caught up with him in 1525. On 25 February, Francis was defeated and captured by the Emperor's forces at Pavia. Suddenly, France seemed to be at his mercy; plans for peace were abandoned, and enthusiastic proposals for partitioning the kingdom canvassed. This time, however, it was Charles who was cautious. He was now in a position to extract real concessions from his prisoner, and in no mood to humour the extravagant greed of a virtually useless ally. So Charles signed an advantageous peace at Madrid, and left Henry to get the best terms he could. His plans to raise extra-parliamentary taxation (the Amicable Grant) having collapsed, Henry made peace in the Treaty of the More in August 1525. The fleet does not appear to have been mobilized at all during that summer, but at some point the *Mary Rose* was moved to Deptford, where she 'lieth in the pond', awaiting caulking (**55**).

Apart from an entirely theoretical war with the Emperor in 1527, the next fifteen years saw no hostilities, largely because the King was totally absorbed by his Great Matter (getting rid of Catherine of Aragon) and its ramifications. Throughout this period, with a few brief exceptions, all the King's Great Ships were kept on a care and maintenance basis, either at Deptford or Portsmouth. Tentative plans to use Dartmouth and Rye for that purpose were not accepted. According to the surviving accounts of Thomas Jermyn (who had succeeded Brigandine as Clerk of the Ships in 1523), the *Mary Rose* was at Portsmouth for virtually the whole period from November 1524 to January 1530. The number of shipkeepers paid for looking after her varied from six to twenty-one for no obvious reason, and the apparently unbroken sequence of accounts may be deceptive. In addition to the Deptford visit mentioned here, she was also recorded as being there, awaiting repair, on 22 October 1526, when according to Jermyn's accounts she was supposed to be at Portsmouth. The only gap in the Clerk's sequence is from 15 to 26 October 1527, and is equally unexplained. Extensive superficial repairs and regular maintenance work was carried out in June 1527 (**56**), and the fact that these accounts were also presented by Jermyn suggests that this work was carried out at Portsmouth. Such overhauls seem to have taken place annually by this time, and between February and June 1528 a new dock was excavated at Portsmouth, specifically for the repair of the *Mary Rose*, and other ships like her. Another overhaul and recaulking was also undertaken at that time.

After 1531, sightings become fewer and fewer. From January 1536 to March 1537 William Gonson accounted for the *Mary Rose*, and several other ships, which were then laid up in the Thames, but there is no reference to her being in service. In 1536 also, Eustache Chapuys, the Imperial ambassador, commented disparagingly that all Henry's Great Ships were in such a poor state of repair that it would take eighteen months to get them to sea. This was probably an exaggeration, born of Chapuys' dislike of, and contempt for, the English; but Thomas Cromwell, now Henry's chief minister, seems to have come to a similar conclusion. Only three ships had been added to the fleet since 1524: the *Trinity Henry* of 250 tons in 1530; the *Mary Willoughby* of 160 tons in 1532; and the *Sweepstake* of 300 tons in 1535. Of these, the *Mary Willoughby* was promptly taken by Scottish pirates in 1533, and only the *Sweepstake* was a significant acquisition. So the navy needed attention, and between 1536 and 1538 eight ships were either built or rebuilt, including the *Mary Rose* and the *Peter Pomegranate*. When and where this happened is unclear. Cromwell recorded the rebuilding of the *Mary* among his achievements in a memorandum of uncertain date (probably towards the end of 1536), but Gonson's accounts, which cover the supposed period of the work, are incomplete. He records only £1,018 13s 3d for unspecified repairs, and that would have been insufficient to cover even one modest rebuild, let alone two thoroughgoing ones. So it is probable that the work was contracted out to one of the several shipyards on the Thames or the Medway, and paid for by a special assignment, which would not have passed through Gonson's accounts.

The archaeological evidence for the work is substantial, but somewhat controversial. What seems to have happened is that the internal structure was altered, possibly to accommodate an increased number of gunports on the lowest gun deck (the main deck). Alterations were made to the side of the ship at upper-deck level, and several of the smaller gunports were blocked. At the same time the ship was strengthened by the addition of large, heavy riders across the keelson, and diagonal braces were added, strengthening the side of the ship and the main gun deck. As we have seen, the effect was to increase her long-range fighting potential, possibly at the cost of her sailing efficiency and stability. In this remodelled form, she probably saw service in the spring of 1537, but as she is not specifically named, we cannot be sure. The fracas that was brought to the attention of the Admiralty Court in June 1539 probably took place when the ship was in commission, and was on standby at Greenwich (**57**). Henry had been acutely alarmed by the Treaty of Nice in 1538 between the Emperor and the King of France. As he was excommunicate, and both his potential opponents wished to secure the support of the papacy, he feared that one, or both of them, would attack him. This fear dominated 1539. The whole fleet was mobilized, and large sums of money (raised by selling off former monastic lands) was spent on coastal defences. A string of modern forts, like Walmer, Deal and Portsea, was hastily erected and armed. Huge musters were held, right across the south of England. The panic passed, and within a year the two great European powers were at each other's throats again, but England was now armed and ready for major war. The antics of Richard Baker and his drunken friends have no particular relevance to this situation, except that they illustrate what could happen when a fully manned warship was left at anchor within easy reach of a populous city. They provide almost the only tangible evidence of the whereabouts of the *Mary Rose* in the summer of 1539, and confirmation that she was, at that point, ready for the call which never came. She was, presumably, laid up again in the winter of 1539/40, but it is not known where. An ordnance list survives from February 1541, which may indicate another spring preparation, but the next firm evidence is from July 1543, when she was again at sea in the context of Henry's last French war.

DOCUMENTS

55. *From a list of ships, 1525 or earlier.*

Mary Rose. Item the *Mary Rose*, being of portage 600 ton, lieth in [the pond] at Deptford beside the storehouse there, which must [be . . .] and caulked from the keel upward, both within and without.

Ceramic cooking pot from a chest on the main deck at the stern. The handle indicates that this pot would have been suspended over the galley fire. (*Mary Rose Trust*)

56. *Extracts from accounts of Thomas Jermyn, Clerk of the Ships, for 1523–30.*

Hereafter ensueth all such payments as hath been paid by Thomas Jermyn, deputy for Thomas Sperte, master of the *Henry Grace à Dieu* since the 26th day of November in the 15th year of the reign of our sovereign lord King Henry the VIIIth for wages and victuals of masters, boatswains, mariners, keeping of the King our sovereign lord's ships within his haven of Portsmouth by the space of 10 months begun the foresaid 26th day of November and to end the first day of September in the 16 year of the reign of our said sovereign lord, as hereafter more plainly doth appear.

The Mary Rose. Paid more to John Conner, master of the *Mary Rose*, for wages and victuals of 21 men, shipkeepers, keeping of the said ship within the haven of Portsmouth by 10 months begun the 26th day of November in the 15th year of the reign of our sovereign lord King Henry the VIIIth and to end the first day of September in the 16th year of the reign of our said sovereign lord, after the rate of 10s 4d every man by the month, with 2 deadshares for the master by like time at 10s a month – £113 10s.

Paid by me Thomas Jermyn, master of the *Mary Rose*, for wages and victuals of 15 men, shipkeepers, keeping of the said ship within the haven of Portsmouth by 7 months begun the 2th day of September in the 16th year of the reign of our sovereign lord King Henry the VIIIth and to end the 16th day of March then next following in the same year, of the rate of 10s 4d every man by the month, with 2 deadshares for the master by like time at 10s a month – £57 15s. . . .

Similar payments by Jermyn as master for eighteen men, 17 March–21 December 1525, and for twelve men, 22 December 1525–25 October 1526. It seems that for this period there was no regular master, and Jermyn was therefore directly responsible for these charges.

. . . Paid more to John Jett, keeper of the *Mary Rose*, for wages and victuals of 11 men, shipkeepers, keeping the said ship within the haven of Portsmouth by 4 months begun the 26th day of October in the 18th year of the reign of our said sovereign lord King Henry the eight and to end the 14 day of February then next following, after the rate of 10s 4d every man by the month, with one deadshare for the keeper at 5s a month by like time, amounteth – £23 14s 8d. . . .

Similar payments to Jett for between six and thirteen men for half-yearly periods between 15 February 1527 and 7 January 1530.

. . . Hereafter followeth all such stuff with other necessaries provided by me Thomas Jermyn, Clerk of our sovereign lord the King's Ships, for the repair of the *Mary Rose* and for caulking of her orlop and decks forth and aft withinboard, and likewise for searching and caulking from the keel upward withoutboard, and repairing and trimming of her boat, the 5th day of June in the 19th year of the reign of our sovereign lord King Henry the VIIIth.

   First paid for 37 foot of plankboard containing 5 inches, at 8s the hundred, the sum maketh – 3s.

Item more for 120 foot of orlop board containing 2 inches, at 3s 4d the 100, sum – 4s.
Item more for 46 foot of square timber at 3s 4d the ton – 4s 10d.

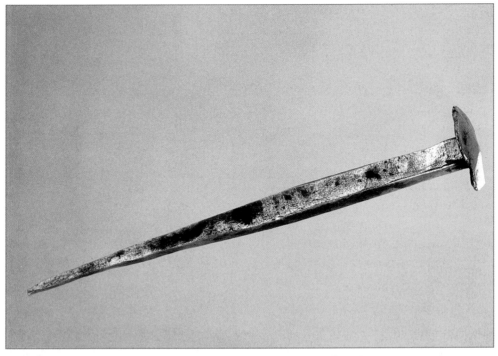

An iron nail, 105 mm long, remarkably preserved in a cauldron of tar. (*Mary Rose Trust*)

Item more for 6 clove boards at 4*d* a board – 2*s*.
Item for 55 lb of carvel spikes, at 1½*d* the lb – 6*s* 10½*d*.
Item for 150 of orlop nail at 3*s* [*the*] 100 – 4*s* 6*d*.
Item more for 150 of orlop nail at 2*s* [*the*] 100 – 3*s*.
Item for 150 of orlop at 16*d* the 100 – 2*s*.
Item more for 600 of 6*d* nail – 3*s*.
Item 100 of 5*d* nail – 5*d*.
Item for 400 of 4*d* nail – 16*d*.
Item for 100 of 3*d* nail – 3*d*.
Item for 600 of scupper nail – 2*s*.
Item for two load of burning – 2*s*.
Item for 600 [6 cwt] 3 quarters of oakum at 7*s* 8*d* the 100 [cwt] – 51*s* 9*d*.
Item for 6 lb of thrums 12*d* – 12*d*.
Item for 2 hoses – 16*d*.
Item more spent in pitch – 8 barrels.
Item in tar – 2 barrels.

Sum of the page – £4 13*s* 3½*d*.

57. *Depositions before the Admiralty Court, June 1539.*

Concerning an alleged assault by sailors from the Mary Rose *against the crew of a Portuguese ship moored in the Thames. The outcome of the case is not known.*

Richard Baker alias Skenthroppe, dwelling in St Nicholas Lane of the city of London, mariner, in which city he hath dwelt about 20 years, now one of the mariners of the *Mary Rose*, examined before Mr Dr [*John*] Tregonwell upon Wednesday the 11th day of June in anno Domini 1539 and in the 31th year of the reign of our sovereign lord King Henry the eight, saith that upon Monday night last, after eight of the clock, when he and his company had supped upon board the said *Mary Rose*, he and certain of his company, mariners of the same ship, with divers other mariners of those ships lying at anchor besides Deptford, went on land to make merry at an honest man's house in Deptford, whose name he knoweth not, and there this examinant, one Robert Grygges of Suffolk, mariner, one William Oram, mariner, of London, and one Marmaduke, all

In the wooden world of the sailing ship, the carpenter was a major figure. Items of his equipment recovered include a caulking mallet (on right), general-purpose mallets, planes, rules, a mortise gauge and a brace. (*Mary Rose Trust*)

These recovered items show that the ship was well equipped to serve food and drink. But an evening ashore was a more tempting prospect. (*Mary Rose Trust*)

mariners of the said *Mary Rose*, sat making merry at the said house in Deptford until 10 of the clock in the night, and then departed from the said house and came down to the water's side and called to the *Mary Rose* for the boat, intending to have gone on board; and their company being on board did not hear them. And then this examinant and the said three other mariners took a wherry which had no oar in her, but only a pair of rafts wherewith they set the wherry up by the shore's side, and at the last they fell down on stream, the boat of the said *Mary Rose* lying at the stern of the same ship. And there one of his company took hold of an oar lying in the same boat, and the stream was so bent downwards that it bare them from the said *Mary Rose*'s boat towards Greenwich, and drove the said wherry athwart the hawse of a Portingale [*Portuguese*] ship riding at her anchors over against the mouth of Deptford Creek; and then the Portingales being within the same ship, threw stones at this examinant and his said company and brake the said Oram's head. And therewith this inquisite and his company were angry, and thereupon they entered the same Portingale ship, purposing to give them a blow or two for throwing of the said stones; and at their entering the said Oram drew his sword and struck flat long at the Portingales, being about three in number, and drove them under hatches and laid the hatches down upon them, and so went into the wherry again, taking nothing with them, nor did no manner other harm unto them, for he saith that they had neither bill, sword nor staff with them, nor any other kind of weapon with them, but only the said Oram's sword. And after that they were into the wherry and gone from the Portingales' ship towards land, the Portingales cried, making a great noise. And therewith this inquisite and his company came on land on the North shore and landed between Greenwich and over against where the said Portingale lay, and so went down to Blackwall, and came from thence to London. And his said company went to St Katharine's, and there lay that night. And this inquisite came home to his own house, and went next morning to his work again on board the said *Mary Rose*, and there was taken as he saith, and otherwise he knoweth not.

Robert Grygges, late of Ipswich, mariner, one of the mariners of the *Mary Rose*, examined the day and year abovesaid, saith that upon Monday at night last, about half an hour at after 10 of the clock in the night, the said Baker, William Oram and Marmaduke Colman, late of Ipswich, mariner, came all together from a house in Deptford, where they had been drinking until some of them were overseen with ale, and so they took a wherry and rowed down with a piece of a board down towards Greenwich, and came athwart the hawse of a Portingale lying over against Belynges Gate at Greenwich in the middle of the stream. And then with that one of his said company said, Vengeance on him, here lyeth a Portingale. But which of them said so he knoweth not, for he saith that he, this inquisite, had well drunk. And soon after that they fell on board the Portingale's boat, lying on larboard side the same ship, and entered the same boat, and from thence the said Oram and Baker entered into the Portingale ship. And soon after that this inquisite heard the Portingales cry, and with that this examinant went into the same ship for fear lest his said fellows Baker and Oram had been hurt. And when this inquisite came on board the Portingales' ship, the Portingales were all under hatches saving one. And he further saith that there was two shirts and two hose cloths [or two remnants of cloth *inserted*] of the Portingales' goods cast into the said wherry, but how it came there he knoweth not, not by whom. And then they came into the same wherry and came on land right over against Greenwich. And [*he*] saith that after they were gone from the said Portingales' ship, the Portingales cried and made such noise that the men of Greenwich cried unto them again; and saith that the said cloth was left on the oose [*mud*] where this inquisite and his company landed. And from thence they came towards London. And this inquisite went into a hay barn at St Katharine's and tarried there till about 10 of the clock next day because he was so foul arrayed with oose, and saith that Oram's head was broken; but whether it were at the entering into the Portingale or after that they were departed from the same ship he knoweth not; and further saith that Marmaduke came not into the Portingale, nor they had no manner of weapons with them, saving that Oram had a sword and this inquisite had a knife called a 'matchan' not half a yard long, the which he did draw because Oram said that he was hurt. And further he sayeth not.

Memorandum that upon Thursday the 12th day of June in the year of Our Lord 1539 and in the 31th year of the reign of our sovereign lord King Henry the eight, in the dwelling house of John Dyes, merchant of Portugal, situate in the parish of St Dunstan's in the East of the city of London, in the presence of me Roger Huntte, notary public, and of these witness under named, did personally appear Gonsalianus Cassado of Villa Viana in the realm of Portugal, pilot of a good ship called Saynte John de Cangas in Galicia now at anchor in the River of Thames at St Katharine's pool, and Petro Falcon of Cangas beforesaid, merchant, and they did allege and say that upon Monday at night last past about 12 of the clock in the night, the abovesaid Richard Baker and Robert Grygges before examined, with four or five persons more, came with a wherry unto the said ship, then lying over against Greenwich in the said River of Thames, at what time the said Gonsalianus and Petro were on sleep under hatches of the said ship, and the master of the same ship, called Roderigo de Pyncta with them, and under the deck abaft the same ship lay two mariners on sleep called John de Vale and Edwarde Roderigus, and upon the hatches lay two boys of the ship on sleep. And then and there the said Baker and his company entered the said ship and beat the said boys with their swords flatlong, and drove them under hatches, and then one of the said Baker's company went abaft the said ship and kept the said John de Vale and Edward, that they could not come forth of their cabin, and another of the same Baker's company stood at the hatch hole with a naked drawn sword in his hand, and kept the said Gonsalianus and his company, then being waked with that noise, under hatches, that they could not come up. And the same thieves tarried searching on board the same ship by the space of an hour, in which time they broke three chests and unlocked another chest, and took and carried away with them £5 6s sterling of the said Petro Falcon's, found wrapped in a clout in one of the said three chests, and 17 yards northern cloth, colour orange, price 17s, and 5 yards northern cloth of orange colour, price 5s, and half a white kersey containing 9 yards, price 10s, and 2 remnants of white kersey containing 6 yards, price

8s 8d, and five yards of broadcloth, colour russet, price 23s 4d, belonging to Anthony Roderycke of Cangas, merchant, and one shirt of the said Petro Falcon's, price 2s 6d, and 2 shirts of Gonsalianus Cassado, price 6s 8d, and £4 2s 8d, and 2 ryals of plate of the same Cassado's, and 2 shirts, price 4s, belonging to Roderigo de Pyncta, and one sugar loaf weighting 8 lb, price 5s 4d, belonging to the said Petro Falcon and to Gregory de Vale, and 3 ells of holland, price 4s 9d, belonging to John de Porto of Cangas in Spain, merchant. And all the said goods were carried away from the said ship by the same thieves, and at their departing from the same ship they loosed the ship's boat and let her drive down the stream, because the company of the said ship should not overtake them, nor make any suit after them at that time. And they further alleged and said that they came up above the hatches of the said ship soon after the thieves were departed, and saw them going away, and perceived them to be six or seven in number, and that all the said parcels of money and other goods be lacking and not received again; albeit they say that the next morning following they found lying on the ooze upon the north shore over against Greenwich 6 yards grey cotton price 3s, of the goods of Gonsalianus before named, and one yard and half of red cloth price 7s 6d, and one yard and an half of broad green cloth price 7s 6d, of the goods of the said Petro Falcon's, and one old shirt, an old cape, and a cap of the said Gonsalianus. In witness of all which premises to be true the said Gonsalianus and Petro gave a corporal oath upon the gospels of God, by them bodily touched, and for the more faith of the premises they have subscribed their firms [*affirmations*] with their own hands; then being present the said John Dyes, who did interpret the sayings of the said Gonsalianus and Petro unto me the notary above written, and Malachias Cogley, notary public, and John Cocke, mariner, witness required by the said Gonsalianus and Petro to bear witness of the premises.

> P. Falcon. Thus it is: by me Roger Huntte, notary public.
> For testimony John Dyaz. [*Signature of Gonsalianus*].
>> [*Sign of an anchor*].
> In the presence of me Malachias Cogley, notary public.

7

THE WAR OF 1543–6, AND THE LOSS OF THE *MARY ROSE*

There are arguments about why Henry decided to return to war in 1542. He is alleged to have wanted to put his advancing years (he was fifty-one) and deteriorating health on one side, and rediscover the zest of youth. He is also alleged to have been humiliated by the infidelities of his fifth wife, Catherine Howard, and keen to restore his self-respect. However, the real reasons, although equally selfish, were probably less introspective. Once Catherine of Aragon was dead, and Anne Boleyn had followed her (January and May 1536), the Emperor had reluctantly come to terms with the King's idiosyncratic religious policy. This in turn meant that when the brief Franco-Imperial entente of 1538–9 fell apart, there was a chance to return to a traditional political orientation. From the end of 1541 onward Henry began to seek a closer alliance with Charles, and this inevitably meant participating in the latter's renewed war with France. In June 1542 they came to a secret understanding, which committed Henry to a joint attack in the summer of 1543. His willingness to do this was fuelled partly by a long-standing desire to increase the size of the English bridgehead in France, an ambition relinquished after the surrender of Tournai in 1518. It was also relevant that he now had the means to pay for such a campaign. The dissolution of the smaller religious houses in 1536, and the surrender of the major ones between 1538 and 1540 had given Henry an enormous disposable wealth. For the first time since 1514, he could actually afford to go to war, and it is not surprising that the temptation was irresistible.

Henry launched his first assault, not to the south but to the north. Working on the assumption that an invasion of France would inevitably bring the Scots over the border behind his back, he decided to take them out first. The Scots had no desire for war, but the Duke of Norfolk's provocative (and hopelessly inefficient) raid in October 1542 could not be ignored. This was supported by a small naval squadron, but since the victualling arrangement totally disintegrated (again), nothing was achieved beyond stimulating a Scots counterattack. As it happened, this served the King's purpose just as well as a victory by Norfolk, for on 25 November the invading Scots army was routed at Solway Moss, and a large part of the Scots nobility carried prisoner to London. The French evaded a rather feeble English naval blockade to convey reinforcement to Scotland, but they arrived too late and, when James V died a couple of weeks later, it was uncertain what role they would be called upon to perform. In the meantime, Henry had concluded another agreement with the Emperor in February 1543, and began to prepare for his promised campaign in France. Sir Francis Bryan managed to get out of the Tyne with a small force of ships in the same month, but was driven back by a combination of weather and superior Franco-Scottish numbers. William Woodhouse fared rather better, and in the easier weather conditions of the summer remained on station in the Firth of Forth, inflicting some damage, and much inconvenience. His ships appear to have been medium-sized or small, and the *Mary Rose* was certainly not among them.

Henry had now decided that the accession of James's daughter, Mary (barely a week old), combined with his victory, had opened a golden opportunity to take over Scotland through a matrimonial union with his own son Edward, aged five. A more diplomatic approach might actually have achieved that, because Scottish representatives did agree to such a treaty at Greenwich in July 1543, but the King's bullying tactics divided his supporters and handed the initiative to their opponents, so the treaty was never ratified. Meanwhile, grasping after a Scottish prize Henry missed his cue to join in the continental war, in spite of having renewed his Imperial treaty in April. The Emperor was not pleased.

In fact there was little real friendship in the Imperial alliance, as each party was trying to use the other for its own purposes. In December 1543 the Scottish Parliament repudiated the Treaty of Greenwich, and after containing his fury for several months in the hope of a diplomatic solution, Henry launched another destructive raid into the Scottish Lowlands in May 1544. This was again supported by a fleet, but again of modest dimensions, not involving any of the Great Ships. Now, though, the great attack on France could not be delayed any longer, and in the middle of June the King himself crossed to Calais with a large army, escorted by most of his fleet. By this time the Navy was expanding rapidly. The *Henry Grace à Dieu* had been rebuilt in 1540 (and somewhat reduced in size), and since then ten other vessels had been built, purchased, or taken as prizes. The total at the time of the summer campaign of 1544 was over forty, and still rising. In one sense, the campaign was a success; by September Henry had taken Boulogne, which had become his prime objective. But in another sense it was a disaster; strategic coordination with the Emperor broke down totally, and recriminations followed. Both sides were to blame, but the result was that Charles felt no obligation to his ally, and signed a separate peace with Francis, just at the time when Henry was entering Boulogne in triumph.

This was extremely bad news for the English, because there was no chance that they could also settle while retaining control of Boulogne. Henry would either have to surrender his cherished conquest, or fight on on his own. He chose to do the latter. So in 1545 he was faced with an unresolved conflict in Scotland, a French King determined to recover what he had lost, and no allies. Although England had a much more efficient naval infrastructure, and Henry had by this time about fifty ships of his own, the resources of France, both in men and ships, were potentially far greater. Peace with the Emperor also meant that the French Mediterranean fleet was available for deployment in the north. This consisted mostly of galleys, and as has already been seen from the events of 1513, they were most effective in the right circumstances. Warship technology had moved on, and the ships of 1545 were not as vulnerable as those of a generation earlier. Nevertheless, Viscount Lisle, the new Lord Admiral, was understandably worried that his opposite number, Claude d'Annebault, had about twenty-five such vessels available, while he had only one or two, together with a dozen very small galleys, known as rowbarges, which did not carry heavy guns. The French strategy was straightforward. As long as the English had the command of the sea, any siege of Boulogne would be doomed to failure, and his prime objective was the recovery of that town. So d'Annebault needed to take out the English fleet, and destroy its advance base at Portsmouth. To that end, he began to assemble a huge fleet of some 200 ships in the Seine estuary.

It was slow work, and the English, as usual, were at sea first. By the end of May their privateers (encouraged by royal proclamation) had taken some fifty prizes, and inflicted heavy damage on French trade. Lisle's main concern, however, was to disrupt d'Annebault's preparations, and it was with that in mind that he led out a warfleet of some thirty to thirty-five ships early in June. It would appear from his letter of the 24th that his flag was not in either the *Henry* or the *Mary Rose*, but there was a fair amount of choice by this time, and both were old ships (**59**). Lisle's tactics, as far as they can be reconstructed, seem to have depended upon using a number of captured merchantmen (hulks) as fireships to destroy as much as possible of the French fleet at anchor in Le Havre. Because of the bad weather, a number of these prizes escaped, but he reckoned that the seven which remained would be sufficient for his purpose. His intelligence was accurate; d'Annebault was still waiting for his galleys and other ships from Brest, and would not be ready to set out for some time. Nevertheless, Lisle failed to turn this initiative to advantage, and when he attacked Le Havre on 6 July, he was repulsed. This was partly due to the continuing bad weather, and partly to the effectiveness of the French galleys, which had by then arrived. Lisle also seems to have been handicapped by the King's insistence that he await specific orders, which were then delayed. Why Henry should have done this is not clear. Perhaps he wanted to feel in control, but the consequences were unfortunate.

However, fate to some extent performed what Lisle had failed to do. As the English retreated and the French celebrated, d'Annebault's 100-gun flagship, the *Philippe*, caught fire and burned to the waterline. The ship to which he then transferred his flag ran aground and had to be abandoned. Quite apart from the loss of two large fighting ships, many would have taken this for an ill omen, but d'Annebault was unperturbed. He put his fleet to sea on 12 July, and having made a diversionary raid on the Sussex coast on the 18th, entered the Solent the following day, landing 5,000 men on the Isle of Wight. He had somewhere between 150 and 200 ships, and between 30,000 and 50,000 men, which was probably the largest invasion armada ever assembled. In naval terms these figures are somewhat misleading, because the great majority of his ships would have been troop transports. He had between 20 and 30 large warships, and 25 galleys. Against him, Lisle had about 80 ships, but they were all fighting ships of various sizes, including about 20 large ones (over 400 tons).

D'Annebault's arrival seems to have taken the English by surprise. The whole fleet was at anchor within Portsmouth harbour, and the King was actually dining on the *Henry* when the alarm was given. Having sent his landing force ashore, the French Admiral then deployed his fleet in three squadrons, keeping the transports well out of the way. The total absence of wind then gave him the initiative. He could not get his sailing warships into Portsmouth harbour, and the English could not get out, but his galleys, being moved by oars, remained mobile. They advanced, firing their basilisks, although to little effect. Then, in the late afternoon, a fitful wind sprang up, and Lisle began to move his big ships forward to attack. The galleys retreated in some haste, because they were no longer a match for the sailing ships in open combat. The *Mary Rose*, possibly leading the fleet, fired guns from one side (it is not clear which, but historical sources favour the starboard); then, in coming about to fire from her other broadside, she was caught by a sudden strong gust of wind. She heeled over and with the gunports being open for action, the water rushed in and she went down like a stone. There were only a handful of survivors, and the captain, Sir George Carew, was among the dead.

There has been much debate about how this tragedy, which the King witnessed from the shore a few hundred yards away, came about. Twenty years later, Martin Du Bellay claimed that she had been sunk by French gunfire (**63**), but nobody thought that at the time, and there is no trace of damage upon the existing remains. There was also a theory that the crew were running riot, and although the Carew family favoured this explanation in order to exonerate Sir George, it is an unnecessary and improbable thesis (**82**). What seems to have happened is that the ship had been to some extent destabilized by her rebuilding ten years before. On top of that, she had been overloaded with guns and men in preparation for battle, and far too many of these men were on the top deck and in the castles. It is also likely that Sir George, in his zeal to show his mettle to the King, attempted to bring her about too sharply. It is known that the weather that summer was unusually squally, and both fleets had already suffered from such conditions (**59**). So it seems that an unstable ship, turning too steeply, was caught at the crucial moment by a fierce, brief squall, and the open gunports did the rest. The enormous loss of life was partly down to the fact that few sixteenth-century seamen could swim, and partly to the deployment of the anti-boarding netting in the waist of the ship. Intended to prevent enemies from jumping down onto the deck, it also effectively prevented those on the deck from leaving the ship. An engraving made in the late eighteenth century from a contemporary painting at Cowdray Park, subsequently destroyed (see p. 119), shows the scene immediately after the disaster. It portrays the top of the *Mary Rose*'s mainmast rising forlornly out of the water, with a solitary survivor clinging to it.

The loss of one ship, however, did not decide a battle, let alone a war. The wind having failed again, Lisle skilfully used the tides and currents to get the rest of his fleet to sea, and in the process frustrated d'Annebault's attempts to manoeuvre his big ships into position. The result was a deadlock, which suited Lisle very well because his strategy was defensive and he had supplies and reinforcements to hand. In reporting this satisfactory situation to the King on 21 July, he rather surprisingly made no allusion to the loss of one of his most powerful ships; perhaps he felt that the King hardly needed reminding (**60**). Over the next two days, the French Admiral sought for some decisive action, but was totally frustrated, by Lisle's skill, the weather, and his lack of local knowledge. Even his landing party on the Isle of Wight made no progress because Henry had reinforced the garrison. With supplies running low, and disease beginning to afflict his overcrowded troop ships, d'Annebault had no choice but to retreat. Evacuating his troops from the Isle of Wight on the 23rd, he quit the Solent the following day. Although unspectacularly achieved, and overshadowed by the loss of the *Mary Rose*, this was in fact a major and decisive English victory.

At first, it seemed that the campaign was not over, and the threat to Boulogne certainly remained. If d'Annebault could deploy his large fleet to prevent the English from supplying the town, it might still fall to a land-based assault. He disembarked about 7,000 of his soldiers to enhance the attacking army, and then returned to the Channel, his galleys carrying out some small-scale raids on the south coast. At the end of the first week of August, and with his fleet enhanced to nearly 100 fighting ships, Lisle came in search of d'Annebault, this time seeking battle. It was in this connection that he drew up his innovative fighting instructions, proposing to use a squadron battle formation, and laying down a system of identifying flags. His intention was to fight, somewhere off Beachy Head, on 10 August, and the fleets did, in fact, encounter on that day. There was an inconclusive exchange of gunfire, and then the wind failed again. This time it was d'Annebault who stalled. Plague already raged in his fleet, and he was in no fit condition to offer battle. On the night of 10/11 August he withdrew under cover of darkness, and returning to the Normandy coast, immediately demobilized. The siege of Boulogne failed and the following spring Francis made peace, leaving Boulogne in English hands. Henry had, in a sense, won his final war, although the Scottish situation remained unresolved when he died in January 1547.

DOCUMENTS

58. *Extract from the Anthony Roll inventory, completed 1546.*

This is the second entry in the roll (the Henry Grace à Dieu *taking first place). It was not presented to the King until after the* Mary Rose *had sunk, but salvage was still in prospect. Anthony's professional concern was ordnance, to which his inventory is restricted. He also painted the illustrations which accompany each entry.*

The *Mary Rose*. Tonnage – 700. Men: soldiers – 185; mariners – 200; gunners – 30; [*total*] – 415.

A bastard culverin, on a precise replica of the carriage on which it was found on the wreck site. (*Mary Rose Trust*)

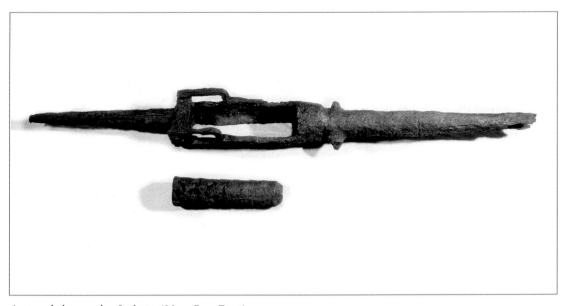

A corroded example of a base. (*Mary Rose Trust*)

For the *Mary Rose*. Ordnance, artillery, munitions, habiliments for the war, for the arming and in the defence of the said ship to the sea.

Guns of brass. Cannons – 2; demi-cannons – 2; culverins – 2; demi–culverins – 6; sakers – 2; falcon – 1; sum – 15.

Guns of iron. Port pieces – 12; slings – 2; demi-slings – 3; quarter-sling –1; fowlers – 6; bases – 30; top pieces – 2; hailshot pieces – 20; handguns complete – 1.

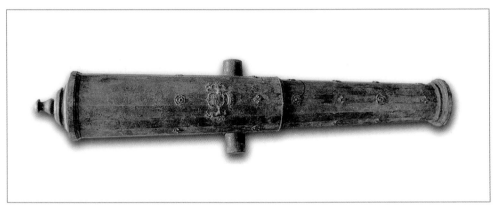

A bronze demi-cannon. The *Mary Rose* is said to have carried six, of which two have been recovered by the *Mary Rose* diving team. (*Mary Rose Trust*)

Hailshot piece, a hand-held gun that fired a type of shrapnel. The hook would fit over the side of the ship to absorb the recoil. (*Mary Rose Trust*)

113

Over 3,500 arrows have been recovered, mostly poplar. Some were held in sheaves of twenty-four by leather spacers, helping to protect the feather flights (of which only fragments, probably swan, have survived). (*Mary Rose Trust*)

Gunpowder. Serpentine powder in barrels – 2 lasts. Corn powder in barrels – 3.

Shot of iron. For cannon – 50; for demi-cannon – 60; for culverin – 60; for demi-culverin – 140; for sakers – 80; for falcon – 60; for sling – 40; for demi-sling – 40; for quarter-sling – 50; dice of iron for hailshot – [*blank*].

Shot of stone and lead. For port pieces – 200; for fowlers – 170; for top pieces – 20; for bases, shot of lead – 400; for handguns, shot of lead – 1,000.

Bows, bowstrings, arrows, morris pikes, bills, darts for tops. Bows of yew – 250. Bowstrings – 6 gross. Livery arrows in sheaves – 400; morris pikes – 150. Bills – 150. Darts for tops, in dozens – 40.

Munitions. Pickhammers – 12; sledges of iron – 8; crows of iron – 12; commanders – 12; tampions – 4,000; canvas for cartridges – 20 ells; paper royal for cartridges – 1 quire; forms for cartridges – 6.

Habiliments for war. Ropes of hemp for woulding and breeching – 10 coils; nails of sundry sorts – 1,000; bags of leather – 8; firkins with purses – 6; lime pots – 10 dozen; spare wheels – 4 pairs; spare truckles – 4 pairs; spare axle-trees – 6; sheep skins for sponges – 12; timber for forelocks and quoins – 100 feet.

59. *John Dudley, Viscount Lisle, Lord Admiral, to the Privy Council, 24 June 1545.*
   This is the last surviving letter to refer to the Mary Rose *afloat.*

After my most hearty recommendations unto your good lordships, I have received your letters of the 21th of this present, perceiving thereby that the King's majesty's pleasure is to have the enterprise whereof I advertised his highness to be put in ure [effect]. These shall be to signify unto the same, that since my said advertisements unto his majesty, we have been so tormented with storms and strainable winds, the like I suppose hath not been seen this time of the year so long continuing, And upon Sunday last, being the 21st of this present, we were all together a quart seas over athwart Beauchef [*Beachy Head*], lying on hulling, the wind veering at North-East, and being very fair weather, having with us the fleet of the hulks, whereof I advertised the King's majesty; thinking thereabouts to remain until answer came from his highness or from your lordships of such advertisements as I had written unto his majesty. And the same night in the dark of the evening, the wind beginning to blow up, divers of the hulks came under their sails, thinking to have stolen from us. Which being perceived, we followed with sundry of the swiftest ships of the fleet, wherof Sir John Berkeley in the *Less Galley* was foremost; who, thinking with the shooting of a piece to have caused them to have turn again, commanded his master gunner to shoot off a saker, which being fired, brake all to pieces; and standing himself at the recoil of the same, one piece, not so much as half the quarter of a hazel nutshell, struck him besides the pap and out at the top of the shoulder; of which misfortune I suppose your lordships be before this advertised from the Captain of Portsmouth. It was the next day, at 9 of the clock in the morning, before we could get all the hulks together, and with following of them, we were put Westwards a kenning beyond the Wight. And that night following there came down so unreasonable pairs of winds at the South and South-South-West that it was as much as many of our ships could do to brook the seas; by reason whereof we were constrained to hold up again with the Narrow Seas or else to put ourselves in with the Wight, which I thought not convenient, conjecturing that with those strainable winds, the rest of the army coming out of Thames, and also the *Henry* with the *Mary Rose*, should be in the Downs. Which place, although it was more painful than to have come in with the Wight, we made towards, where we arrived in safety yesterday at afternoon. Finding there the *Harry* and the *Mary Rose*, and none of the ships that cometh out of the Thames, neither small nor great, saving only the small shallop that conveyed my lord Great Master [*Suffolk*] to Queenborough, which came unto me upon Saturday last in the morning, and hath been with me ever since. The residue remained at Gravesend, upon payment, which I would had been deferred until their arrival in the Downs, for they had no winds since to bring them about the Foreland. In this foul night we lost the company of all the said hulks, saving seven, which I trust shall serve for the purpose, that shall be put in ure with as much diligence as wind and weather will serve, God willing. It may please your good lordships also to understand that, by sundry hoys which since my coming into the Narrow Seas have passed out of Rouen into Flanders, whereof I have advertised your lordships of sundry of them, I had intelligence of certain Breton ships that came with the Bordeaux fleet, which should be ready to depart from Rouen with the next easterly wind, newly freighted with merchandise for the parts of Brittany. Whereupon I appointed two of the ships of Bristol and my two ships, with one handsome bark, which a servant of Mr Southwell's hath here upon his own adventure, and John Winter's bark, and two of the boats of Rye, which departed from us upon Sunday last, the wind being at North-East, to lie in wait upon the coming forth of the said Breton ships; of whom as yet I hear no word; but if the weather hath done them no harm, there is no doubt of them, for there is not a man of war abroad on this side Brest. And the same day I sent the *New Bark* and the *Jenet* with two of the boats of Rye to scour the coast as far as Dieppe; who met with two hoys laden with canvas coming from Rouen, which seemeth to be free men's goods; and they met also three Flemish pinks laden with powdered cod, bound for Rouen, and chased them 5 miles before they could take them; which hoys be brought into Rye for that they were not able to hold up to this place. And the masters of them being examined of the towardness of the French navy in Newhaven [*Le Havre*] and those parts, saying that the same will not be ready to come forth this month and more, and that they tarry for the coming of the galleys and army from Brest, which they look for daily. The said pinks, with the fish, I intend to cause to be delivered unto Thomas Rolf, the King's majesty's purveyor of victuals, until your lordships shall advertise him of his highness's pleasure therein. And as touching the said hoys with the canvas and the like, when they shall be met withal, I beseech your lordships that I may be advertised of the King's majesty's pleasure in that behalf. And thus etc.

Endorsed: Copy for my lord of Hertford.

60. *Lord Admiral Lisle to the King, 21 July 1545.*

The first letter written from the fleet since the sinking of the Mary Rose *on 19 July, to which no reference is made.*

It may please your most excellent highness to understand that I do perceive by my lord of Surrey it is your majesty's pleasure that I should declare unto the same by writing the effect of a certain purpose which, by occasion of a little gale of wind that he had for a while yesternight, came in my mind, which is after this sort; in case the same gale of wind had grown to be stable, being then at 'plank weste', and had blown too a course and a bonnet off, which were the terms that I examined the masters by, whether then the French fleet were able to ride it out in that place where they lie, and they said, very well they might do it. And then I asked whether if they saw or perceived us to come under sail making towards them, whether they would bide us at anchor or not; and they said, if they did bide us at anchor, they were cast away; for we, coming with a fore-wind, should bear over whom we listed into the sea, and therefore they would not sure bide that adventure, but rather come under their small sails to abide us lose, for that were their most advantage. I asked, if they were once loose and put from their anchor with that strainable wind, whether they could seize any part of the Wight again, and they said it was not possible for them to do it, but of force must go roam with the high seas, and much ado to escape a danger called the 'Avers'; and that some of them, of likelihood, would rest there, if such a wind should come, and that if they were put from their anchors as is before said. So thought I, and said then to my lord of Surrey that these Frenchmen which be here, if they land, they may happen find such a blast that they shall never see their own country again. This is the effect of this purpose, serving to none other end, but, if such a wind should chance, this I doubt not would follow. If it shall so like your highness that we shall endeavour us to the same, wherein neither in no other enterprise to be done upon them being never so feasible, I will not attempt, your majesty being so near, without first making your highness privy thereunto, and not without your grace's consent to the same, albeit that I would for my own part little pass to shed the best blood in my body to remove them out of your sight. But have your grace no doubt in any hasty or unadvised or presumptuous enterprise that I shall make, having the charge of so weighty a matter under your majesty, without being first well instructed from your highness. For if I have any knowledge how to serve you in any kind of thing, I have received the same from your self, and being so near the fountain, and would die for thirst, it were little joy of my life. And thus I wish all joy and continual felicity unto your most excellent majesty's person. In the *Harry Grace à Dieu*, the 21th of July at 8 of the clock in the evening.

Your majesty's most humble and obedient subject and servant, John Lisle.

61. *John, Lord Russell, to Sir William Paget, Principal Secretary, 23 July 1545. Extracts.*

Right worshipful, after my most hearty commendations. This is to signify to you that I received your letters yesternight late, dated the 19th of this instant at Portsmouth, for which your most gentle remembrance of me I heartily thank you. . . . I am very sorry of the unhappy and the unfortunate chance of the *Mary Rose*; which, through such rashness and great negligence should be in such wise cast away, with those that were within her; which is a great loss of the men and the ship also, notwithstanding you give me good hope by your letters that the ship shall be recovered again, which I pray God may be so. I understand also that there are besides St Helen's Point to the number of 8 score sail, and that the King hath determined that my lord Admiral shall give them battle if they abide. And that even then, at the writing of your letters, 17 of the galleys came in the order of battle to the fight, of the which one was sunk, and the ships began to retire, which I believe will not come again. . . .

  Thus I bid you heartily well to fare. From Bodmin, the 23th of July. Your own assured,

J. Russell.

62. *François van der Delft, Imperial ambassador to Charles V, 23 (postscripted 24) July 1545.*

  This ciphered dispatch from Portsmouth is the closest contemporary account of the loss of the Mary Rose. *It establishes the explanation, confirmed by archaeological evidence and evaluation, that she sank because she went about with open gunports. Enemy action is not mentioned as a factor.*

. . . On the following day, Sunday [*19 July*], whilst the King was at dinner on the flagship, news came that the French were only five short leagues away. This turned out to be true, for within two hours their fleet in great force was seen in front of this port, and the King hurriedly left the flagship, The English fleet at once set sail to encounter the French, and on approaching them kept up a cannonade against the galleys, of which five had entered well into the harbour, whilst the English could not get out for want of wind, and in consequence of the opposition of the enemy.

  Towards evening, through misfortune and carelessness, the ship of Vice-Admiral George Carew foundered, and all hands on board, to the number of about 500, were drowned, with the exception of about five and twenty or thirty servants, sailors and the like, who escaped. I made enquiries of one of the survivors, a Fleming, how the ship perished, and he told me that the disaster was caused by their not having closed the lowest row of gunports on one side of the ship. Having fired the guns on that side, the ship was turning in order to fire

118

This eighteenth-century picture was made from a painting, since destroyed, at Cowdray House in Sussex. It shows the engagement of 19 July 1545, with (centre of this detail) the *Mary Rose* already beneath the waters of the Solent, survivors clinging to her mainmast. Below, the King passes outside Southsea Castle. The accurate topography of this image gives authority to its depiction of the fleet dispositions. (*Mary Rose Trust*)

from her other, when the wind caught her sails so strongly as to heel her over, and plunged her open gunports beneath the water, which flooded and sank her. They say, however, that they can recover the ship and guns.

63. *Account of Martin Du Bellay, 1569.*
   This extract represents the widespread belief (or propaganda) on the French side.

In the morning, with the aid of the sea which was calm, without wind or force of current, our galleys could be steered and managed at their pleasure and to the damage of the enemies, who, being unable to move for lack of wind, lay openly exposed to the hurt of our artillery, which had more impact on their ships than they could on them, the more because they are higher and stouter, and also by their use of oars, our galleys could withdraw, avoid danger, and gain the advantage. Fortune supported our army in this way for more than one hour,

119

during which time, among other damages the enemy received, the *Marirose*, one of their principal ships, was sunk by cannon fire, and out of five or six hundred men who were on board, only thirty-five were saved. The *Grand-Henry*, which carried their Admiral, was so damaged that, had she not been supported and assisted by nearby ships, she would have had the same end; there would have been more memorable losses if the weather had not changed in their favour, and not only freed them from this danger, but was most propitious for attacking us, as a land wind rose which, with the current, bore them under full sail upon our galleys. And this change was so sudden that our people had barely time or facility of turning our prows; for, during the calm weather and in the heat of battle, the galleys were so close that, when the ships came at them so suddenly and with such speed, they would have been caught and sunk without any remedy, had it not been for the boldness of our chiefs and the skill and experience of our mariners and oarsmen, who forcibly and quickly turned the galleys. And by these means our people, having turned our prows with agility of oars and help of sails, distanced themselves in a short time from the range of the cannon and started to change their stroke and slow down in order to attract the enemies, as were their orders, out of range and away from the difficulties of the place just described.

64. *From the chronicle of Charles Wriothesley, Windsor Herald, 20 July 1545.*

This entry in one of the best-known Tudor chronicles is in line with the explanation given by the Imperial ambassador. The chronicler was a kinsman of one of the Privy Councillors on the scene (cf. **74** *below).*

The 20th day of July the *Mary Rose*, one of the King's Great Ships, by great misfortune by leaving the port holds open, as she turned sank, and all the men that were in her, saving a 40, were drowned, which were above 500 persons; Sir George Carew, knight, captain, which was drowned; this was done before Portsmouth haven.

8
SALVAGE ATTEMPTS (1546–9)

It was at first assumed that the *Mary Rose* would be recovered without much difficulty, because of the relatively shallow water in which she had gone down. Indeed, when the Duke of Suffolk, who had overall responsibility for the defence of Portsmouth, reported to Sir William Paget on 31 July, he was more concerned about the shortage of pioneers for fortifying the haven than he was about the ship (**65**). It was not appreciated at that point that the French threat had gone away, and Suffolk was still anticipating an attack. Work upon the *Mary* was planned, and would be undertaken as soon as might be convenient. In fact a Venetian salvage expert had already been consulted (he must have been on the spot), and had drawn up a list of requirements which Suffolk passed on to Paget the next day (**66**). From this it appears that the intention was to run cables between two large merchant ships (great hulks), passing the cables under the sunken ship, which had not yet settled into the silt, possibly at low water. Perhaps the intention was merely to wait for the rising tide to lift the *Mary Rose* clear of the seabed, or to half submerge the hulks and then raise the wreck by pumping them out, or perhaps to draw it up by tightening the cables with winches. Possibly a combination of all three methods was envisaged. The presence of ten new capstans on the equipment list suggests as much.

Over the next few days Suffolk and Lisle both reported progress to Paget (**67–9**), and the work clearly acquired a higher priority as the French threat receded. The first target date for the attempt was 3 August, and at first there was complete confidence of success. However, it appears that the Italian experts were not quite as skilful as had been thought. Their first intention seems to have been to set the wreck upright by pulling on the masts (the tops of which were above the water), and then, having got her clear of the bottom by tightening the cables under her, to ease her into the shallows on the high tide. When the tide retreated, it would then have been possible to close the ports and pump out the remaining water. As the hull was undamaged, she should then have refloated. The *Jesus* and the *Sampson* are the hulks named as being used for the purpose. The former was probably the *Jesus of Lübeck*, which had been recently purchased for the navy; the identity of the latter is not known, but if she was to match the *Jesus*, she must have been of 600–700 tons. However, these plans did not work out. Firstly it took longer than anticipated to prepare the hulks and get them into position; the date of the attempt was put back from 3 to 8 August. By the 5th they had managed to recover her sails and some of her rigging, and had attached cables to her masts (**70**), but when they attempted to pull her upright on the 8th, the foremast, and possibly part of the mainmast, were broken. On the 9th permission was asked to try again, this time aiming to move her into shallower water without attempting to set her upright first (**73**). Lisle agreed to allow the hulks, which should have departed on that day with the fleet, to remain at the disposal of the salvors for a further six days. What happened then is not clear. In spite of (or because of) the consumption of 22 tuns of beer, the attempt to 'weigh' the *Mary Rose* failed, and her hull remained on the seabed for another 437 years. However, salvage attempts continued; anchors were recovered, more tackle, and some of her ordnance (**77**). An unnamed Italian diver was paid £20 for this work (**78**), and Peter Pawlo or Paule (who may have been the same man) a further £50. Pawlo was subsequently imprisoned for attempting to remove some unidentified salvage illicitly (**80**). The efforts continued for about four years, at a total cost of nearly £560, and in 1552 the value of the ordnance lost was put at £1,723 – about £1¼ million in modern money (**81**).

DOCUMENTS

65. *Charles Brandon, Duke of Suffolk, to Sir William Paget, 31 July 1545.*

Master Secretary, I commend me right heartily unto you, advertising the same that where I perceive that the King's majesty is informed that there hath been great shot heard upon the sea about the Hurst, I promise you we have heard no such thing here in these parts, yet have we laid wait and hearkened for such purpose. And as for the western fleet, I can hear nothing of them. Finally, as

The Duke and Duchess of Suffolk, artist unknown. Charles Brandon and the *Mary Rose* were among the more enduring objects of Henry VIII's affection, and there is a persistent tradition that the ship was named after, if not actually by, the Duchess, the King's sister Mary. (*Marquess of Tavistock and the Bedford Settled Estates*)

Sir William Paget, later 1st Baron Paget of Beaudesert, whose competent service as principal secretary (of state) to Henry VIII led to promotion under Edward VI and Mary I. Artist unkown. (*The Most Honourable the Marquess of Anglesey*)

touching the going forward of his grace's things here, I assure you I never saw things so far out of order, for here have we nothing in a-readiness, neither pick-axes, mattocks [. . .] else to set men a-work. And as touching [. . .] for the *Mary Rose*, we intend with all speed to set men in hand for that purpose as shall appertain. Thus fare you heartily well. From Portsmouth, the last of July 1545.

Your assured friend, Charles Suffolk.

[*Postscript*]: But as touching his grace's works here, there is and shall be as much done as is possible, as difficult it is almost to get pioneers as tools; yet will we do our best to accomplish all things I doubt not to his grace's contentation.

66. *Suffolk to Paget, 1 August 1545.*

Extract from a further letter from Portsmouth, with an enclosed paper listing the equipment required for the salvage operation.

. . . And as concerning the *Mary Rose*, we have consulted and spoken together with them that have taken upon them to recover her, who desireth to have for the saving of her such necessaries as is mentioned in a schedule herein enclosed. Not doubting, God willing, but they shall have all things ready accordingly, so that shortly she shall be saved . . .

[*Schedule*]

A remembrance of things necessary for the recovery, with the help of God, of the *Mary Rose*,

First, 2 of the greatest hulks that may be gotten.

More, the hulk that rideth within the haven.

Item, 4 of the greatest hoys within the haven.

Item, 5 of the greatest cables that may be had.

Item, 10 great hawsers.

Item, 10 new capstans with 20ty pulleys.

Item, 50 pulleys bound with iron.

Item, 5 dozen ballast baskets.

Item, 40 lb of tallow.

Item, 30 Venetians, mariners, and one Venetian carpenter.

Item, 60 English mariners to attend upon them.

Item, a great quantity of cordage of all sorts.

Item, Symond, patron and master in the foist doth agree that all things must be had for the purpose abovesaid.

67. *Suffolk to Paget, 1 August 1545.*

Conclusion of a letter dealing with other business.

. . . I trust by Monday or Tuesday, at the furthest, the *Mary Rose* shall be weighed up and saved. There be two hulks, cables, pulleys and other things made ready for the weighing of her. Fare your most heartily well. From Portsmouth, the first of August 1545.

Your assured friend, Charles Suffolk.

A whetstone (centre) and two holders. Whetstones were used for sharpening tools as well as weapons. (*Mary Rose Trust*)

68. *Suffolk to Paget, 2 August 1545.*

Master Secretary, I commend me most heartily unto you. Forasmuch as I have thought it very expedient and necessary once a day to write unto you during mine abode here, to the intent you may thereby from time to time signify unto the King's majesty how his things goeth forward here, which I will not fail, God willing, to accomplish accordingly. First, as touching the enemies, I can hear no more of them but as I have seen in a letter from Sir John Gage which I opened this morning, addressed to the lords of the Council.

And as concerning the *Mary Rose*, all things [is *deleted*] be put in good readiness for the weighing of her, which shall go in hand tomorrow, and so speedily done as may be for the serving of the tides.

Also for the fortifications here, as much diligence as is possible is made, and men working as fast as may be, so that I trust all things shall proceed to his grace's contentation. Thus fare you most heartily well. From Portsmouth, the second of August 1545.

Your assured friend, Charles Suffolk.

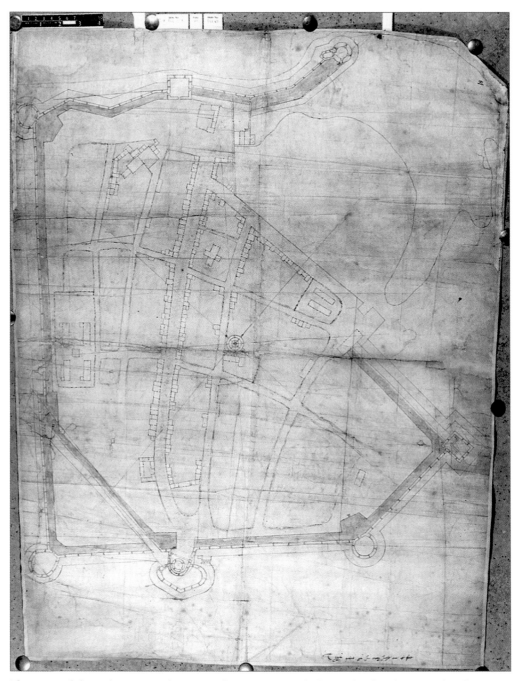

This groundplan of Portsmouth was made in 1545, and shows the fortifications that letter **68** mentions as under construction. Its very ordinariness represents a cartographic revolution, as it is the earliest scale plan of any British town, a world away from pictorial mapping such as on pp. 42 and 90. From British Library Cotton MS Augustus I, i, 81. (*British Library*)

69. *Lord Admiral Lisle to Secretary Paget, 2 August 1545.*
   Conclusion.

. . . We have much ado to frame everything for the *Mary Rose*, but all that may possibly be done is done for the same; the worst is we must forbear three of the greatest hulks of the fleet till the thing be done, which must be emptied of all her victuals, ordnance and ballast during the business, which will be a great weakening to the Navy if anything in the mean time shall happen. And where his majesty, as it appeareth by your said letter, in passing yesterday over Portisdown, found a disorder with lying of the ships, and that his majesty's pleasure is they shall repair to the strait a-this-side St Helen's Point, I require you to signify unto his majesty that the whole fleet remaineth in the same place that they came unto anchor by his majesty's commandment the same day his highness departed from this town, saving the great Venetian [which is brought near the haven to take the ballast *inserted*] and the two hulks the *Jesus* and the *Sampson* which is brought unto the *Mary Rose* because they must weigh her up. Resting these, all the whole fleet abideth as his majesty left them. And thus I bid you farewell. Tomorrow I will visit you with my . . . book of the ships and the captains. Scribbled at Portsmouth in haste, this present 2nd of August.
   Yours assured friend, John Lisle.

70. *Suffolk, Lisle and William Paulet, Lord St John (Lord Chamberlain) to Paget, 5 August 1545.*
   Extract.

. . . And as touching the *Mary Rose*, her sails and sail yards be laid on land, and to her masts there is tied three cables with other engines to weigh her up, and on every side of her a hulk to set her upright, which is thought by the doers thereof, God willing, to be done tomorrow one time in the day. And that done, they purpose, [God willing *deleted*] to discharge her of water, ordnance and all other things with as much diligence as is possible, and by little and little to bring her near to the shore; and as we shall from time to time work with her to save her, his majesty shall be advertised accordingly. . . .

71. *Lisle to Paget, 5 August 1545.*
   Extract.

. . . But the *Mary Rose* (which I trust, with the leave of God, shall be brought upright once tomorrow) hath so charged all the King's majesty's shipwrights with making engines for the same, that they have had no leisure to attend any other thing since his majesty's departure hence, which I beseech you to signify unto his highness. And thus I wish you heartily well to fare. At Portsmouth, the 5th of August.

72. *Suffolk to Paget, 7 August 1545.*
  Conclusion.

. . . My lord Admiral being this present Friday [*that day*] at dinner with me, told me that he had a good hope of the weighing upright of the *Mary Rose* this afternoon or tomorrow. Thus fare you well. From Portsmouth, the 7th of August 1545.
        Yours assured loving friend, Charles Suffolk.

73. *Lisle and St John to Paget, 9 August 1545.*

Master Secretary, after our right hearty commendations. These shall be to advertise you that this day the Italians which had the doing for the weighing of the *Mary Rose* have been with my lord Chamberlain and me to signify unto us

A seaman's chest recovered from the orlop deck. (*Mary Rose Trust*)

that, after this sort which they have followed hitherto, they can by no means recover her, for they have already broken her foremast, which they were coming to declare unto my lord Great Master. But his lordship were departed from hence a little before, and now they desire to prove [*try*] another way, which is to drag her as she lieth until she come into shallow ground, and so to set her upright, and to this they ask six days' proof. And forasmuch as these great hulks which have been occupied all this while about the weighing of her may not well be spared out of this army if we should chance to meet with the enemies, and considering nevertheless the importance of the thing if she may be recovered, as well for the ship as also for the goodly ordnance that is in her, I the lord Admiral have appointed those two hulks which were stayed to have gone forth with the fleet to attend and to serve for the recovery of the said ship and ordnance, wherein assuredly they shall stand the King's majesty in more stead than though they should go with the army; and also they would not be put in order for us to any purpose, for they must have spar decks and waist netting with ports cut, which appeareth unto us now that the same will not be overcome so soon as we thought it would. Wherefore, in our poor opinions, they cannot be so well employed as to be set on work about the recovery of this ship.

And as touching the book of the ships with the captains' names, I the lord Admiral do stay the return of the same until I have word again from you concerning the King's majesty's pleasure to be known for the placing of one captain or two to have the charge of his highness's rowing pieces, whereof I beseech you that I may be advertised with speed. And thus we bid you right heartily well to fare. At Portsmouth, the 9th of August.

Your assured loving friends, John Lisle, W. St John.

74. *Thomas, Baron Wriothesley, Lord Chancellor, to the King, 25 August 1545.*

. . . Tomorrow or the next day we shall send to your majesty a particular declaration how the money received since my going hence hath been defrayed. It shall please your highness also, order is taken that by Wednesday there shall be laden and trussed in two rafts about 50 masts of all sorts; the rafts be made of the great masts which are too long to lie in any ship, and we have two boats ready for the lading of them, whereof the one shall serve for the *Mary Rose* and the other for necessary things to remain as a lighter at Portsmouth. They shall not depart till we hear from your majesty because of the danger of passage. . . .

And this I beseech Our Lord to preserve your majesty in perpetual felicity. From Ely Place the 25th of August,

> Your majesty's most humble and bounden subject and
> servant, Thomas Wriothesley, chancellor.

75. *Edmond Harvel, English agent in Venice, to Paget, 3 September 1545.*
  Opening.

Honourable Master Paget, I salute you reverently. And by your letters of the 24 of July I have been certified of the occurrences in our country much copiously, which was to me passing grateful, not only for the repulsion of our enemies both by sea and land by great valour and virtue, but also to see the intolerable crakes of Frenchmen reduced to vain ostentation and cowardness, and their galleys (wherein they gloried so much) to have served them in small use and moment. The burning and sinking of both the French Admiral's ships is undoubtedly *malum omen* to the enemies, and portendeth victory to Englishmen by the favour of God, although the infortunable case of Sir George Carew is by negligence so miserably successed; but the fortune of war is inevitable of sundry damages, and hereto, thanks to God, the King's majesty hath continually had prosperous success in his wars, and like to have more, and more sustaining. This braw and last efforce [*attempt*] of the French King, who by the judgement of all men being totally exhausted, cannot sustain longer war, but shall be constrained to pacify with his majesty. And at the present is great bruit [*rumour*] that the things between both princes tendeth to agreement, which should be joyful news, being to the satisfaction of the King's majesty our prince. . . .

76. *Extract from the register of the Privy Council, meeting at Westminster, 8 December 1545.*

Warrant was addressed to the Treasurer of the Chamber to deliver to Petre de Andreas and Symone de Maryne, Venetians, 40 marks sterling, to be divided betwixt them by way of the King's majesty's reward for their pains taken about the weighing of the *Mary Rose.*

77. *Extract from the account of the Treasurer for Marine Causes, 1547.*

Charges in recovering of divers anchors and ordnance out of the *Mary Rose.*

The early salvors, interested mainly in the guns and the hull itself, would have paid no attention to everyday objects such as these ceramic pots. (*Mary Rose Trust*)

Also paid by the same accountant to Edward Vaughan, Captain at Portsmouth, for so much money by him paid to one Peter Pawlo, stranger, for the recovering of certain anchors and ordnance out of the *Mary Rose*, who was sent purposely by the King's most honourable Council for the recovering thereof, as by the same particular book doth appear – £37 11s 5d.

78. *Extract from the register of the Privy Council, meeting at Somerset Place, 17 May 1547.*

Warrant to . . . Sir John Williams for £20 to a certain Italian, being a diver, undertaking the recovery of the ordnance of the *Mary Rose*.

79. *Extract from the register of the Privy Council, meeting at Westminster, 3 August 1549.*

Mr Carew had warrant for £50 imprest of the relief of spirituality, to Peter Paule, Italian, for recovering of certain ordnance out of the *Mary Rose*.

80. *Extract from a list of prisoners in the Tower of London, 22 October 1549.*

Peter Pawle, Italian, a diver into the sea, was committed to the Tower about five weeks past by the Duke of Somerset because he departed from Portsmouth (where he had taken certain guns out of the ship drowned) toward the Earl of Arundel's to take certain of his stuff out of the sea, as he saith. To be examined by Mr Wotton etc. My lord Great Master can inform.

81. *Extract from an account of military and naval expenses temp. Henry VIII and Edward VI, September 1552.*

. . . Charges of the *Mary Rose* with wars. Drowned at Portsmouth, the weighing whereof, with the recovery of some part of her tackling, anchors and ordnance, cost in the said late King's time – £559 8*s* 7*d*.

Ordnance with munition and habiliments of war. Spent, lost and employed in the King's majesty's ships serving upon the seas within all the time of the said wars, viz. in the said late King's time, with £1,723 as of the price of certain ordnance lost in the *Mary Rose* at Portsmouth, and with £566 for like ordnance lost in the *Lion Lübeck* – £19,276 13*s* 10½*d*.

9

THE AFTERMATH

COMMENTARY

The fate of the *Mary Rose* passed into history. When John Hooker came to write the life of Sir Peter Carew (Sir George's brother) in the 1580s, he presented a highly circumstantial account of the event, which seems to have been handed down in the Carew family (**82**). This is the source of the notorious story about Sir George calling his crew 'a sort of knaves', a remark not recorded by anyone else, and savouring of special pleading on the captain's behalf. Hooker also set the death toll at 700, instead of the 500 which most contemporaries thought. The most accurate account was almost certainly that given by the anonymous Flemish survivor to François van der Delft, and that was also the most generally accepted (**62**). Nearly eighty years later, Sir Richard Hawkins, writing his memoirs of a voyage he had made in 1593, wrote of 'the *Great Harry*' lost at Portsmouth when her captain and crew were drowned 'with a little flaw of wind, for that her ports were all open' (**83**). Apart from mistaking the name of the ship, it is clear that the warning example to seamen had been taken to heart. Sir William Monson, writing at about the same time, got the name right but mistook the venue of the King's dinner party (**84**). William Harrison's chronology even recorded the sinking as a prime event of 1545, at the cost of the battle of which it was a part. How Monson could have seen any part of the wreck itself, which was covered by some 30 feet of water even at low tide, is an unsolved mystery. Perhaps he saw a piece that had broken away.

The site of the wreck was then forgotten for over 200 years, until it was stumbled upon accidentally by the pioneering diver John Deane in 1836. Deane and his associates recovered several bronze and wrought-iron guns, including a bronze cannon, demi-cannon and bastard culverin, all of which attracted great interest at the time, and led to the wreck being correctly identified. However, the interest did not persist. Deane wrote a book which may never have been published (see Postscript below, p. 142), and his drawings were mostly scattered and lost. At that time wrecks were commonly blown up as hazards to navigation, and that was the fate of another nearby ship at the hands of the Royal Engineers in the 1840s. In fact the *Mary Rose* barely protruded above the sea floor, and was no hazard to anyone, but it came to be believed that Deane's discovery had been destroyed. It was not until the Southsea Branch of the British Sub-Aqua Club began a systematic survey of the historic sites of the Solent in 1965, that it began to be suspected that Henry VIII's Great Ship was still there.

DOCUMENTS

82. *Extract from John Hooker's 'The dyscourse and dyscovery of the lyffe of Sir Peter Carewe'. This is the fullest account of the loss of the* Mary Rose *written within living memory. But Hooker was not an eyewitness, and his loyalty to the Carew family inclined him to blame a disorderly crew rather than a negligent captain.*

. . . The King, as soon as his whole fleet was come together, willeth them to set all things in order and to go to the seas; which things being done, and every ship cross sailed, and every captain knowing his charge, it was the King's pleasure to appoint Sir George Carew to be Vice-Admiral of that journey, and had appointed unto him a ship named the *Mary Rose*, which was as fair a ship, as strong and as well appointed as none better in the realm. And at their departure the King dined aboard with the lord Admiral in his ship named the *Great Henry*, and was there served by the lord Admiral, Sir George Carew, this gentleman Peter Carew, and their uncle Sir Gawain Carew, and with such others only as were appointed to that voyage and service. The King, being at dinner, willed someone to go up to the top of the ship and see whether he could see anything at the seas. The word was no sooner spoken but that Peter Carew was as forward, and forthwith climbeth up to the top of the ship, and there sitting the King asked of him what news; who told him that he had sight of three or four ships, but, as he thought, they were merchants; but it was not long but he had escried a great number, and then he cried out to the King that there was as he thought a fleet of men-of-war. The King, supposing them to be the French men-of-war, as they were indeed, willeth the board to be taken up, and every

S.G.Carow Knight

Sir George Carew. Appointed to command the *Mary Rose* on what was to be her final mission, he allegedly found the crew unmanageable. His wife looked on as the ship went down and took him to his death. This drawing is by Holbein. (*The Royal Collection © 2002, Her Majesty Queen Elizabeth II*) man to go to his ship, as also a longboat to come and carry him on land; and first he hath secret talks with the lord Admiral, and then he hath the like with Sir George Carew, and at his departure from him took his chain from his neck, with a great whistle of gold pendant to the same, and did put it about the neck of the said Sir George, giving him also therewith many good and comfortable words.

The King then took his boat and rowed to the land, and every other captain went to his ship appointed unto him. Sir George Carew, being entered into his ship, commanded every man to take his place, and the sails to be hoisted; but the same was no sooner done but that the *Mary Rose* began to heel, that is, to lean on the one side. Sir Gawain Carew, being then in his own ship and seeing the same, called for the master of his ship and told him thereof, and asked him what it meant; who answered that [if she did heel *inserted*], she was like to be cast away. Then the said Sir Gawain, passing by the *Mary Rose*, called out to Sir George Carew, asking him how he did; who answered that he had a sort of knaves, whom he could not rule. And it was not long after, but that the said

Linstocks, used to fire the guns by extending a lighted taper. These examples are ornamented with fine carvings, each gunner having a personalized design. (*Mary Rose Trust*)

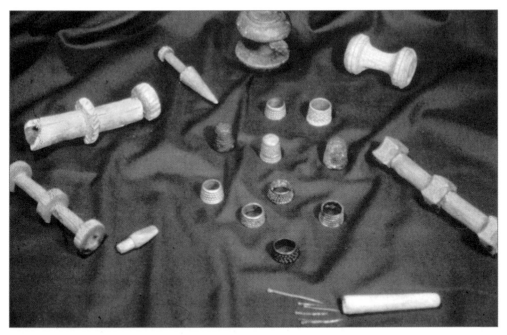

Items of sewing equipment. (*Mary Rose Trust*)

Mary Rose, thus heeling more and more, was drowned with 700 men which were in her, whereof very few escaped. It chanced unto this gentleman, as the common proverb is, the more cooks the worse pottage. He had in his ship a hundred mariners, the worst of them being able to be a master in the best ship within the realm, and these so maligned and disdained one the other, that, refusing to do that which they should do, were careless [also *inserted*] to doth that [they ought to do *deleted*] which was most needful and necessary, and so contending in envy, perished in frowardness.

The King this meanwhile stood on the land and saw this tragedy; as also the lady, the wife to Sir George, who with that sight fell into a sounding. The King, being oppressed with sorrow of every side, comforted her and thanked God for the other, hoping that of a hard beginning there would follow a better ending. And notwithstanding this loss, the service appointed went forthward as soon as wind and weather would serve, and the residue of the fleet, being about the number of one hundred and five sails, took the seas. . . .

83. *Extract from the* Observations *of Sir Richard Hawkins, 1593.*
The writer identifies the Mary Rose *as the* Henry Grace à Dieu *alias* Great Harry.
He also perhaps refers to the Grand Guy, *taken when Drake captured San Domingo on*

1 January 1586 and renamed New Year's Gift, *and abandoned elsewhere when, overloaded with spoil, she began to ship water.*

. . . the eight of April 1593, I caused the pilot to set sail from Blackwall . . . and coming to Barking, we might see my ship at an anchor, in the midst of the channel, where ships are not wont to moor themselves; this bred in me some alteration. And coming aboard her, one and other began to recant the peril they had past of loss of ship and goods, which was not little; for the wind being at East-North-East, when they set sail and veered out Southerly, it forced them for the doubling of a point to bring their tackle aboard, and luffing up, the wind freshing, suddenly the ship began to make a little heel, and for that she was very deep loaden and her ports open, the water began to enter in at them; which nobody having regard unto, thinking themselves safe in the River, it augmented in such manner as the weight of the water began to press down the side more than the wind. At length, when it was seen and the sheet flown, she could hardly be brought upright. But God was pleased that, with the diligence and travail of the company, she was freed of that danger; which may be a gentle warning to all such as take charge of shipping, even before they set sail, either in river or harbour, or other part, to have an eye to their ports, and to see those shut and caulked which may cause danger, for avoiding the many mishaps which daily chance for the neglect thereof, and have been most lamentable spectacles and examples unto us. Experiments in the *Great Harry* [sic], admiral of England, which was over-set and sunk at Portsmouth with her captain, Carew, and the most part of his company drowned in a goodly summer's day, with a little flaw of wind; for that her ports were all open, and making a small heel, by them entered their destruction; where, if they had been shut, no wind could have hurt her, especially in that place.

In the River of Thames, Master Thomas Cavendish had a small ship over-set through the same negligence. And one of the fleet of Sir Francis Drake, in San Domingo harbour, turned her keel upward likewise, upon the same occasion; with many others, which we never have knowledge of.

And when this cometh to pass, many times negligence is cloaked with the fury of the wind, which is a double fault; for the truth being known, others would be warned to shun the like neglects. For it is a very bad ship whose masts cracked not asunder, whose sails and tackling fly not in pieces, before she over-set, especially if she be English-built. And that which over-setteth the ship is the weight of the water that presseth down the side, which, as it entereth more and more, increaseth the weight, and the impossibility of the remedy. For the water not entering, with easing of the sheet or striking the sails, or putting the ship before the wind or sea, or other diligences, as occasion is offered (and all expert mariners know), remedy is easily found.

84. *Extract from the* Naval Tracts *of Sir William Monson, 1623.*

Another inaccurate recollection: it was the Henry Grace à Dieu *aboard which the King dined (***82***).*

The *Mary Rose*, next to the *Regent* in bigness and goodness, after this was cast away betwixt Portsmouth and the Isle of Wight, the very same day King Henry boarded her, and dined in her. Parts of the ribs of this ship I have seen with my own eyes; there perished in her four hundred persons.

POSTSCRIPT
THE RESURRECTION OF
THE *MARY ROSE*

THE DEANE BROTHERS

As has been seen, the wreck was accidentally discovered in 1836. That part of the Solent was full of sunken remains, the most notable being those of a large warship, the *Royal George*, which had gone down in 1782. It was the possibility of recovering some of her guns, and earning a substantial bounty for so doing, which had brought Charles and John Deane to the site. John Deane was the inventor of a pioneering diving system, and it was with the aid of his invention that they hoped to succeed where others had failed. While they were on site, their assistance was requested by some fishermen whose nets had become snagged a short distance away. The Deanes knew exactly where the *Royal George* was, and she was clearly not the culprit. Upon investigation, it was discovered that the snag was a small piece of timber, not rising much above the seabed. However, it appeared that this insignificant object was actually part of a larger mass completely buried in the silt. Exploring further, John Deane discovered near at hand another object, projecting about a foot out of the mud, which proved on investigation to be a large gun. This they recovered, and found to their surprise that it was a bronze 12-foot demi-cannon, bearing a foundry mark of 1542, and the name of Henry VIII. This find was duly reported to the Ordnance Office, where it aroused considerable interest, and led to a correct identification of the wreck. Inspired by thoughts of profit, the Deanes risked their lives to raise several other guns from the same site: a massive bronze cannon cast by Robert and John Owen in 1535, a demi-cannon, a culverin and a bastard culverin, together with three complete wrought-iron port-pieces on their massive elm beds, and up to fifteen other portions of wrought-iron guns. These discoveries led to energetic exchanges between learned gentlemen, and enlightened encouragement by the Ordnance Office.

John Deane planned to write a book, and gathered some material for it, but it appears never to have been published under his name. The pioneering collection of documents published in the 1840s was well beyond Deane's antiquarian competence, and was evidently the work of its publisher, S. Horsey. Something of Deane's literary project may have been accomplished by this means, but only the fact that it was bound in wood recovered from the site specifically acknowledges a connection with the Deane brothers' diving efforts. The profit margins of further work were not encouraging. The Deanes spent one more season on the site, in 1840, and recovered a wide range of objects, including bows, glass bottles, and numerous pieces of structural timber. They were unable to sell the larger complete guns, which were declared to be Crown property, but most of the other discoveries were auctioned at Portsmouth on 12 November 1840. In a bid to hasten the proceedings, and reduce his costs, John Deane also ignited some small charges of gunpowder. The intention seems to have been to make a crater in the seabed and excavate within using conventional picks and shovels. Although they claimed to have been successful, the steady stream of objects appears to have declined, and working the site became unprofitable. At that point the Deanes gave up, and went off after other projects, and it came to be generally believed that the *Mary Rose* had been blown up. As this was the fate eventually inflicted upon the neighbouring *Royal George* (which was a hazard to navigation) at the hands of the Royal Engineers, this belief is understandable.

ALEXANDER MCKEE

In January 1965 the Southsea Branch of the British Sub-Aqua Club set up 'Project Solent Ships'. Inspired by Alexander McKee, then an enthusiastic amateur diver and historian, although not a young man, the original intention had been to disprove the theory that the *Mary Rose* had been destroyed. However, as further investigation threw up a quantity of conflicting evidence as to her possible whereabouts, McKee decided to go for a wider project, seeking to locate and map just over a dozen historic wrecks in the Solent area. The original scientific purpose was to facilitate the exact calculation of timber deterioration.

The team decided to start by looking for whatever might be left of the *Royal George*, after the attentions of the Royal Engineers, knowing, of course, that the *Mary Rose* (if there was anything left of it) was in roughly the same area. There was at that time no legislation protecting historic sites, so it was important that the investigators should keep any possible discoveries away from the eyes of potential treasure hunters. Starting in April 1966, the team began a systematic exploration of the surrounds of the *Royal George* debris. Visibility was poor, and there was more than a suspicion that explosive devices of a much more recent date might still be lying around. A frustrating season produced no positive results, beyond the discovery that the seabed in the immediate vicinity of the site they were reconnoitring appeared to be undisturbed. Whatever signs the Deanes might have left of their presence seemed to have been long since removed by the processes of nature.

In 1982 McKee published a detailed account of the manoeuvrings and frustrations that followed. Marine archaeology in the 1960s was an infant discipline, and those who had some experience in it had worked mainly in the Mediterranean. There were disagreements about techniques, about equipment, and even about the possibility of carrying out any serious investigation in such unpromising conditions. Then there was a breakthrough, of a sort, when the team found an exact location for the wreck plotted on a naval chart of 1841. It was not quite where they had been looking, but they had been close enough to be reasonably sure that there was nothing to be seen. Was the chart inaccurate, or had they been looking for the wrong things? In 1967, using sonar sounding equipment, McKee's team detected some irregularities in the sea floor for which there was no obvious explanation, in more or less the charted place. These irregularities would have meant nothing to the naked eye, particularly one inhibited by poor visibility, but now they began to look significant. McKee negotiated a lease to the seabed to work on the site, and formed the Mary Rose 1967 Committee in collaboration with the Hampshire and Sussex Archaeology Committee. There was now genuine interest, and a fair amount of practical help, but funds remained extremely short, and virtually the whole of the summer of 1968 was wasted because of lack of money. It was not until 1970 that McKee's persistence was finally rewarded, and weeks of fruitless digging and probing on the identified site began to recover objects which positively located a Tudor warship.

The corner had now been turned, and a gun recovered in 1970 attracted a great deal of interest and attention. Excavation continued at an enhanced pace in 1971, and more artefacts were recovered, but as yet there was no sign of the ship itself, and it began to look as though it had completely disintegrated. Then finally, later in 1971, large timbers were located, and it was clear that a part, at least, of the *Mary Rose*'s hull had survived. By 1973 the management of the project had been reorganized into a special branch of the British Sub-Aqua Club, with McKee as Chairman and Director of Excavation. High-profile sponsors began to appear, and British Petroleum gave the project a diving platform, which greatly facilitated the work, for a while. Unfortunately it sank in a storm the following year. By this time, however, with tangible results being achieved almost every working day, a level of public interest had been created which guaranteed the future of the work. For five years, from 1973 to 1978, the outline of the great ship was slowly and painstakingly uncovered. It was lying on its starboard side at an angle of 60 degrees, and most of the upper port side had collapsed into the interior. Part of the bow had broken away, but in the circumstances the integrity of what remained was remarkable. No doubt for years after it had originally sunk, the timbers of the upper side had stood proud, but once they had collapsed, the entire wreck had been covered in silt, leaving virtually nothing to break the surface and attract the attention of an investigator. The small timber which had caught the fisherman's net in 1836 had long since disappeared.

THE MARY ROSE TRUST

By 1978 it was clear that something more than a maritime excavation was in progress. A major national treasure, of international significance, was being uncovered, and it was necessary to decide what to do about it. In 1979 the Mary Rose Trust was established, with a mandate to excavate, raise and conserve the wreck for posterity, and the power and responsibility to raise the necessary funds. An Executive Committee was established, upon which McKee served, and Margaret Rule was appointed as Archaeological Director. The Prince of Wales became a very active and involved President. Four years of intensive excavation followed on the site, using a large team of volunteer and professional divers, supervised by diving archaeologists. The hull was painstakingly excavated and her contents raised, after which the hull was prepared for salvage. On 11 October 1982, with the assistance of an enormous floating crane, the bulk of the 437-year-old warship was raised to the surface. The recovery and conservation of objects from the site continued, but the main focus now became the conservation and display of the hull itself.

Just after 9 am on the morning of 11 October 1982 the hull of the *Mary Rose* broke the surface of the Solent, lifted in a steel cradle by the floating crane *Tog Mor*. The Prince of Wales, President of the Mary Rose Trust, and King Constantine of the Hellenes were spectators, as their remote kinsman Henry VIII had been of the sinking 437 years before. (*Dr M.H. Rule*)

When it was brought ashore to the Naval Dockyard in Portsmouth, a customized workshop was erected over it. The location was No. 3 Dry Dock, itself a scheduled monument dating from 1799. There then followed twelve years of passive holding, during which the timber was sprayed with re-cycled and chilled fresh water for twenty hours a day, maintaining a humidity level of about 95 per cent. During this period various scientific tests were carried out to establish the most satisfactory methods of long-term conservation, and a number of the deck timbers recovered earlier from the site were reinstated in the hull. These internal structures were also supported by the insertion of vertical props and horizontal struts made of titanium, which is light, strong, and resistant to corrosion. In 1985 the hull was turned upright, an attitude not achieved since 1545. All this work was completed by December 1993.

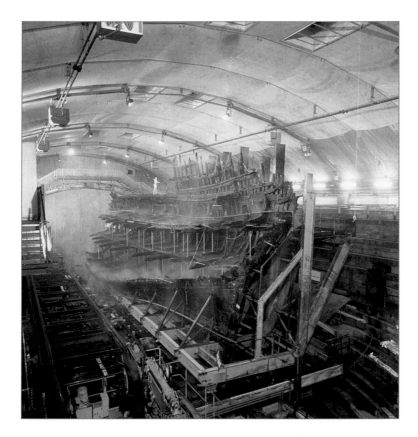

The ship during the conservation process in the ship hall built over No. 3 Dry Dock in the Portsmouth Historic Dockyard. The stern is to the right. (*Mary Rose Trust*)

Active conservation began in September 1994, and for that purpose a new spray system was built, monitored and controlled by a computerized management system designed to maintain a stable environment and give warning of any problems. Using this system, the hull is presently being sprayed with heated Polyethylene Glycol (PEG) in a steadily increasing concentration, designed to avoid damaging the cell walls of the timber. Starting at 5 per cent, this concentration was increased to 50 per cent over a period of six years. The progress of the penetration of PEG is being constantly monitored. When this stage is completed in about 2005, the hull will be treated with PEG of a different molecular weight, intended to seal the penetrated timbers and to enable the whole structure to be dried without disintegration. It is expected that the second phase will take a further five years, after which will follow a process of controlled air drying, taking three to five years. When that is complete, the humidity will be reduced to 55 per cent. If all goes well, in about 2014 the conservation machinery will be finally switched off, although the temperature and humidity in the Ship Hall will still have to be carefully controlled.

In addition to the ship itself, a total of over 19,000 objects have been found on or near the site, and brought ashore. The task of identifying, cataloguing and conserving all this material has been, and continues to be, an enormous one. In association with the Ship Hall, the Trust has also established a museum nearby, where many of these objects are displayed, and aspects of the ship's active life are reconstructed. The museum contains large guns (some with reconstructed carriages), small arms, bows and other munitions. It also displays samples of rigging, navigational equipment, household utensils, remnants of shoes and clothing, board games, musical instruments, devotional objects, and the famous barber-surgeon's chest. Copies of documents and illustrations help to establish the context, and constitute a remarkable capsule of sixteenth-century history.

The Trust is a registered charity and a limited liability company. It operates its own trading company, and an information group of volunteer speakers. It is also supported by a Mary Rose Society, and by a group of American Friends. The immense task of publishing a full report of the archaeological work which has been undertaken on the site is in hand, and will appear in five volumes, the first of which is expected in the autumn of 2003. The present collection of documents is published with the full support of the Trust, and as a contribution to its activities.

The tomb of an unknown sailor from the *Mary Rose* in Portsmouth Cathedral. Burial was preceded by a requiem mass sung according to the Sarum rite. The stone of Welsh slate was cut by John Skelton. (*Mary Rose Trust*)

LIST OF ABBREVIATIONS

All works listed here or elsewhere cited are published in London or by the issuing society unless otherwise stated.

APC   *Acts of the Privy Council of England*, new series, ed. J.R. Dasent (1890–1907)
BL   British Library
CSPD EdVI   *Calendar of State Papers, Domestic Series, Edward VI*, ed. C.S. Knighton (1992)
CSP Span   *Calendar of Letters, Despatches, and State Papers, Relating to the Negotiations between England and Spain*, ed. G.A. Bergenroth et al. (1862–1954)
Ellis   *Original Letters Illustrative of English History*, ed. Sir H. Ellis (1824–46, repr. 1969)
LP   *Letters and Papers, Foreign and Domestic, of the reign of Henry VIII*, eds J.S. Brewer, J. Gairdner and R.H. Brodie (1862–1932) (references are to entry numbers)
NRS   Navy Records Society
PRO   Public Record Office
Spont   *Letters and Papers Relating to the War with France, 1512–1513*, ed. A. Spont, NRS no. 10 (1897)
St. P.   *State Papers during the Reign of Henry VIII*, Record Commission (1830–52)

APPENDIX I
KEY TO DOCUMENTS

No.   Source of Text/Other Printings

1   *MS*: PRO, E/404/87/2, no. 121
        Printed (extract): Spont, p. 4, n. 3 (on pp. 4–5)

2   *MS*: PRO, SP 1/2, f. 178 (old f. 162)
        Calendared: *LP*, i, I, 1393 (viii)

3   *MS*: PRO, SP 1/2, f. 179 (old f. 163)
        Calendared: *LP*, i, I, 1393 (ix)

4   *MS*: PRO, E 36/1, ff. 25v, 27v, 29, 29v, 31v
        Calendared: *LP*, i, II, 3608 (pp. 1496–9)

5   *MS*: PRO, E 36/12, p. 17
        Calendared: *LP*, i, I, 1453 (v) (p. 663)
        Printed (extract as here): Spont, pp. 4–5

6   *MS*: BL, Cotton MS Galba B.III, f. 22
        Calendared: *LP*, i, II, 1387

7   *MS*: BL, Add. MS 48012 (Yelverton MS 12), f. 17r–v (Latin)

151

8   *MS*: BL, Harleian MS 309, f. 37
          Calendared: *LP*, i, II, 3615
          Printed (extracts as here): Spont, pp. 35, 36

9   *MS*: PRO, E 36/12, pp. 151, 172
          Calendared: *LP*, i, II, 3318 (p. 1396)

10   *MS*: PRO, SP 1/4, f. 226 (old f. 322)
          Calendared: *LP*, i, II, 2305 (i) (p. 1032)

11   *MS*: PRO, E 36/12, p. 32
          Calendared: *LP*, i, II, 3318 (p. 1396)

12   *MS*: PRO, 1/229, f. 133 (old. f. 128)
          Calendared: *LP*, i, I, 1688, where dated by association with
          Howard's patent as Admiral of the fleet on 16 March: ibid.
          1732 (32)

13   *MS*: BL, Cotton MS Caligula D.VI, ff. 101v–103
          Calendared: *LP*, i, I, 1698
          Printed: Ellis, 2nd ser., vol. 1, pp. 213–17; Spont, pp. 94–8

14   *MS*: PRO, SP 1/3, ff. 149–150v (old ff. 182–183v)
          Calendared: *LP*, i, II, 1748
          Printed: Ellis, 3rd ser., vol. 1, pp. 145–51; Spont, pp. 103–7

15   *MS*: BL, Cotton MS Caligula D.VI, ff. 344–5 (old ff. 337–8)
          Calendared: *LP*, i, I, 1771
          Printed: Spont, pp. 122–4

16   *MS*: BL, Cotton MS Caligula E.I, ff. 9–10
          Calendared: *LP*, i, I, 1786
          Printed: Spont, pp. 126–9; *The Lisle Letters*, ed. M. St C. Byrne
          (Chicago, 1981), vol. 1, pp. 158–9 (extract, with editorial
          supply of *lacunae* improving readings in *LP* and Spont)

17   *MS*: BL, Cotton MS Caligula D.VI, ff. 106–7 (old ff. 104–6)
          Calendared: *LP*, i, II, 1851
          Printed: Spont, pp. 154–9

18   *MS*: PRO, SP 1/3, f. 201r–v (old f. 200r–v)
    Calendared: *LP*, i, II, 1852
    Printed: Ellis, 3rd ser., vol. 1, pp. 154–6; Spont, pp. 159–61

19   *MS*: PRO, SP 1/4, f. 208 (old f. 267)
    Calendared: *LP*, i, II, 2305 (ii) (p. 1032)

20   *MS*: PRO, SP 1/4, f. 210 (old f. 272)
    Calendared: *LP*, i, II, 2305 (ii) (p. 1032)

21   *MS*: PRO, SP 1/229, ff. 169–70 (old ff. 163–4)
    Calendared: *LP*, i, II, 1870

22   *MS*: PRO, SP 1/229, f. 172 (old f. 166)
    Calendared: *LP*, i, II, 1875

23   *MS*: BL, Cotton MS Caligula D.VI, ff. 104–5 (old ff. 102–3)
    Calendared: *LP*, i, II, 1883
    Printed: Spont, pp. 163–6

24   *MS*: PRO, SP 1/229, f. 173 (old f. 167)
    Calendared: *LP*, i, II, 1886

25   *MS*: PRO, SP 1/229, ff. 174v–175 (old ff. 168v–169)
    Calendared: *LP*, i, II, 1894

26   *MS*: PRO, SP 1/229, f. 176r–v (old f. 170r–v)
    Calendared: *LP*, i, II, 1907

27   *MS*: PRO, SP 1/229, f. 183 (old f. 178)
    Calendared: *LP*, i, II, 1936

28   *MS*: PRO, SP 1/4, ff. 79–80 (old ff. 114–15)
    Calendared: *LP*, i, II, 1965
    Printed: Ellis, 3rd ser., vol. 1, pp. 157–60; Spont, pp. 168–70

29   *MS*: PRO, SP 1/229, f. 190r–v (old f. 184r–v)
    Calendared: *LP*, i, II, 1971

30   *MS*: PRO, SP 1/229, ff. 193–194v (old ff. 187–188v)
Calendared: *LP*, i, II, 1978

31   *MS*: PRO, SP 1/229, f. 213 (old f. 205)
Calendared: *LP*, i, II, 1992

32   *MS*: PRO, SP 1/4, f. 208 (old f. 268)
Calendared: *LP*, i, II, 2305 (ii) (p. 1032)

33   *MS*: PRO, SP 1/4, ff. 125–8 (old ff. 162–5)
Calendared: *LP*, i, II, 2305 (ii) (p. 1033)

34   *MS*: PRO, 1/4, f. 206 (old f. 264)
Calendared: *LP*, i, II, 2305 (ii) (p. 1033)

35   *MS*: PRO, E 101/56/10/3, f. 179, with warrant attached
Calendared: *LP*, i, II, 3614 (p. 1520)

36   *MS*: PRO, SP 1/4, f. 186 (old f. 183)
Calendared: *LP*, i, II, 2305 (iii) (p. 1034)

37   *MS*: PRO, E 101/61/27, f. 1
Calendared: *LP*, i, II, 2652

38   *MS*: BL, Stowe MS 146, f. 129r–v
Calendared: *LP*, i, II, 2865

39   *MS*: BL, Cotton MS Caligula D.VI, f. 108r–v (old f. 106r–v)
Calendared: *LP*, i, II, 2946
Printed: Spont, pp. 202–5

40   *MS*: PRO, SP 1/230, f. 167r–v (old f. 188r–v)
Calendared: *LP*, i, II, 2959

41   *MS*: BL, Cotton MS Caligula D.VIII, f. 250r–v (old f. 146r–v)
Calendared: *LP*, i, II, 3001

42 *MS*: BL, Cotton MS Caligula D.VIII, f. 249r–v (old f. 245r–v)
Calendared: *LP*, i, II, 3000; placing follows arrangement of MS, but context indicates dispatch after **41**

43 *MS*: PRO, SP 1/230, f. 208 (old f. 229)
Calendared: *LP*, i, II, 3137(11)

44 *MS*: BL, Add. Charter 6289

45 *MS*: PRO, E 36/11, ff. 104, 117v (old ff. 101, 114v)
Calendared: *LP*, iii, I, 1009 (p. 372)

46 *MS*: Bodleian Library, Oxford, MS Ashmole 861, p. 331

47 *MS*: PRO, SP 1/24, f. 220r–v
Calendared: *LP*, iii, II, 2302

48 *MS*: PRO, SP 1/24, f. 325r–v
Calendared: *LP*, iii, II, 2337

49 *MS*: PRO, SP 1/24, f. 322
Calendared: *LP*, iii, II, 2341

50 *MS*: PRO, SP 1/25, f. 1
Calendared: *LP*, iii, II, 2342

51 *MS*: PRO, SP 1/25, f. 16
Calendared: *LP*, iii, II, 2351

52 *MS*: BL, Cotton MS Caligula D.VIII, ff. 251–2
Calendared: *LP*, iii, II, 2355

53 *MS*: SP 1/25, f. 22
Calendared: *LP*, iii, II, 2362

54 *MS*: SP 1/25, f. 64r–v
Calendared: *LP*, iii, II, 2419

55   *MS*: BL, Cotton MS Otho E.IX, f. 68
        Calendared: *LP*, iv, I, 1714 (3)

56   *MS*: PRO, E 315/317, ff. 43, 45v, (48, 49v), 51v, (52v, 53, 54, 55, 55v,
        56), 73; material from bracketed ff. given in abstract only
        Calendared: *LP*, iv, III, 6138 (p. 2740)

57   *MS*: PRO, HCA 1/33, ff. 133–8

58   *MS*: Magdalene College, Cambridge, Pepys Library no. 2991, pp. 6–7
        Printed: *The Anthony Roll of Henry VIII's Navy*, ed. C.S. Knighton and D.M.
        Loades, NRS, Occasional Publication no. 2 (2000), p. 43

59   *MS*: PRO, SP 1/202, ff. 163–4 (old ff. 170–1)
        Calendared: *LP*, xx, I, 1023
        Printed: St. P., vol. 1, pp. 790–2

60   *MS*: Hatfield House, Cecil Papers 1/35–6
        Calendared: *LP*, xx, I, 1237; Historical Manuscripts Commission, *Calendar
        of the Manuscripts of the Most Hon. the Marquis of Salisbury, K.G.* (1883–),
        vol. 1, no. 185 (p. 45)
        Printed: *A Collection of State Papers . . . left by William Cecill Lord Burghley*,
        ed. S. Haynes (1740), pp. 51–2

61   *MS*: PRO, SP 1/204, f. 101–101v (old f. 106r–v)
        Calendared: *LP*, xx, I, 1255
        Printed: *St. P.*, vol. 1, pp. 793–4

62   *MS*: Vienna, Österreichisches Staatsarchiv, Haus-, Hof- und Staatsarchiv,
        Staatenabteilungen, England – Diplomatische Korrespondenz, K.12, Konv.
        Berichte an Karl V, f. 182.
        Text: *CSP Span*, vol. 8, p. 190

63   *Text*: M. Du Bellay, *Memoires . . . de plusieurs choses advenües au
        Royaume de France depuis l'an MDXIII jusques au trespas du roy
        François premier* (Paris, 1569), repr. in *Mémoires de Martin et
        Guillaume du Bellay*, eds V.-L. Bourrilly and F. Vindry (Paris,
        1908–19), vol. 4, pp. 289–90; this translation kindly made by
        Mrs J.T. Fitzsimons

64   *Text*: Charles Wriothesley, *A Chronicle of England during the Reigns of the Tudors, from ad 1485 to 1559*, ed. W.D. Hamilton, vol. 1, Camden Society, new ser., no. 11 (1875), p. 158 (spelling modernized)

65   *MS*: PRO, SP 1/204, f. 187 (old f. 190)
            Calendared: *LP*, xx, I, 1325

66   *MS*: SP 1/205, ff. 1v, 5
            Calendared: *LP*, xx, II, 2, 2 (2)
            Printed: *St. P.*, vol. 1, p. 796 and n. 2

67   *MS*: PRO, SP 1/205, f. 6
            Calendared: *LP*, xx, II, 3
            Printed: *St. P.*, vol.1, pp. 798–9

68   *MS*: PRO, SP 1/205, f. 28 (old f. 27)
            Calendared: *LP*, xx, II, 14

69   *MS*: PRO, SP 1/205, ff. 32v–33 (old ff. 31v–32)
            Calendared: *LP*, xx, II, 16
            Printed: *St. P.*, vol. 1, p. 801

70   *MS*: PRO, SP 1/205, f. 76r–v (old f. 75r–v)
            Calendared: *LP*, xx, II, 38
            Printed: *St. P.*, vol. 1, p. 803

71   *MS*: PRO, SP 1/205, f. 80 (old f. 79)
            Calendared: *LP*, xx, II, 39
            Printed: *St. P.*, vol. 1, p. 806

72   *MS*: PRO, SP 1/205, f. 117 (old f. 113)
            Calendared: *LP*, xx. II, 61
            Printed: *St. P.*, vol. 1, pp. 807–8

73   MS: PRO, SP 1/205, f. 154r–v (old f. 146r–v)
            Calendared: *LP*, xx, II, 81

74   *MS*: PRO, SP 1/206, f. 159v
          Calendared: *LP*, xx, II, 211

75   *MS*: PRO, SP 1/207, f. 85v
          Calendared: *LP*, xx, II, 288

76   *Text*: *APC*, vol. 1, p. 285

77   *MS*: PRO, E 351/2588

78   *Text*: *APC*, vol. 2, p. 92

79   *Text*: *APC*, vol. 2, p. 308

80   *MS*: PRO, SP 10/9, no. 48
          Calendared: *CSPD Ed VI*, no. 418 (p. 152)

81   *MS*: PRO, SP 10/15, no. 11
          Calendared: *CSPD Ed VI*, no. 721 (4) (p. 261)

82   *MS*: Lambeth Palace Library, MS 605, ff. 16–17 (old ff. 12–13)
          Printed: *Calendar of the Carew MSS in Lambeth Palace Library 1515–1574*,
          ed. J.S. Brewer and W. Bullen (1867), pp. lxxx–lxxxi

83   *Text*: *The Observations of Sir Richard Hawkins Knight, in his Vojage into the
          South Sea. Anno Domini 1593* (1622), pp. 5–6 (spelling modernized)

84   *Text*: *The Naval Tracts of Sir William Monson*, ed. M. Oppenheim, vol. 2,
          NRS, no. 23 (1902), p. 265

APPENDIX II
LIST OF PERSONS

DNB or *ODNB* signifies an existing entry in the *Dictionary of National Biography* or one forthcoming in the successor *Oxford Dictionary of National Biography*.
HP signifies an entry in *The House of Commons, 1509–1558*, ed. S.T. Bindoff (History of Parliament, 1982).

Anne of Brittany, Queen of France. Duchess of independent Brittany, she had married Charles VIII of France and, in 1500, his cousin and successor Louis XII. Her death in January 1514 allowed for the marriage of Louis to Mary Tudor as part of the peace treaty with England.

Annebault, Claude d'. Marshal of France 1538. From 1542 one of Francis I's two principal councillors. Admiral of France, February 1544. Admiral of the fleet, 27 June 1545 (for the force sent to invade England), though without actual experience of sea command. Lost political power after the accession of Henry II in 1547. He died in 1552.

Anthony, Anthony. Son of a Flemish immigrant, he became a clerk of the Ordnance Office and, in 1549, its Surveyor. Best known for the illuminated MS of the Royal Navy which he presented to Henry VIII in 1546; he also compiled a chronicle and other works. He remained in office until his death in 1563 (*ODNB*).

Atclif, William. A long-serving court official. One of the clerks of the Green Cloth and Avener of the Stable. Victualler of the army and of the King's ships during the war of 1512–14. Died by May 1519.

Berkeley, Sir John. Eldest son of Richard Berkeley of Stoke, Somerset, from a cadet branch of a noble family. Standard-bearer in the 1544 campaign, and knighted by the King at the taking of Boulogne. Died by September 1545, perhaps as a result of the injuries received at sea earlier that year. Succeeded as standard-bearer by his younger brother Sir Maurice.

Bidoux, Prégent de. Knight of Rhodes, French admiral in the Mediterranean. Born near Tarbes in Gascony, he had a distinguished naval career going back to 1500. In 1513 he was commander of the French galleys at Brest.

Brandon, Sir Charles, becoming Viscount Lisle, then Duke of Suffolk. Jousting companion and favourite of Henry VIII. Born about 1484, he was knighted by April 1512 and became Master of the Horse in October that year. He was appointed Knight of the Garter in April 1513, was created Viscount Lisle in the following month, and was High Marshal of the army invading France. He was created Duke of Suffolk in February 1514. At the beginning of 1515 he was sent to France to bring back the King's sister Mary, by then the dowager Queen. The couple were secretly married in France, without the King's permission. Suffolk recovered Henry's favour, but paid a heavy price in money. In 1540 he became Lord Great Master of the Household. In 1545, at the time of the loss of the *Mary Rose*, he was commander of the land forces at Portsmouth; he died that year (*DNB*).

Bray, Sir Edward. Born by 1492 at Eaton Bray, Bedfordshire, nephew of Henry VII's minister Sir Reginald Bray. Captain of the *Mary Rose* from May 1513; served in the army at Tournai and knighted 13 or 14 October 1513. Subsequently held several other naval and military commands. Lieutenant of Calais 1541–52. Edward VI gave him the reversion of the post of Constable of the Tower of London, to which he succeeded in 1556. Although he had helped to defeat Wyatt's rebellion, his loyalty to Mary was compromised by the suspected treason of his cousin Lord Bray. He resigned his Tower place in 1557 and died the next year (*HP*).

Brigandine, Robert. Born about 1465 into a Kentish yeoman family, he entered the service of Henry VII and by 1495 was a Yeoman of the Crown. In that year he was appointed Clerk of the King's Ships, at a fee of 12*d* a day. He retained this position until 1523, although his influence diminished after Henry VIII's accession, and during the latter part of his career his activities were confined to Portsmouth. He lived about two years after his retirement, dying (probably) in 1525 (*ODNB*).

Browne, John (master). One Browne occurs as master of the *Great Bark* 1513; possibly this is the John Browne first mentioned as master of the *Mary Rose* in a warrant of 2 March 1514, and who still held that position in 1522.

Browne, John (painter). Heraldic painter for state occasions from 1502. Appointed King's painter in 1512. Alderman of London in 1523. Promoted Serjeant Painter in 1527. He died in 1532.

Browne, Sir Wystan. From a West Country family, settled at Abbess Roding, Essex. Esquire of the Body by 1509. Served in Spain against the Moors, and personally knighted by Ferdinand II of Aragon at Burgos on 11 September 1511. One of the King's Spears. Captain of the *Peter Pomegranate* 1512–13, and of the *Trinity* 1514. Granted reversion of the treasurership of Calais in March 1513, but never succeeded to the post. Appointed to review naval expenditure in 1519. In the following year had many responsibilities in preparation for the Field of the Cloth of Gold, including rigging and victualling the *Mary Rose*. Also in 1520 customer of London and chamberlain of Princess Mary's household. Said to have been near to death in November 1521, but may still have been living in December 1532.

Bryan, Sir Francis. Born by 1492, son of Sir Thomas Bryan of Ashridge, Hertfordshire, well connected at court. Held a naval command in 1513 under his kinsman, Lord Admiral (Thomas) Howard. Served in the 1522 expedition and knighted after the capture of Morlaix. In 1543 Lord Lisle appointed him as his Vice-Admiral. He died as acting Viceroy in Ireland in 1550 (*DNB*, *HP*).

Bull, Sir Stephen. Of Old Radnor on the Welsh border. Uncompromisingly described as a 'man of war', he held several naval commands. Captain of the *Regent* in 1512, and knighted at sea by Sir Edward Howard in June that year. Captain of the *Less Bark* jointly with Thomas Cheyne (q.v.) 1513, and alone, 1514. Captain of Carisbrooke Castle, Isle of Wight. Died by January 1515.

Calthrop, Richard. Captain of the hired merchantman *Mary of Brixham* serving with the King's ships in 1513. Captain of the *Sabyne* in 1514.

Carew, Sir Gawain. Born *c.* 1503, the fourth son of Sir Edmund Carew of Mohun's Ottery, Devon, and uncle of Sir George (q.v.). MP for Devon, perhaps first in 1542 and several times thereafter. Active in the suppression of the south-western rising of 1549. Imprisoned for his part in Wyatt's plot against Mary (1554) but resumed his parliamentary career under Elizabeth. He died in 1585 (*HP*).

Carew, Sir George. Born by 1505, eldest son of Sir William Carew, son of Sir Edmund. MP for Devon in 1529. Knighted in 1536. Sheriff of Devon, 1536–7, 1542–3. Helped Vice-Admiral Dudley patrol the Channel in 1537. Captain of Rysbank Tower at Calais in 1539. Taken prisoner by the French in 1543. Gentleman of the Privy Chamber in 1544. Elected again for Devon in January 1545, but did not live to take his seat. Vice-Admiral of the fleet and Captain of the *Mary Rose*, in which he drowned on 19 July 1545. His wife Mary, who witnessed the disaster, later married Sir Arthur Champernon (*HP*).

Carew, Sir Peter. Born *c.* 1510, third son of Sir William. MP for Tavistock in 1545, and subsequently for other Devon constituencies. Sheriff of the county in 1546–7; soon afterwards Vice-Admiral of Devon and Cornwall. Followed his uncle Sir Gawain against the rebels in 1549, but took the lead in the plot against Mary, after which he fled to France. Subsequently captured, he was eventually pardoned by Mary, and served Elizabeth in Ireland. His life was written by the sixteenth-century Exeter historian, John Hooker (*HP*).

Carew, Sir Wymond. Son of John Carew of Antony, Cornwall. An official of the Duchy of Cornwall, and to Queens Jane Seymour, Anne of Cleves and Catherine Parr. Knight of the Bath at Edward VI's coronation. He died in 1549 (*HP*).

Catherine of Aragon. Daughter of Ferdinand II of Aragon and Isabella of Castile. She married Henry VIII in 1509. Her failure to provide a male heir prompted the King to seek annulment of the marriage on grounds of pre-contract with his elder brother Arthur. After eventually being set aside in 1533 she was given the title Princess Dowager; she died in 1536 (*DNB*).

Cavendish, Thomas. Born in Suffolk in 1560, he sailed in the first attempt to colonize Virginia (1585). He won renown by becoming, in 1586–8, the second Englishman to circumnavigate the globe. He died at sea on another expedition in 1592 (*DNB*).

Chapuys, Eustache. A native of Savoy, who entered Charles V's service, *c*. 1527. Appointed ambassador to England in 1529, he was almost continually resident until 1544; during his final visit in 1544–5 he accompanied his accredited successor François van der Delft (q.v.). He died in 1556.

Charles V. Hereditary ruler of the Netherlands, much of Italy, and the Habsburg lands in Austria, King of Spain (as Carlos I) from 1516, and elected Holy Roman Emperor in 1519; he thus held a unique concentration of power, but it would have been unmanageable even without the divide which the Reformation cut through his dominions. From 1556 he abdicated his thrones, entering a monastery where he died in 1558. He twice visited England; on the second occasion, in 1522, he went aboard the *Mary Rose* at Dover.

Cheyne, Sir Thomas. Entered royal service as a henchman to Henry VII. In 1513 was Captain of the *Less Bark* jointly with Stephen Bull (q.v.), and alone, of the *Christ*. Knighted by November that year. Held many public offices in his native Kent. Lord Warden of the Cinque Ports from 1536, becoming Knight of the Garter in 1539, Treasurer of the Household and a Privy Councillor from the same year until his death in 1558 (*DNB*, *HP*).

Clere, Sir Thomas. Second son of Robert Clere, of Stokesby, Norfolk. Serving at sea by 1522; in 1523–4 as captain of the hired merchantman *Edmund of Hull*. JP for Norfolk in 1538. In 1544 commanded the *Jesus of Lübeck*. Knighted by Lord Hertford at Leith in May that year. Vice-Admiral in July 1545; confirmed in this position (also called Lieutenant) on the establishment of the Navy Board in April 1546, retaining office until 1552; he died the following year.

Clermont, René. Lieutenant-General (or Vice-Admiral) of the French fleet. Taken prisoner at the battle of the Spurs (16 August 1513).

Clogge, John. Master of the *Peter Pomegranate* in 1512, as he was ten years later.

Coke, William. Yeoman of the Chamber to the Queen (Catherine of Aragon). Captain of the rowbarge *Catherine Pomegranate* then of the *Sweepstake* in 1514. Despite censure of his conduct during the action of 25 April that year, he continued to hold naval commands.

Compton, Sir William. Son of Edmund Compton of Compton, Warwickshire, born *c*. 1482. A personal favourite of the King, and one of the first Gentlemen of the Privy Chamber. Knighted at Tournai in 1513, and subsequently Chief Gentleman and Groom of the Stool. He was an arch-enemy of Wolsey, but died, conveniently for the latter, in 1528. Among other appointments, he served as Sheriff of Hampshire in 1512–13, and of Somerset and Dorset in 1513–14 (*DNB*).

Coo, Christopher. Shipowner of King's Lynn and (by 1518) a collector of customs there as deputy to the Chief Butler of England. Captain of the *Lizard* and other ships in the war of 1512–14. In 1522–3 a principal supplier of ships to the Crown, with a reputation for plundering others.

Cromwell, Thomas, Earl of Essex. Born *c*. 1475. A former servant of Wolsey, he became Henry VIII's chief minister after the Cardinal's fall in 1529. Principal Secretary in 1534. Lord Privy Seal in 1536. Directed the suppression of the monasteries and the other processes by which the Church in England became an agency of the Crown. Created Earl of Essex in 1540, but fell from power and was executed for treason later that year.

Daunce, Sir John. Teller of the Exchequer in 1505. Appointed Treasurer at War, July 1511, playing a key role in Henry VIII's first French war, and generally in developing the Crown's financial administration; his accounts survive profusely in the Public Records. Knighted in October 1513, a member of the Council in the Star Chamber by 1516 and of the King's Council for legal affairs in 1526. He died in 1545 (*HP* as 'Dauntesey').

Dawtrey, John. Customer (collector of customs) for Southampton. Under-Treasurer of the war 1512–14.

Delabere, James. Captain of the victualler *Antony de Montygro* in 1513. Detached from the navy to lead 100 men in the aborted assault on Brittany.

De La Fava, Ludovico. Merchant of Bologna. In 1509 and on several previous occasions chartered the King's ship *Regent* for export of wools and other merchandise.

Delft, François van der. Replaced Eustache Chapuys as Imperial ambassador in England in 1544. He was withdrawn on grounds of ill health in June 1550, and died shortly after. His extensive dispatches to Charles V and others are a major, though necessarily partisan, source of information.

Devereux, Walter, Lord Ferrers, later Viscount Hereford. Born *c.* 1489 and succeeded as 3rd Baron Ferrers in 1501. As a youth he waited at Henry VII's table where he was a close companion of Charles Brandon, the future Duke of Suffolk. He served with the Marquess of Dorset in 1512. After his time with the fleet in the summer of 1513, as Captain of the *Trinity*, he fought at Flodden (9 September). He accompanied Suffolk to France in 1523 and was elected to the Garter the same year. He served with the King at Boulogne in 1544, and was created Viscount Hereford in 1550. He died in 1558 (*DNB*).

Don, Sir Griffith. Soldier. Occurs as a Sewer of the Chamber at Henry VII's funeral (1509). One of the band of King's Spears in 1511. Captain of the *Mary John* in 1512; knighted by Sir Edward Howard on 7 June that year. Ambassador to Mantua in 1514. Knight of the Body in 1516. Magistrate in Hertfordshire.

Draper, Robert. From the north-east. Captain of a ship of 160 tons originally the *Nicholas Nevill*, then called *Nicholas Draper*, hired by the King. In 1512 joint captain with William Keby (q.v.), but in sole command of the same ship from 1513 until at least 1529.

Du Bellay, Martin. Younger brother of Jean Du Bellay, Bishop of Bayonne, who was sent as French ambassador to England at the height of Henry VIII's divorce crisis in 1533. Author of *Memoires . . . de plusieurs choses* (1569).

Dudley, John, Viscount Lisle, later Duke of Northumberland. Born 1504, elder son of Edmund Dudley, minister of Henry VII, who was executed in 1509. Trained as a soldier, he was knighted during the campaign of 1523, and served the King mainly as an administrator. In 1542 he was created Viscount Lisle after the death of his step-father Arthur Plantagenet (q.v.), the previous holder of the title. In the following year he became Lord Admiral, serving in that capacity, and with conspicuous success, throughout the war of 1543–6. On the accession of Edward VI in 1547 he was created Earl of Warwick, and seized control of the minority government after the fall of the Duke of Somerset in October 1549; in November 1551 he became Duke of Northumberland. He eventually over-reached himself in trying to exclude Mary from the accession on Edward's death in July 1553, and died on the scaffold in the following month (*DNB, HP*).

Edgecombe, Sir Piers. From Meavy, Devon; born *c.* 1469. Esquire of the Body by 1489, Knight of the Bath at the creation of the future Henry VIII as Duke of York, 1494. Among much public service in the south-west, he was several times pricked Sheriff for Devon and Cornwall between 1494 and 1534. He fought against Warbeck's rebellion in 1497, and with Henry VIII in France in 1513 (receiving the honour of Knight Banneret on 16 August). He died in 1539 (*DNB*, under 'Edgcumbe, Sir Richard' (d. 1489) (father); *HP*, as 'Sir Peter').

Ferdinand II. King of Aragon 1479–1516; also (as Ferdinand V) King of Castile 1506–16. His marriage to Queen Isabella of Castile established the united Spanish monarchy. Their daughter Catherine was Henry VIII's first Queen.

FitzAlan, Henry, Earl of Arundel. Born in 1512, succeeded his father in 1544. Lord Chamberlain, 1546–50. Lord Steward, 1553–64. Privy Councillor to Henry VIII, Edward VI, Mary I and Elizabeth. On his death in 1580 his title and estate passed to the Howard family.

Fitzwilliam, William, Earl of Southampton. Born *c.* 1490, younger son of Sir Thomas Fitzwilliam of Aldwark, Yorkshire. A childhood companion of the future Henry VIII, with court appointments from 1509. Served with the Marquess of Dorset in 1512. Held naval command in 1513, wounded at Brest, and knighted 25 September for service at Tournai. Treasurer of Wolsey's household in 1518. Treasurer of the King's Household, 1525–37, also Comptroller 1526–32. Vice-Admiral in 1525–36, Lord Admiral in 1536. Knight of the Garter in 1526. Created Earl of Southampton in 1537 and died in 1542 (*DNB, HP*).

Flemyng, James. Comptroller of customs for Southampton in 1509. Captain of the *Nicholas of Hampton* in 1512, of the *Katherine Fortileza* in 1513 (at first in partnership with William Gonson, q.v.), and of the *Great Nicholas* in 1514.

Fox, Richard. Bishop of Exeter, 1487–92; of Bath and Wells, 1492–4; Durham, 1494–1501; and Winchester, 1501–28. Keeper of the Privy Seal, 1487–1516. Founder of Corpus Christi College, Oxford. A major figure in Henry VII's government, and a moderating influence in the early years of his son's reign (*DNB*).

Francis I. King of France, succeeding his cousin Louis XII on 1 January 1515, and reigning until 1547. In maritime history his main achievement was the creation, from 1517, of the port of Le Havre. In July 1545, as he surveyed his fleet from the clifftops, he came close to death when Lord Lisle's ships bombarded his position.

Freman, —. Master of the *Katherine Fortileza* in 1513.

Gage, Sir John. Born in 1479, and an Esquire of the Body by 1509; knighted by 1519. Privy Councillor and Constable of the Tower from 1540. Comptroller of the Household 1540–7. Knight of the Garter, 1541. Lord Chamberlain from 1553 to his death in 1556 (*HP*).

Gonson, William. Merchant and seaman. Joint captain with John Flemying (q.v.) of the *Katherine Fortileza* in 1513; held various other commands in the war of 1512–14. Became Keeper of the Storehouses at Erith in 1524, and unofficial treasurer of the navy. He was trusted by both Wolsey and Cromwell, and was described in 1537 as 'Master of the King's Ships' (a title never officially bestowed). He died in 1544. His son Benjamin became the first Surveyor of the navy in 1546, and died as Treasurer in 1577.

Grey, Thomas, 2nd Marquess of Dorset. Born in 1477, grandson of Edward IV's Queen. Jousting companion of Henry VIII. Lieutenant-General of an expedition to conquer Guyenne (Aquitaine) in June 1512. Nothing came of a planned alliance with the King of Aragon, and Dorset was obliged to bring his force home empty-handed. He served in the subsequent French war, but was never given another high command. He died in 1530.

Guildford, Sir Henry. Younger son of Sir Richard Guildford, Comptroller of the Household to Henry VII. Jouster and boon companion to Henry VIII. Knighted in March 1512. At the engagement off Brest in August that year he served jointly with Sir Charles Brandon as captain of soldiers aboard the *Sovereign*. Esquire of the Body by 1513, standard-bearer to the King, and one of the original Gentlemen of the Privy Chamber. Councillor from 1516. Comptroller of the Household, 1522–6.

Gurney, Thomas. Captain of the *Jenet Purwyn*, 1512–13.

Gybson, Christopher. Master gunner of the *Mary John* in 1512. Granted a permanent place as a King's gunner, December 1514, still holding this appointment in 1534.

Harper, William. Captain of the *Baptist of Harwich*, the victualler for the *Mary Rose* in 1513. Subsequently a supplier for the navy.

Harvel, Edmond alias Sigismund. German by birth; represented Henry VIII and Edward VI as Agent in Venice. Died there in 1550 and given a magnificent funeral; although he was described as 'the most noble lord, the ambassador of England', the Signory did not attend because he was not a proper ambassador, only an Agent. He had nevertheless been long-serving and reliable.

Hawkins, Sir Richard. Son of the famous Elizabethan seaman, Sir John Hawkins. He commanded the *Swallow* against the Armada of 1588, and in 1593 set out on a voyage intended to surpass the exploits of Drake and Cavendish, but was captured by the Spanish and spent many years in their prisons. His *Observations* on this voyage, published just after his death in 1622, brought him renown. Unfortunately much detail was imperfectly remembered, as in the extract about the *Mary Rose* given above (*DNB*).

Heron, Sir John. Treasurer of the Chamber, 1492–1521 and Treasurer of the war, 1512–14. Clerk of the Hanaper of Chancery in 1514.

Hooker, John. Chamberlain of Exeter in 1555, and a prolific antiquarian writer. Solicitor to Sir Peter Carew, in whose service he went to Ireland in 1568 and became a member of the Irish Parliament. His life of Carew, with its account of Sir George Carew's death in the *Mary Rose*, was not printed until the nineteenth century (*DNB*).

Hopton, John. Yeoman of the Chamber by 1501 and Gentleman Usher by 1511. Served the King at sea from at least 1510, and owned several ships of his own. Presented naval accounts with John Dawtrey and Robert Brigandine (qq.v.) in 1512, and became Clerk Comptroller of the navy in the same year. Responsible for rigging the fleet which went to the Field of the Cloth of Gold in 1520. Retired 1524 and died before July 1526 (*ODNB*).

Howard, Sir Edward. Second son of Thomas Howard, Earl of Surrey and subsequently 2nd Duke of Norfolk. Born about 1478, he gained his first experience of sea service with Sir Edward Poynings in 1492. In 1497 he accompanied his father to the Scottish border, and was knighted by him. He was a prominent jouster, and was appointed standard-bearer to the King in May

1509. By 1511 he was commanding ships in the Channel, and in 1512 was appointed Admiral of the King's war fleet, with an elaborate indenture and instructions. He was also granted the reversion of the office of Lord Admiral, to which he succeeded on the death of the Earl of Oxford on 10 March 1513. He was killed in action on 25 April in the same year (*DNB*).

Howard, Sir Thomas, styled Lord Howard, becoming Earl of Surrey, later 3rd Duke of Norfolk. Eldest son of the Earl of Surrey, born in 1473. He served with his father in 1497, and was knighted by him. Until becoming a peer in his own right, he was known as Lord Howard, a courtesy title he had held in the time of his grandfather, the 1st Duke of Norfolk (though the barony from which it derived was forfeited in 1485 and never restored). He succeeded his brother as Lord Admiral in April 1513, and served in that capacity until 1525. He was created Earl of Surrey when his father was promoted to the dukedom of Norfolk in 1514, and succeeded him in the latter title in 1524. He was a prominent courtier and politician during the later part of Henry VIII's reign, and Lord Treasurer from 1522, but fell from favour in 1546, and was attainted of high treason. Saved from execution by the King's death in January 1547, he remained in prison during Edward VI's reign, and was released and restored by Mary on her accession in 1553. He died in 1554 (*DNB*).

James IV. King of Scotland, 1488–1513. In 1503 he married Henry VII's elder daughter Margaret. He strengthened Scottish naval power, in particular by building warships designed to mount heavy artillery. It can be argued that Henry VIII, in building the *Mary Rose* and her sister the *Peter*, Henry VIII was following his brother-in-law's lead.

Jenyns, John. Servant to Sir John Heron as Treasurer of the Chamber from 1513.

Jermyn, Thomas. Master of the *Mary Walsingham* in 1513. Became Clerk of the Ships following the retirement of Robert Brigandine in March 1523, but did not have his predecessor's role in advising the King. In office until February 1538.

Jerningham, Sir Richard. Second son of John Jerningham of Somerleyton, Suffolk. A member of the Band of Spears, 1511. Esquire of the Body, 1512. Knighted at Tournai on Christmas Day in 1513, and later Deputy there during the English occupation. Resident ambassador in France 1520–1; subsequently undertook several special missions. He died in 1525.

169

Keby, William. Yeoman Usher of the Chamber in 1509. Also customer of Boston, and jointly captained a ship with Robert Draper (q.v.). Promoted Serjeant of Arms in May 1513. Had a part in the flotilla escorting Charles V on his visit in 1522.

Legge, Robert. Appointed Treasurer for Marine Causes in the patent establishing the Navy Board, 24 April 1546. Died in office in 1548.

Le Roy, Guyon, Sieur du Chillou. Vice-Admiral of Brittany and Admiral of France. Responsible for the construction of the new port at Le Havre from 1517.

Louis XII. King of France, 1498–1515. In 1514 he married, as his second wife, Henry VIII's sister Mary.

Margaret of Savoy. Also known as Margaret of Austria, she was the aunt of the Emperor Charles V, and served as his Regent in the Low Countries from 1509 to 1513, and from 1519 to her death in 1530.

Monson, Sir William. Born in Lincolnshire in 1569. Left Balliol College, Oxford at an early age and went to sea. Served against the Armada of 1588 and in the continuing Spanish war. Admiral of the Narrow Seas in 1604. Retired in 1635 and died in 1643. His extensive compilation of 'Naval Tracts' (published posthumously, and reissued by the NRS in 1902–14), is an important source of naval and maritime history, if occasionally inaccurate.

Paget, Sir William, later Lord Paget. Clerk of the Privy Council, 1540-3, and Secretary to the King, April 1543–June 1547. He played a leading part in setting up the Protectorate in 1547, and became Comptroller of the Household later in the same year. In 1549 he was created Baron Paget of Beaudesert, but fell out with the Earl of Warwick and was dismissed from office. Appointed to the Privy Council by Mary in July 1553, he became Lord Privy Seal in December 1555, probably at the suggestion of King Philip, whom he supported. His services were not employed by Elizabeth, and he died in retirement in 1565 (*DNB, HP*).

Palshide, Richard. Appointed customer of Southampton in June 1509. Under-Treasurer of the war, 1512–14.

Paulet, William, Baron St John, later Marquess of Winchester. Son of Sir John Paulet of Basing, Hampshire. Knighted by 1525. Comptroller of the Household in 1532. In 1537 he was promoted to Treasurer of the Household, and was raised to the peerage as Lord St John of Basing in March 1539. He was appointed Lord Chamberlain in 1543. From 1545 to 1550 he served as Lord Great Master of the Household, and in 1550 was created Earl of Wiltshire and appointed Lord Treasurer. In 1551 he was promoted to the marquisate of Winchester. He remained Lord Treasurer under both Mary and Elizabeth, dying in 1572 (*DNB, HP*).

Pawne, William. Served with Henry Tudor at Bosworth, and became his Clerk of the Stable. Received many further offices at the start of Henry VIII's reign, including Bailiff of Guines in 1509, Receiver of Berwick in 1511 and Master of the Ordnance there in 1514.

Peryn, John. Master, of the *Swallow* in 1513, and of the *Barbara* in the following year.

Plantagenet, Arthur, later Viscount Lisle. Illegitimate son of King Edward IV by Elizabeth Lucy. Born *c.* 1462 and first known by his mother's maiden name of Wayte. Captain of the ill-fated *Nicholas of Hampton* in 1513, and knighted the same year. Created Viscount Lisle in 1523. Vice-Admiral of England in 1525. Lord Warden of the Cinque Ports and governor of Calais from 1526. Councillor in 1540, but fell from favour and died in prison in 1542. His family correspondence, confiscated on his arrest, survives among the State Papers, a comprehensive edition published as *The Lisle Letters* (1981) (*DNB*).

Poyntz, Sir Anthony. Son of Sir Francis Poyntz of Iron Acton, Gloucestershire, born *c.* 1480. Knighted by Sir Edward Howard during the 1513 campaign. Captain of an unspecified ship of Bristol that year, and of the *Katherine Fortileza* in 1514. He undertook an embassy to France in 1518, and attended the Field of the Cloth of Gold in 1520. He served again at sea in 1522, and became Vice-Admiral. Sheriff of Gloucestershire, 1527. He died 1533 or 1535 (*DNB*, under father's entry).

Radcliffe, Robert, Baron Fitzwalter, later Earl of Sussex. Born *c.* 1483, son of John Radcliffe, Baron Fitzwalter, whom he had succeeded by 1509. Created Viscount Fitzwalter in 1525, and Earl of Sussex in 1529. He died in 1542.

Rogers, Thomas. Captain in the private fleet of Richard Neville, Earl of Warwick. In Edward IV's service by 1475, and appointed Clerk of the King's Ships in 1480. Reappointed by Richard III and Henry VII. He died early in 1488.

Rolf, Thomas. Esquire of the Body. Customer of Sandwich and victualler to the navy. Also one of the auditors of the Court of General Surveyors.

Rouville, Louis de. Huntsman to Louis XII. Lieutenant-General (or Vice-Admiral) of the united Franco-Scottish fleet, appointed September 1513.

Russell, John, Baron Russell, later Earl of Bedford. Born *c*. 1485 at Weymouth, Dorset. An early competence as linguist is said to have enabled him to interpret for Archduke Philip of Austria, forced ashore at Weymouth in 1506. This brought Henry VII's favour and a place at court, leading to his long service as soldier, diplomat and politician. Served in the naval expedition of 1522; lost his right eye at the capture of Morlaix. Knighted by Lord Admiral Surrey after the battle. Created Baron Russell in December 1542, on appointment as Lord Privy Seal. He was reappointed to the same office in 1547, and was created Earl of Bedford in 1550. Mary retained him in office until his death in 1555. He acquired the estate at Woburn which in later generations would become the seat of the political dynasty he founded (*DNB, HP*).

Sabyne, William. Merchant of Ipswich, and shipmaster in the King's service. Captain of his own ship *Sabyne* in 1512–13. Appointed one of the King's Serjeants of Arms in 1518. Served with the King's ships again in 1522–3.

Seaman, Peter. Pilot of the *Katherine Fortileza* in 1513. Captain of the *Gabriel* in 1523.

Seymour, Edward, Earl of Hertford, later Duke of Somerset. Eldest son of Sir John Seymour of Wolf Hall, Somerset. Prospered when his sister Jane became Henry VIII's third Queen in 1537. On the accession of his nephew Edward VI he had himself made Lord Protector, setting aside the collective regency which Henry had designed for his son's minority. Overthrown in October 1549. Although allowed to resume his place in the Privy Council, he was suspected of plotting to recover full control of the government, and was executed for treason in 1552.

Sherborne, Sir Henry. Born in 1474, eldest son of John Sherborne (or Shernborne), of Shernborne, Norfolk. Knighted in 1511. Captain of the *Martinet* in 1512, joint captain of the *Great Bark* in 1513, and captain of the *Mary Rose* in 1514. Marshal of the King's Bench in 1515. Customer of Drogheda in 1522. Vice-Admiral of the North Sea by February 1523. Killed in action against the French on 11 June that year. His son Thomas, serving with him, suffered permanent deafness from the noise of the guns.

Sidney, Sir William. Esquire of the Body by 1512. Soldier. Captain of the *Dragon of Greenwich* 1512. Joint-captain of the *Great Bark* in 1513. Special ambassador to France in 1515. Chamberlain of the household of Prince Edward in 1538. Among much property granted to him in Edward's reign was Penshurst Place, Kent, which became the family seat. He died in 1553.

Southern, Lewis. Captain of the *Elizabeth of Newcastle* in 1512.

Southwell, Sir Richard. Born in Essex *c.* 1503. Receiver of the Court of Augmentations 1536–42, active in the suppression of the monasteries. Treasurer of the wars from August 1544. Privy Councillor under Edward VI (briefly) and Mary. Master of the Ordnance, 1554–9. He died in 1564 (*DNB, HP*).

Sperte, Sir Thomas. An experienced sea captain, and the first master of the *Henry Grace à Dieu*, he became Clerk Comptroller of the navy when John Hopton retired in 1524. He was knighted in 1535, in which year he was also described (like Gonson) as 'Master of the King's Ships'. By 1538 he was also Captain of Portsmouth, and was responsible for the additional fortifications built there in 1539. He seems to have retired in 1540, and died soon after (*ODNB*).

Stewart, John, 2nd Duke of Albany. Born 1481, grandson of James II of Scotland, and brought up in France. Following the death of his cousin James IV at Flodden in 1513, he was declared Regent for and heir to James V. This led to a power struggle with the dowager Queen Margaret, and Albany intermittently took refuge at the French court. He left Scotland finally in 1524, when the regency was formally terminated. He died in 1536.

Swanne, John. Master of the *George of Rye*, among those escorting Princess Mary to France for her marriage to Louis XII in 1515.

Symmond, William. Captain of the *Mary Christopher of Bristol* in 1513, of the *Magdalen of Poole* in 1517, and of the *Mary Boleyn* in 1523. Sewer of the Chamber in 1520.

Tooley, William. Captain of the *Sweepstake* in 1513. His brother Sir Robert, who served with him, had no naval appointment.

Tregonwell, Sir John. Born by 1498. DCL of Oxford University. Commissioner for piracy in 1527. Principal judge of the Admiralty Court by 1535. Master in Chancery by 1536. Played a prominent part in suppression of the monasteries, but accepted the restoration of Catholicism by Mary, at whose coronation he was knighted and in whose Privy Council he sat. He died in 1565 (*DNB, HP*).

Trevelyan alias Trevanion, Sir William. Soldier. Knight of the Body by 1512. Captain of the *George of Falmouth* in 1512, of the *Henry Grace à Dieu* in 1513 and of the *Gabriel* in 1514. Pricked Sheriff of Cornwall in 1515. Auditor of the Duchy in 1518.

Vaughan, Edward. Occurs as Gentleman Pensioner from 1540. Served as one of the captains at Guines from April 1541. Captain of Portsmouth from 1545, and responsible for the fortifications under construction there at the time the *Mary Rose* was lost.

Vaughan, Thomas. Bailiff of Dover. Captain of the *Fortune of Dover* in 1514.

Veysey, John. Bishop of Exeter, 1519–51 and 1553–4. (*DNB*)

Wallop, Sir John. Son of Stephen Wallop of Hampshire. Soldier and diplomat; probably knighted in the Low Countries by Sir Edward Poynings, 1511. Served at sea through the war of 1512–14; captain of the *Sanchio de Gara* in 1513 and of the *Great Barbara* in 1514. Sent on a diplomatic mission to Portugal in 1516, and expressed a wish to serve against the Infidel. Was sent as a soldier to Ireland in 1518–20, and served in France in 1522–3. Gentleman Pensioner in 1518. Undertook missions to the Low Countries (1526) and to Germany. Gentleman of the Privy Chamber by 1540, and Ambassador in Paris, 1540–1. Captain of Guisnes, 1541. Knight of the Garter, 1543. He served in France in 1544, and died at Guisnes in 1551 (*DNB*).

West, Sir Thomas, later Baron West and De La Warr. Born about 1472. Soldier and courtier. Esquire of the Body by 1503. He served at Tournai in 1513 and was created Knight Banneret at Lille in that year. Sheriff of Surrey and Sussex, 1524. Succeeded to his father's baronies in 1526. He was implicated in the alleged Exeter conspiracy in 1539, and briefly imprisoned. He returned to court in 1540, was Lord Lieutenant of Sussex in 1551, but declared for Mary in 1553, and died in the following year (*DNB*).

Weston, Sir Richard. Esquire of the Body. Captain of Guernsey in 1509.

Westowe, John. Appointed one of the gunners of the Tower of London in 1509. Searcher of the port of Bristol in January 1513. Served as Master Gunner of the Middle Ward of the army in France that year. Sent with ordnance to Tournai in 1514.

Williams, Sir John, later Baron Williams of Thame. Born by 1503, younger son of Sir John Williams of Burghfield, Berkshire. Associate of Thomas Cromwell, and prominent in suppression of the monasteries. Treasurer of the Court of Augmentations, the department which handled the proceeds of the dissolution, 1544–54. Received his barony from Mary in 1554, and was appointed Chamberlain to King Philip. He died in 1559.

Willoughby, Robert, Baron Willoughby de Broke. Born in 1472 and succeeded his father in 1502. Also de jure Baron Latimer, but summoned to Parliament in the Willoughby barony, and known informally as Lord Broke. Knighted by 1504. Knight of the Bath at Henry VIII's coronation in 1509. Served under the Marquess of Dorset in 1512 and at Tournai in 1513. Died in 1521.

Windsor, Sir Andrew. Lawyer. Son of Thomas Windsor of Stanwell, Middlesex. He was born in 1467, and succeeded his father in 1485. He was a Bencher of the Middle Temple in 1500, and Keeper of the Great Wardrobe in 1506. Created Knight of the Bath at the coronation in 1509, he was a treasurer on the campaign of 1513, and commissioner for the navy in 1514. Became a Councillor in 1525/6. He was created Baron Windsor in 1529, and died in 1543 (*DNB*).

Wingfield, Sir Richard. Son of Sir John Wingfield of Letheringham, Suffolk. Born about 1469, he studied briefly at Cambridge and Ferrara. Esquire of the

Body by 1500, and knighted by 1511. In 1512 he was a commissioner for negotiating the Holy League against France, and undertook missions to the Low Countries between 1514 and 1516. He was Treasurer of Calais in 1518, and Ambassador to France in 1520. He died in 1525 (*DNB, HP*).

Winter, John. Merchant and sea captain of Bristol. Possibly related to Wolsey's mistress. He was intended as Treasurer of the navy in 1546, but died in the same year. His son Sir William Winter was a distinguished naval commander and administrator.

Wiseman, Edmund. Captain of the *Christopher Davy* in 1512, and of the *Mary George* in 1514. One of the King's Spears by 1514. Captain in the garrison at Tournai in 1515.

Wodeshawe, Thomas. Customer of Southampton in the reign of Henry VII, vacating office on the appointment of Richard Palshide in June 1509. Received a pension from the customs in September 1510.

Wolsey, Thomas. Born about 1472, and educated at Magdalen College, Oxford. He served as chaplain both to the Archbishop of Canterbury, and to Sir Richard Nanfan, the governor of Calais, before entering the royal household in the same capacity in 1507. He undertook several modest diplomatic missions before Henry VII's death. Henry VIII appointed him as Almoner towards the end of 1509. While thus nominally in charge of royal charity, his main occupation was managing the logistics of the campaigns of 1512 and 1513, gaining the King's favour in the process. In reward he received several middle-ranking ecclesiastical preferments, culminating in the deanery of York in 1513. Thereafter his rise was meteoric. In 1514 he became Bishop of Lincoln, then of Tournai, and Archbishop of York in September of that year. In September 1515 he was created Cardinal on the King's petition, and in December became Lord Chancellor. In 1518 he was created Legate *a Latere*. From 1515 until his fall in 1529 he was the King's chief minister, and his influence was unchallenged. However, Henry's confidence began to wane after the fiasco of the 'Amicable Grant' in 1525, and he was dismissed eventually for failing to secure the King's divorce. (*DNB*)

Woodhouse, Sir William. Born by 1517, second son of John Woodhouse of Waxham, Norfolk. At sea from an early age. In February 1543 appointed

Admiral of a squadron of four ships in the North Sea. Vice-Admiral of the fleet which assisted the invasion of Scotland in 1544 and knighted that year. Master of naval ordnance, 1545–52. Lieutenant of the Admiralty in 1552 until his death in 1563 (*HP*).

Worsley, James. Groom of the Chamber, and of the Wardrobe of the Robes in 1509. Among many other grants from Henry VIII, he held customs collectorships at Poole, Southampton and Calais. Keeper of the lions and leopards at the Tower of London in 1513. Constable of Carisbrooke Castle, Isle of Wight, 1520.

Wotton, Sir Edward. Eldest son of Sir Robert Wotton of Boughton Malherbe, Kent. Appointed Treasurer of Calais in 1540 and Privy Councillor in 1547. Was in London September–November 1549, lending support to the coup against Protector Somerset. He died in 1551. His brother Nicholas, Dean of Canterbury and of York (d. 1567), was resident ambassador in France and a Privy Councillor from 1546. Like his brother he was in London at the time of Somerset's fall, one consequence of which was his own appointment as a Principal Secretary (of State) in October 1549. It is likely that the 'Mr Wotton' mentioned in the document here printed is Sir Edward; his brother was usually distinguished as 'Dr'.

Wriothesley, Charles. Son of Sir Thomas Wriothesley (cousin to the following), born about 1508. He became Rouge Croix Pursuivant in 1525 and Windsor Herald in 1534. He entered Gray's Inn in 1529. Later in life he compiled the chronicle which bears his name, and died in 1562.

Wriothesley, Thomas, Baron Wriothesley, later Earl of Southampton. Born December 1505, he became Keeper of the Great Seal in April 1544. Raised to the peerage as Baron Wriothesley in January 1544, he became Lord Chancellor in the following May. He retained his office on the accession of Edward VI in January 1547, and was created Earl of Southampton, but immediately after fell out with Protector Somerset, and was dismissed in May. Defeated in a bid to recover power after Somerset's fall in October 1549, he was finally dismissed from the Council in December and died in July 1550 (*DNB*, *HP*).

Wyatt, Sir Henry. Born about 1460, he entered the service of Henry Tudor in about 1483, and was immediately named to the Council on Henry's accession in 1485. By 1492 he was established in Kent. He served Henry VII both in Scotland and Ireland, and became a Knight of the Bath at Henry VIII's coronation. He served at the Battle of the Spurs in 1513, and became Treasurer of the Chamber in 1523. He retired in 1528, and died in 1537. The poet Sir Thomas Wyatt was his son (*DNB*)

Wyndham, Sir Thomas. Son of Sir John Wyndham of Felbrigge, Norfolk, and Margaret, daughter of the 1st Duke of Norfolk; he was thus first cousin to Lord Admirals Edward and Thomas Howard. He served at sea from about 1510, and was Vice-Admiral throughout the war of 1512–14. He was knighted at Crozon Bay by Sir Edward Howard in June 1512. He was with Howard (somewhat as now would be called flag captain) aboard the *Mary Rose* at the assault on Brest in August. In March 1513 he was appointed Treasurer of the fleet. Captain of the *John Hopton* that year, and of the *Henry Grace à Dieu* in 1514. Reappointed Vice-Admiral in 1516. He died in 1522. His son Thomas (d. 1553) also had a distinguished naval career (*DNB*, entry for son).

APPENDIX III
GLOSSARY

bandog literally, a dog kept on a chain or rope as a guard; generally used for mastiffs or similar types.

base a small gun, usually of wrought iron and breech-loading; of 1-in to 6-in bore; firing cast lead shot; usually mounted on a wooden block, with a drop-in chamber. An anti-personnel weapon.

basilisk a large gun, generally bronze, defined as a bastard (or reduced) demi-culverin, instanced as having a 5-in bore and firing shot of 15¼ lb.

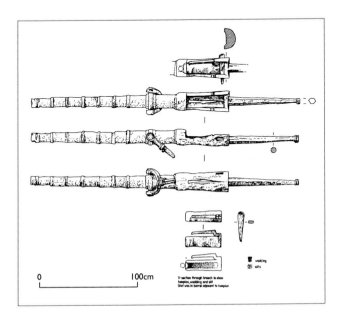

A drawing of a corroded base. (*Mary Rose Trust*)

179

bastard culverin smaller type of culverin, q.v.

bolt cylindrical pin of iron or copper to hold a movable object in place.

bonnet an additional part laced to the bottom of a sail, usually one-third of its depth.

bouging staving in of a ship's hull to cause a leak.

bowline a rope leading forward, which is fastened to the perpendicular edge of the sail. Used to keep the weather edge of the sail tight.

breeches, breeching ropes used to secure a gun to the structure of the ship; sometimes attached to the gun itself, and sometimes to the carriage.

buckram a coarse linen cloth.

bumkin a vessel for carrying water.

cagger a kedge anchor; a small anchor used for mooring or warping.

camlet a fine fabric made from the hair of Angora goats.

cannon the largest type of cast mounted gun, usually of bronze and muzzle-loading; bore of at least 7 in, and weighing 7,000 lb. Firing mostly cast-iron shot of 45 lb or more.

cat ropes used for hauling cat hooks.

cat hook strong hook used to retain the ring of an anchor when it is raised.

charter party an indenture, or contract, written in duplicate.

chief of iron 'chief', meaning principal. In this case an iron sheathing for the prow of a boat.

commander large wooden mallet, used for removing or replacing wedges.

crayer a small single-masted trading vessel.

culverin cast-iron or bronze muzzle-loading gun; long in relation to its bore (14 ft, bore 5–5½ in), weighing approximately 4,770 lb; firing cast-iron shot of between 7 and 26 lb weight.

curtal large gun firing shot up to 40 lb, with bore of approximately 6 in.

deadshare the wage due to a fictitious or non-existent seaman; these shares were recognized perquisites distributed among the officers pro rata.

Deeps, or Black Deeps an area in the North Sea, between Harwich and Margate.

demi-cannon cast bronze or iron muzzle-loading gun; approximately 12 ft long, with a bore of 6–6½ in; weighing 5,800 lb; firing cast-iron shot of 33–4 lb weight.

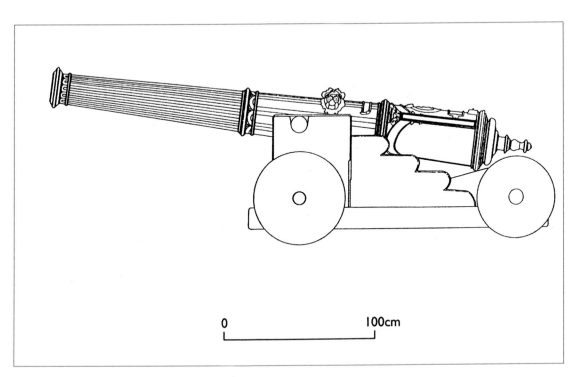

0   100cm

Demi-culverin on carriage. (*Mary Rose Trust*)

demi-culverin cast bronze or iron muzzle-loading gun; approximately 13 ft long, with a bore of 4–4½ in; weighing 4,760 lb; firing cast-iron shot of 10–15 lb weight.

demi-sling a small sling, but it is not known whether the half dimension refers to the bore size, or weight of shot.

Downs a sea area off the Sussex coast, in the neighbourhood of Dogger Bank.

falcon cast bronze or iron muzzle-loading gun; approximately 7 ft long, with a bore of 2¾ in; weighing 700 lb, and firing cast-iron shot of a little over 2 lb weight.

foist a light galley, propelled by oars and sails.

fowler a small breech-loading gun; sometimes cast bronze, but usually wrought iron; carriage-mounted; of uncertain dimensions, but with a bore of more than 2 in; fired stone shot.

garland collar of rope wound around the head of a mast to prevent the shrouds from chafing.

garnet (1) a hinge. (2) a purchase fastened to the main stay, for hoisting cargo in and out.

gunstones shot of all descriptions, including iron as well as stone.

hackbut portable matchlock firearm with a large hook beneath the barrel to attach to a rail as a recoil mechanism, heavy enough to require support; also known as an 'arquebus'.

hailshot piece breech- or muzzle-loading gun, cast or wrought iron, with rectangular bore, weighing about 30 lb; firing dice (iron cubes).

harness body armour (set of).

hoses either in the common sense, to convey water, or possibly sockets to hold shafts.

Drawing of hailshot piece. (*Mary Rose Trust*)

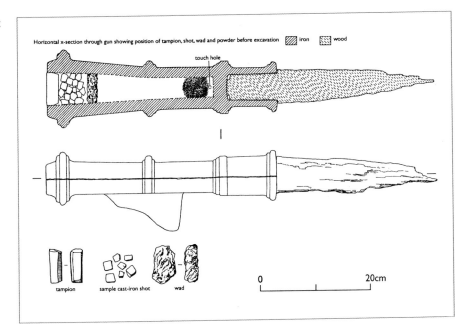

Horizontal x-section through gun showing position of tampion, shot, wad and powder before excavation ▨ iron ▨ wood

touch hole

tampion   sample cast-iron shot   wad

0   20cm

junk remains of pieces of old cable, used for making oakum.

kenning distance of ordinary vision at sea (about 20 miles).

knight and ramshead two principal blocks of timber securing running rigging.

leech hook as leeches were the borders or edges of sails, these hooks were probably used to attach bowlines.

lift ropes which reach from each mast head to their respective yard arms.

luff hook a luff tackle was composed of a double and a single block, the fall coming from the double. The hook was used to secure the tackle to a strong point.

marline small line of two strands.

murderer a general name for a large gun firing loose fragments of iron.
parrel a loose collar of iron or rope fitted around the mast, retaining the yard to the mast, but able to slide up and down with the yard.

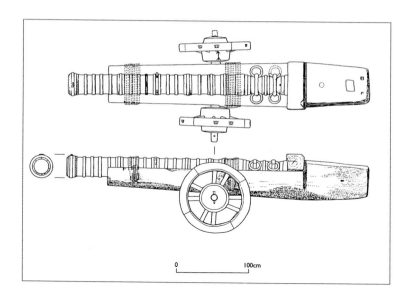

Drawing of a port-piece. (*Mary Rose Trust*)

polancre a combination of pulleys connected by rope; a hoisting or hauling device.

port-piece a large breech-loading gun, usually of wrought iron, with a bore of up to 10 in; weighing (with its breech chamber) about 1,200 lb; usually mounted on a large sledge, with a single pair of wheels.

prest advance of money for public service.

quarter-sling a form of sling; it is uncertain whether the dimension refers to the bore or the shot size.

raft wooden spar or plank (the original meaning of the word, subsequently applied to an assembly of such).

ramshead *see* **knight**

saker muzzle-loading gun, usually bronze but sometimes of cast iron; approximately 9 ft long, with a bore of 3½ in; weighing 2,000 lb, and firing iron shot of about 4 lb 12 oz.

serpentine wrought-iron breech-loading gun, usually long in relation to bore, and commonly mounted.

sheet ropes fastened to one or both the lower corners of a sail to retain the clew down to its place.

shiver wheel upon which the rope runs in a block.

sling wrought-iron breech-loading gun, long in relation to bore, which was from 1 to 5 ft. Usually carriage-mounted.

spike a large headless nail, usually of iron.

stay strong ropes extending from the upper end of each mast towards the stem of the ship.

swifting tackle pairs of shrouds, fitted to the port and starboard sides of the lower masts.

swivel gun gun such as a base (q.v.) rotated on a pin to increase arc of fire.

tacks any arrangement of blocks used to increase purchase or lifting power.

thring usually a verb, meaning to bind tightly together; as a noun, probably a bundle (unspecified).

thrum section of coarse woollen or hemp yarn used for mops etc.

top armours cloths tied about the tops of masts for show.

Trade, the the sea area around Brittany, centred on the port of Brest.

truss a parrel used on the lower yards to bind them to the masts.

tuke canvas.

warping moving a ship by hauling on a cable from the shore.

wildfire incendiary mixture directed, used as projectile, especially against sails or rigging.

APPENDIX IV
MAP OF FLEET DISPOSITIONS,
19 JULY 1545

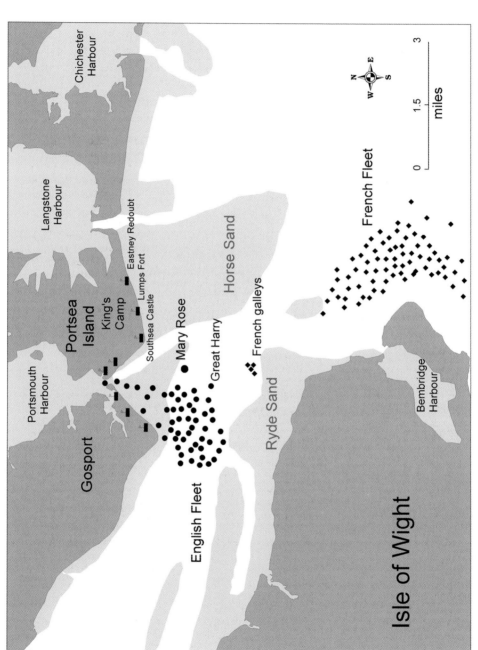

Chichester Harbour

Langstone Harbour

Portsmouth Harbour

Gosport

Portsea Island

King's Camp

Eastney Redoubt

Lumps Fort

Southsea Castle

Mary Rose

Great Harry

English Fleet

Horse Sand

French galleys

Ryde Sand

Bembridge Harbour

French Fleet

N
W E
S

0   1.5   3
miles

Isle of Wight

(D. Fontana, University of Portsmouth)

INDEX

Page references in italic are to the black and white illustrations and their captions; the coloured plates and their captions are referred to by number preceded by pl. The references App. II and App. III denote entries in List of Persons or the Glossary; these appendices are not otherwise indexed.